Learning to Learn

DONALD E. P. SMITH   GENERAL EDITOR

CARL HAAG

RODERICK A. IRONSIDE

ROSEMARIE E. NAGEL

ANNE R. CROSS

DANIEL G. SAYLES

JOHN E. VALUSEK

Learning to Learn

General Editor: **DONALD E. P. SMITH,** *University of Michigan*

CARL HAAG, *University of Michigan*
RODERICK A. IRONSIDE, *College of William and Mary*
ROSEMARIE E. NAGEL, *Delta College*
ANNE R. CROSS, *Fraser High School, Fraser, Michigan*
DANIEL G. SAYLES, *University of Michigan*
JOHN E. VALUSEK, *Western State College of Colorado*

Harcourt, Brace & World, Inc.
New York, Chicago, San Francisco, and Atlanta

Printed in the United States of America

Library of Congress Catalog Card Number: 61-17784

Preface

Reading instruction for mature students has been one of education's most notable advances since World War II. Colleges, adult education centers, high school evening divisions, executive training programs, and public libraries have undertaken such instruction with striking success.

And with increased experience, we have come to realize that mature students are capable of accomplishing more than increased reading skill. They are able to improve their learning efficiency, that is, they can learn how to learn.

Demand for instruction in reading and learning now far exceeds the supply of instructors. There is need now for a book which is self-instructional, which provides in a detailed way both the *how* of improvement and the *why*.

The specifications for this book are based on the foregoing considerations. The staff of the University of Michigan's Reading Service has tried to prepare material which focuses on the problems and skills of college learning, which gives attention to the reading skills most involved in the learning process, and finally, which is largely self-instructional. The material has been used by some two thousand students in a number of institutional settings and revisions made in accordance with that use. Instructors report that the book can be used as a starting point for their own creative teaching or as a complete program in itself.

Professional readings by a number of people resulted in substantial improvement of this book. The authors wish to acknowledge their debt to Professors Paul W. Smith, Pasadena City College, David R. Stone, Utah State University, Claude Buxton, Yale University, and Peter M. Milner, McGill University. Deficiencies which remain reflect limitations of the authors.

DONALD E. P. SMITH
General Editor

August, 1961
Ann Arbor, Michigan

Contents

III HOW TO READ

IV MASTERING THE CONTENT

V TIMED READINGS

APPENDICES

A Note to the Student on the Systematic Nature of Learning

This book is designed for students in reading improvement classes wherein the main emphasis is the development of effective academic skills. It may also be used, however, by those who desire a guide for independent self-improvement.

At one time or another, most college students worry about their ability to succeed academically. One or two low grades are enough to make many begin to doubt themselves. Some who are panic-prone face likely defeat even before the battle begins.

When you begin to doubt, it will be comforting to remember that most college students do succeed. They manage somehow to meet the requirements for the degree, to win most of the battles and, finally, the war.

To an experienced observer, the most surprising element in this academic combat is the student's adversary. It's not the professor who gives the examination; it's not even his classmates who are competing with him for grades. The student's worst enemy is *himself.* Somehow, he manages to learn an overwhelming number of self-defeating habits, ways of interfering with the smooth functioning of his learning mechanism.

The rules by which we learn are not mysterious. They need not be discovered through trial and error, through trying this recommendation and that advice until we find something that works. Many of the procedures which lead to efficient learning are known and need only to be understood and followed systematically.

Certainly, even under optimum conditions, people differ widely in the speed and thoroughness with which they learn. Nevertheless, the regularities, the rules of learning, hold for everyone. Minor variations in procedure or differences in emphasis ordinarily take care of differences in learning style.

It should not be surprising to find that there are regularities or "laws" of learning. The changes in behavior which we call learning are actually changes in the operation of the body. As you know, physical functioning is systematic. The nervous systems and glandular system interact in predictable ways: when an examination looms up, the emotion center in the brain becomes more active, thus stimulating a series of glandular changes which, in turn, have a particular effect on thinking. The mind begins to race and over-all muscle tension increases as the body becomes ready to handle the threat. Sometimes the body overreacts to threat, a condition which is experienced as disorganized thinking or as the blankness of examination panic.

By knowing how we operate, we can set up conditions which facilitate—or impede—learning. In the following pages you will learn procedures which facilitate efficient use of your learning capacity, conditions necessary for creative thinking, skills which reduce time and energy expenditure during learning, theories about how concepts develop, techniques which reduce forgetting and which aid concentration. You will learn about "styles of learning," about relationships between personality and learning, about the effects of motivation, anxiety, and cramming on the learning product. You will learn that some students, who have excellent imaginations, cannot organize their ideas while others, who organize very well, seem to lack imagination. You will learn that weaknesses in some skills do not mean weaknesses in all and that the people whom you envy because of their outstanding skills also envy you because of yours.

With all this talk of "weaknesses," we must not lose sight of "strengths." The lyric, "accentuate the positive," contains an important truth. For the most part, you will improve most in those skills which are already strong, a simple fact of development. On the other hand, it is necessary for you to provide conditions which will bring other skills to a level which will allow you to take advantage of your strengths. For example, A's and B's in math and physics may come easily, but they won't come at all if you are asked to leave school because of E's in English and French.

The first three parts of the book contain materials which are of general interest. Part I (Diagnosis) will help you to learn more about your strengths and weaknesses in skills which contribute to good reading and learning. Part II (How to Learn) presents a detailed explanation of a learning technique that *works.* Part III (How to Read) explains how to increase reading rate, how to improve comprehension and vocabulary, how to read critically, and how to improve spelling. These three parts should be studied *in sequence* for the best results.

The remainder of the book contains materials which are designed to help those with specific problems. If you are having trouble with a certain subject area, you will find helpful suggestions in Part IV (Mastering the Content), including materials in five subject areas for practicing the learning technique described in Part II. Part V provides timed readings to help increase efficiency in reading. Students who have difficulty organizing and writing research papers will find some useful and time-saving ideas in Appendix 2, and additional exercises designed to help in developing your vocabulary are provided in Appendix 3.

The lessons are self-explanatory. Read the directions carefully. Read them again. Then *follow* the directions *exactly*—and you will be on your way toward becoming an efficient learner.

Understanding Directions

Before You Begin. You may think you know how to follow directions. But try taking the following test to discover whether you really do possess this ability.

Read the following directions and follow through with the specified behavior. (Write on the page.) Work rapidly, but accurately. You must finish within *two* minutes.

1. Cross out all the letters in this sentence.

2. If a brother is older than his sister and his sister is older than her brother, what is the least number of children in the family?

3. Write the abbreviation for the shortest month in the year at the end of this sentence.

4. Write the first letter of the last name of the oldest living president of the United States now in office.

5. Is the temperature at zero degrees Fahrenheit or freezing cold higher on a thermometer?

6. If there are 62 weeks in the year, underline the third word in this sentence.

7. If the hour hand of a clock is at 7 and the minute hand at 4, what time is it?

8. Draw a circle around the longest word in this sentence.

9. If awkward and graceful mean the same, write the figure seven after this sentence; if they are the opposite, write twice seven.

If you made any errors, you can be certain that reading directions is a problem area for you. The reasons for it will be discussed in Lesson 7 on Test-Taking Techniques. In the meantime, *read the directions in this book twice* before following them.

Turn to page 10 for the answers.

I

Diagnosis

In the following pages are a series of diagnostic tests.* *Do not open those pages until directed to by your instructor.* It is necessary to follow instructions *exactly* in order to be sure what the results mean. Even a casual preview will invalidate the results. Remember, this is a self-diagnosis. It is for your information, to tell you how your learning apparatus is functioning.

Directions: The following tests must be taken in the order in which they appear. Some are timed tests and others are not. Observe time limits exactly. Scoring is done after all the tests are completed.

1. Learning Style

I-S SCALE

Directions: Your answers to the following questions will enable us to do a better job of instruction. There are no right or wrong answers, for each person's nature is different. Begin at question one and read on at your own rate, circling on this page the choice for each one which is true for you. Do not spend time "pondering" questions. There are three alternatives, usually *Yes, ?, No.* You should mark the middle answer only when it is impossible to say *Yes* or *No. Be sure to answer every question.* (Guess an answer if you are not absolutely sure.)

1. Are you good at repartee, quick retorts, snap judgments?   Yes ? No
2. When you meet someone new, do you usually wait for him to start the conversation?   Yes ? No
3. Are you inclined to express your wishes without much hesitation?   Yes ? No
4. Are you apt to say anything—though you may regret it later—rather than keep still?   Yes ? No
5. Do you think much and speak little?   Yes ? No
6. Do you get very excited by new ideas or new people?   Yes ? No
7. Would you say that you have (a) many friends or (b) just a few close friends?   a ? b
8. Do you often find yourself making comments to a friend while listening to a lecture?   Yes ? No
9. In a discussion with friends, do you think better when you are challenged to defend your position?   Yes ? No
10. Would you rather take an (a) oral test or (b) written test?   a ? b
11. Does it sometimes irritate you to listen to someone who speaks slowly?   Yes ? No
12. Do you recover your composure rapidly after a sudden upset?   Yes ? No
13. Are you inclined to be quick and a little careless in your actions?   Yes ? No

* For information on test validity, see pages 121-22.

14. Would you rather talk than listen in a social situation?   Yes ? No

15. Can you turn out a large amount of work in a short time if you are under pressure?   Yes ? No

16. Do you usually start to work on a new academic subject with great enthusiasm?   Yes ? No

17. Do you hesitate to volunteer remarks in class?   Yes ? No

18. Do you quickly form larger concepts from a few disconnected ideas?   Yes ? No

19. Do you find that your recall of past conversations is more accurate than that of most of your friends?   Yes ? No

20. Do you usually find that you understand a complex situation with a minimum of explanation? (For example, a TV drama turned on late.)   Yes ? No

21. Do you tend to be submissive and apologetic (a) often or (b) seldom?   a ? b

22. Are you likely to complain about your sufferings and hardships?   Yes ? No

23. Do you sometimes have a feeling of anxiety as though you had done something wrong?   Yes ? No

24. Do you often have trouble falling asleep at night?   Yes ? No

25. Do people tell you that you worry unnecessarily?   Yes ? No

26. Do you become discouraged when things go wrong?   Yes ? No

27. Are you usually tired when you get up in the morning?   Yes ? No

28. Do you have nightmares (a) seldom or (b) often?   a ? b

29. Do you usually have a feeling of being able to handle minor crises?   Yes ? No

30. Do you sometimes feel that life would be happier if people only treated you better?   Yes ? No

31. Do you sometimes perspire or feel tense without any reason?   Yes ? No

32. Do you think of yourself sometimes as neglected and unloved?   Yes ? No

33. Would you say that one is wise to be very careful about whom one trusts?   Yes ? No

34. Are your ideas generally well organized and systematic?   Yes ? No

35. Are you frequently troubled by pangs of conscience?   Yes ? No

36. Are you often concerned that you may not have done the right thing in social situations?   Yes ? No

37. Do you feel sometimes that people disapprove of you?   Yes ? No

38. Is the control of your emotions (a) easy or (b) difficult?   a ? b

39. Are you easily discouraged when people make fun of you?   Yes ? No

40. Are there times when you can't help feeling sorry for yourself?   Yes ? No

2. Rate Flexibility

FLEXIBILITY SCALE

Part 1

You will find below several lines of Greek letters. In a box at the side is one of those letters. When your instructor gives a signal, he will begin timing. Your task is to count the exact number of times that letter appears on the page. You may go over each line only *once*. When you finish counting, record the number in the space provided and *record the time which has elapsed.* Then wait before turning to Part 2, page 5.

```
Ψ Β Μ Λ Ι Π Ξ Φ Δ Ε Ζ Γ Η Μ Ω Χ Δ Ι Ο Π Λ Ω Χ
Π Μ Η Φ Ε Δ Ψ Β Μ Κ Λ Π Ι Θ Ο Υ Ε Α Σ Χ Ω Ν Ξ
Ε Ι Κ Λ Ψ Ν Σ Φ Ε Ξ Π Ζ Χ Ψ Σ Α Δ Γ Μ Κ Ξ Τ
Ο Π Λ Μ Β Ψ Ζ Σ Φ Η Κ Ε Τ Θ Ο Π Κ Η Φ Χ Δ Β Μ
Δ Σ Ι Λ Κ Μ Β Ω Φ Γ Ξ Ι Π Χ Σ Φ Ε Ν Ω Ψ Λ Α Ζ
Σ Κ Ι Υ Φ Ψ Χ Μ Π Λ Β Ζ Α Δ Η Ξ Λ Ρ Ε Π Μ Β Ζ
Α Μ Ζ Ψ Φ Ι Θ Κ Ε Γ Μ Σ Π Μ Γ Ε Ξ Κ Λ Ζ Α Δ Κ
Μ Ζ Δ Θ Π Λ Ξ Α Δ Μ Γ Υ Ο Λ Ζ Μ Ψ Φ Ε Λ Π Α Λ
Θ Γ Λ Μ Β Ζ Δ Ε Σ Α Κ Γ Ξ Θ Ν Λ Δ Χ Ω Ψ Ν Β Ζ
Ε Ι Π Α Δ Ξ Γ Κ Λ Χ Β Μ Ζ Α Δ Λ Ι Υ Ρ Π Δ Γ Κ
Ε Λ Α Ψ Ν Μ Ζ Α Δ Ε Ι Ο Π Λ Φ Μ Χ Θ Τ Ε Π Α Ζ
Α Λ Ψ Ν Μ Ζ Χ Ε Ι Π Λ Φ Γ Τ Κ Ν Φ Γ Α Σ Χ Ω Ψ
Π Μ Κ Ι Δ Η Γ Ρ Υ Ε Ι Ζ Χ Ψ Ν Μ Α Σ Δ Η Ο Λ Π
Ψ Ν Β Η Υ Ι Π Α Μ Ν Κ Λ Α Γ Α Ρ Υ Ι Θ Π Λ Μ Ζ Α
Ξ Λ Π Ε Υ Α Ψ Β Λ Κ Ζ Ι Ε Ι Π Β Γ Ξ Δ Ψ Γ Λ Α
Γ Λ £ Ι Ψ Λ Α Λ Δ Ι Ο Π Μ Ψ Ν Χ Ω Ψ Ξ Ι Λ Σ Γ
```

Δ

Number _____
Record your time
_____ Min. _____ Sec.

Part 2

Following are several paragraphs, each preceded by a question. When the signal to start is given, read the question, find the answer given in the paragraph, record it in the space provided, and *go right on* to the next. When you have completed *all five*, look up and record the time which has elapsed.

1. In what part of the brain does CO_2 affect respiration?

Respiration is controlled in three ways: first, by the nervous system, through the respiratory center in the medulla of the brain and through a number of reflexes; second, by chemicals, especially the exciter effect of CO_2 on the activity of the respiratory center; and third, by training. Just as systematic muscular exercise increases muscle size and the heart's volume of blood output per stroke, so also does training affect the rate of breathing. The trained person breathes more slowly and more deeply than the novice, with a net result of increased oxygen, increased energy, and increased work per unit of time. In addition, practice of a muscular process results in a smoother coordination of movements so that less energy, and thereby less oxygen, is required of the trained person per unit of work.

(1) temporal lobe (2) central part (3) reflex center (4) medulla ( )

2. What was the man's comprehension score?

The story is told of an elderly gentleman who was visiting a reading center at an Eastern university. A technician was demonstrating a pacing device which forced attention and rapid reading by bringing a shade down the page at a predetermined rate. Asked whether he wished to try it, he said, "All right. Set it at 200 words a minute. That's my limit."

He struggled to keep ahead of the shade but managed to murmur to himself and to keep his thumbs twirling rhythmically as he read. He scored 70 per cent on a test of comprehension following the exercise. When the technician suggested setting the machine at 300 words a minute, he protested vigorously. "I couldn't possibly do it. Look how poorly I read the article." But he tried it.

(1) 70% (2) 200 (3) 300 (4) does not say ( )

3. What position does the author take on the right of the majority to exercise coercion?

Furthermore, though the law of England on the subject of the press is as autocratic today as it was in the Tudor period, there is little danger of its being actually enforced against political discussion. An exception to this is the possibility of some temporary panic, when fear of revolt drives ministers and judges to irrational acts.

In general, then, it would be surprising if a constitutional government should attempt to control expression of opinion, except when, in doing so, it represents the general intolerance of the public.

Let us suppose, therefore, that the government is entirely representative of the people, and never thinks of coercion unless in agreement with what it conceives to be the popular voice. *But I deny the right of the people to exercise such coercion* either by themselves or by their government.

(1) denies it (2) defends it (3) states that the law upholds it (4) hasn't decided on a position ( )

4. What writer is mentioned?

The rash of "panty raids" on college campuses in recent years has come to the attention of psychologists. What aberration in orderly development could bring about such a display of immaturity, they ask? Or is it, rather, an outburst of libido energy, the beast in man insisting on his due for the last time before culture and taboo drown him in propriety? One college professor has suggested that the panty raid is the twentieth century's answer to Thoreau. But surely this isn't what Thoreau was advocating in his essay on "Civil Disobedience."

(1) Freud (2) Adler (3) Marx (4) Thoreau ( )

5. What is the source of this selection?

The First Hypothesis[1]

But the world of any individual means the part of it with which he comes in contact: his party, his business, his church, his social class. The man to whom it means anything so comprehensive as his own country or his own age may be called "liberal" by comparison. Moreover, his faith in this collective authority is not shaken even when he knows that other ages, countries, churches, classes, and parties have thought, and even now think, the exact reverse.

Yet it is as evident in itself as any amount of argument can make it that ages are no more infallible than individuals. Every age has held many opinions which later ages have considered not only false but absurd. Furthermore, it is as certain that later ages will reject many opinions now general as it is that many, once general, are rejected by the present . . .

(1) *Critical Thinking* (2) *On Liberty* (3) "Defining a Liberal" ( )

[1] Mill, J. S. *On Liberty.*

Record your time_____Min. _____Sec.

3. Vocabulary in Context

CONTEXT TEST

Directions: This is a test of your ability to understand the meaning of a word by the way it is used in a paragraph.

The difficult English words in the article have been replaced by blanks, which can take on any meaning you give them. Read the article rapidly to get the general sense, and then from the choices given below select the word which you think gives the best *meaning* for each blank.

The test is untimed, but go through it quickly. Most students find that the first response is the best. You may refer to the article as much as you wish.

Mark your choices of meaning for the following items in the spaces in the left-hand column.

( ) 1. (a) passionate (b) mournful (c) tired (d) brief

( ) 2. (a) repentently (b) slowly (c) frankly (d) guiltily

( ) 3. (a) to hesitate (b) to shake (c) to decline (d) to submit

( ) 4. (a) lawyers (b) mayors (c) country squires (d) clerks

( ) 5. (a) to educate (b) to conduct (c) to cover (d) to praise

( ) 6. (a) lavishness (b) ease (c) good taste (d) rich foods

( ) 7. (a) to talk glibly (b) to be brilliant (c) to liven up (d) to hurry

( ) 8. (a) free (b) godly (c) profound (d) superficial

( ) 9. (a) humble (b) pearly (c) secluded (d) sensible

( ) 10. (a) followers (b) mimics (c) subjects (d) grandsons

( ) 11. (a) outcome (b) size (c) loudness (d) clarity

( ) 12. (a) relief (b) disaster (c) illness (d) weakness

( ) 13. (a) momentarily (b) dimly (c) intellectually (d) second hand

( ) 14. (a) bony (b) enormous (c) circular (d) adequate

( ) 15. (a) stationary (b) talkative (c) athletic (d) slow

( ) 16. (a) round (b) large (c) classic (d) strong

( ) 17. (a) dejectedly (b) offensively (c) passively (d) heavily

( ) 18. (a) great force (b) urgent need (c) human interest (d) literature

( ) 19. (a) sequence (b) complexity (c) importance (d) readability

( ) 20. (a) fear (b) outline (c) agitation (d) consistency

( ) 21. (a) to exhibit (b) to produce (c) to continue (d) to retract

( ) 22. (a) developing (b) mimicking (c) soothing (d) competing

( ) 23. (a) justifiably (b) reasonably (c) always (d) undeniably

( ) 24. (a) solid (b) lazy (c) lenient (d) independent

( ) 25. (a) wisdom (b) wrangling (c) practice (d) bias

( ) 26. (a) endorsement (b) prestige (c) prediction (d) blueprint

( ) 27. (a) cereal (b) earthen (c) vast (d) metal

( ) 28. (a) bitter (b) whining (c) sarcastic (d) serious

( ) 29. (a) accusation (b) tiredness (c) robbery (d) hatred

( ) 30. (a) lovable (b) clear-sighted (c) sarcastic (d) one-sided

( ) 31. (a) presumptuousness (b) humorousness (c) haughtiness (d) sleepiness

Wouter Van Twiller, a Careful Doubter

The historian who writes the history of his native land is deserving of sympathy. He is in need of this understanding since he discovers that he cannot recall the most prosperous and blissful eras without a __1__ sigh at the reflection that the good old days are gone forever! As for me, I will not attempt to deceive you; let me __2__ confess that I cannot look back on the happier days of our city without great dejection of spirit. I am cautious of jumping into its history because I know the state of melancholy I will be subjected to. Thus it is that with __3__ hand I draw back the curtain of history that veils our beloved ancestors. For these are the men who have made our history notable and who deserve our very deepest respect and humility.

Having begun, however, haltingly, let me now proceed to tell you about Wouter Van Twiller, the first governor of New Amsterdam, who was sent in 1629 by the West India Company to manage the affairs of this thriving colony, most notable for keeping full the treasuries of Holland. The renowned Van Twiller was descended from a long line of Dutch __4__ who had one after the other dozed away their lives and grown fat upon their magistrates' seats back in Rotterdam and other Dutch cities; and who had __5__ themselves with such notable __6__ that there is no known scandal in all their careers. In fact, despite all their wisdom, they have scarcely been heard of! There are two opposite types of men who become famous: one, the __7__, who talk faster than they think and acquire the reputation of men of quick wits; the other, who hold their tongues and don't think at all, and like the owl, the stupidest of birds, these come to be mistakenly considered perfect examples of __8__ thinkers.

These by the way are casual remarks, which I would not for the universe have it thought I apply to Governor Van Twiller. It is true that he was a withdrawn, __9__ oyster of a man and rarely spoke, except in monosyllables; but then it was also noted that he seldom said a foolish thing. With all his reflective habits, he never made up his mind on a subject. His __10__, those young men who aspired one day to resemble

Wouter, accounted for this by the astonishing __11__ of his ideas. He conceived every subject on so grand a scale, they said, that he had not room in his head to turn it over and examine both sides of it. (This is a __12__ which all men experience, but for most of us it comes when we are just about to fall asleep.) In short, it might be said in all seriousness that Wouter Van Twiller perceived the world about him only __13__.

Wouter's person was as distinctive as his habits. He was exactly five feet six inches tall, and six feet five inches in circumference. His head was a perfect sphere, and of __14__ dimensions; similarly, his body was surprisingly large at the bottom, and this indeed suited his __15__ habits since he made it clear that he was averse to walking and preferred to sit. His legs were short, but sturdy enough to support his __16__ frame. His face, that reflection of the mind, presented a vast expanse uninterrupted by those lines and angles which we normally call expression.

The governor's day was well regulated. He took his four stated meals, appropriating exactly one hour to each; he smoked and doubted eight hours; and he slept the remaining twelve. He was a true philosopher, for his mind was either quietly elevated above or __17__ settled below the cares and __18__ of this world. Nay, it has even been said that when any problem of some length, difficulty, or __19__ was on the carpet, the renowned Wouter would shut his eyes and doubt for a full two hours; and at such times the internal __20__ of his mind was made clear. This inner turmoil was __21__ by certain regular snore-like sounds, which his followers declared were merely the noises of conflict made by his __22__ doubts and opinions as they strove to come to the surface.

I have been very anxious to describe fully the character and habits of Wouter Van Twiller, almost as a playwright would, because Wouter was not only the first, but also the best governor New Amsterdam ever had. Throughout the whole of his career not one offender was brought to punishment; and this is __23__ the sign of a merciful and __24__ ruler. Of his kindness and fairness there can be no question. Wouter was not a stupid man. In fact, the very outset of his career as governor was distinguished by an example of legal __25__ which gave a flattering __26__ of the wise and lenient administration which he would handle throughout his term of office. On this occasion, Wouter was eating his enormous breakfast from a __27__ bowl, when he was interrupted by one Wandle Schoonhavoen, who complained sourly that Berent Bleecker owed him money. Wandle's ferocious appearance and __28__ tone of voice made it clear that he was serious in his __29__ of Berent. Whereupon Governor Van Twiller, after carefully finishing his meal, summoned said Berent Bleecker and had the two men produce their account books. The __30__ Wouter took the books one after the other, and having poised them on his hands and counted their pages, fell at once into a very great doubt. A half-hour later, with that usual __31__ with which you are already familiar, Wouter announced groggily that it was found that one book was just as heavy and had just as many pages as the other; therefore it was the final opinion of the court that the accounts were equally balanced; and therefore, Wandle should give Berent a receipt, Berent should give Wandle a receipt, and the constable should pay the costs.

Page 6 lists all the numbered spaces above, in the same order. There are four multiple-choice alternatives for each. Choose the meaning which you think best fits and mark your choice in the answer space. Remember, you may refer to the story as much as you wish, but work rapidly.

4. Reading Rate and Comprehension

READING TEST

Directions: This is a measure of your ability to read difficult material silently under timed conditions. Do not begin reading until your instructor gives you the signal to start. Read at a steady rate, being sure you understand what you read. When you finish the selection, record your time in the space provided. Then answer the questions.

J. S. Mill: "On Liberty"
Introduction*

The time is past, it is hoped, when "liberty of the press" needs any defense as a security against corrupt or tyrannical government. It is no longer necessary to argue that a legislature that does not represent the common interest should not be allowed to determine what doctrines or what arguments the people should be allowed to hear.

Other writers have made this point so well that it needs little attention here. Furthermore, though the law of England on the subject of the press is as autocratic today as it was in the Tudor period, there is little danger of its being actually enforced against political discussion. An exception to this is the possibility of some temporary panic, when fear of revolt drives ministers and judges to irrational acts.

In general, then, it would be surprising if a constitutional government should attempt to control expression of opinion, except when, in doing so, it represents the general intolerance of the public.

Let us suppose, therefore, that the government is entirely representative of the people, and never thinks of force or coercion unless in agreement with what is

* Adapted.

conceived to be the popular voice. But I deny the right of the people to exercise such coercion either by themselves or by their government.

The power itself is unlawful. The best government has no more right to it than the worst. It is as evil, or more evil, when exerted in accordance with public opinion. If all mankind minus one were of one opinion, and only one person were of the contrary opinion, mankind would be no more justified in silencing that one person than he, if in power, would be justified in silencing mankind.

If an opinion were a personal possession of no value except to the owner, if to be deprived of enjoying it were only a private injury, it would make a difference only to the few involved. But the singular evil of silencing the expression of opinion is that it is larceny against the human race: not only existing generations but posterity as well; not only those who hold the opinion but, still more, those who disagree.

Why? If the opinion is right, they are deprived of the chance of exchanging error for truth; if it is wrong, they lose almost as great a benefit, the clearer perception and more emphatic impression of truth produced by its collision with error.

We can never be sure that the opinion we are trying to stifle is a false opinion. It may possibly be true. Of course those who desire to suppress it deny "its truth," but they are not infallible. They *could* be wrong. They have no authority to decide the question for all mankind and exclude every other person from the opportunity of judging.

To refuse a hearing to an opinion, because they are sure it is false, is to assume that their certainty is the same thing as absolute certainty. All silencing of discussion is an assumption of infallibility. Condemning it rests on this common argument, no worse for being common.

Unfortunately for the good sense of mankind, the fact of their fallibility seldom lessens their certainty in practical judgments. While everyone well knows himself to be fallible, few think it necessary to take any precautions against their own fallibility. Few admit the possibility that an opinion, of which they feel very certain, may be one of the examples of the error to which they admit themselves liable.

Absolute princes, who are accustomed to unlimited deference, usually feel this complete confidence in their own opinions on nearly all subjects. People more happily situated, who sometimes hear their opinions disputed, are used to being set right when they are wrong. Nevertheless, they place the same unlimited reliance on those of their opinions which are shared by those around them. In proportion to a man's lack of confidence in his own judgment, he usually relies with

implicit trust on the infallibility of "the world" in general.

But the world of any individual means the part of it with which he comes in contact: his party, his business, his church, his social class. The man to whom it means anything so comprehensive as his own country or his own age may be called "liberal" by comparison. Moreover, his faith in this collective authority is not shaken even when he knows that other ages, countries, churches, classes, and parties have thought, and even now think, the exact reverse.

Yet it is as evident in itself as any amount of argument can make it that ages are no more infallible than individuals. Every age has held many opinions which later ages have considered not only false but absurd. Furthermore, it is as certain that later ages will reject many opinions now general as it is that many, once general, are rejected by the present.

When we consider the number of eminent men of past generations who held erroneous beliefs, how is it that there is on the whole a preponderance of rational opinions and conduct? It is because man is capable of correcting his mistakes by discussion and experience. Not by experience alone. There must be discussion to show how experience is to be interpreted.

Wrong opinions gradually yield to fact and argument. But facts and arguments, to produce any effects on the mind, must be brought before it.

Record your time_____Min. _____Sec.

COMPREHENSION

Answer the following questions without referring to the essay. In the spaces provided, record the letter corresponding to the appropriate choice.

_____ 1. Expression of opinion should be allowed
    a. when there are facts supporting each position
    b. when there is no danger of an uprising
    c. when the government is expressing the will of the people by allowing discussion
    d. at all times

_____ 2. The autocratic British laws concerning the press will be enforced
    a. whenever they are violated
    b. when the press criticizes the majority opinion
    c. when judges fear an uprising
    d. never

_____ 3. A second reason given for allowing expression of opinion is
    a. judges sometimes make mistakes
    b. truth is more striking when contrasted with error

c. historically, free speech has shown its value
d. none of these

_____ 4. Which of the following is implied in the selection?
   a. the rights of man bear no relation to the rights of government
   b. it is of the greatest importance that we agree on what is fact and what is opinion
   c. the minority must not be allowed to dominate the majority
   d. by depriving others we may deprive ourselves

_____ 5. How best could this passage be described?
   a. explanation
   b. description
   c. illustration
   d. argumentation

_____ 6. The selection implies that one proper method for resisting a corrupt legislature is
   a. constitutional government
   b. insurrection
   c. a free press
   d. fearless judges

_____ 7. It can be assumed that Mill would take this position on minority groups. They should
   a. be allowed to sell their ideas
   b. be allowed expression only when the ideas will not hurt others
   c. be given a fair hearing before qualified persons who would evaluate their ideas
   d. think as they like, keep their ideas to themselves, and act in accordance with majority decision

_____ 8. It may be concluded that Mill believes
   a. the public is intolerant
   b. it is better to allow people to hold erroneous opinions than to teach them correct ones
   c. the public should have an opportunity to weigh the evidence before forming its opinions
   d. the government is not the caretaker of individual rights

_____ 9. To refuse to let an opinion have a hearing is to assume that
   a. it is false
   b. we cannot possibly be wrong
   c. experience alone is sufficient for knowing truth
   d. agreement by the majority determines what is true or false

_____ 10. Since most men know they are fallible
   a. the world has a preponderance of rational beliefs

b. they do not commit themselves to definite opinions
   c. they discuss their beliefs with others
   d. they depend on what they believe to be the infallibility of the world

_____ 11. When people realize that other ages have thought the opposite of their beliefs, they
   a. continue to hold their beliefs
   b. modify their beliefs accordingly
   c. reconsider their position at the least
   d. bolster their confidence by asking their friends' opinions

_____ 12. Mill assumes that
   a. most men are incapable of acting rationally
   b. his ideas on liberty are the only correct ones
   c. most of the ideas and conduct of the world are satisfactory
   d. the majority is more likely to be correct than is the individual

_____ 13. The author would describe a liberal man as one who
   a. considers himself subject to error
   b. arrives at a belief through experience and discussion
   c. is in contact with contemporary and historical world events
   d. allows others to think as they wish

_____ 14. Mill has made a plea for an important ingredient of the philosophic attitude. It is
   a. clear thinking
   b. historical perspective
   c. caution
   d. the search for absolute truths

_____ 15. The bulk of the selection is devoted to
   a. how we can know the truth
   b. methods for avoiding error
   c. the value of having a broad view
   d. how man manages to ignore his fallibility

Scoring the Tests

On page 12 is a Diagnostic Chart. To use it, you must first score each test, then compare your score with those of a "norm group" (a sample of people representing scores from the lowest to the highest; most of them are average). The comparison will show how you rank in a representative population, ranked from 1 to 99, from lowest to highest.

Determine your rank by drawing a circle around your score in the appropriate vertical column. Then look across at the ranks to the left of the chart. By connecting the circles in each column, you will produce a profile of scores. We will discuss the meaning of the profiles later.

1. Learning Style. On this page you will find the Key for I-S (Impulsivity-Stability) Scale. The first twenty items measure impulsivity, while items 21 through 40 measure stability. Count all the agreements between your responses and the Key up to item 20 and record this number.

Begin counting over again at item 21. Again, record your total.

Now write in your I and S scores where indicated on the Diagnostic Chart and then, chart them. Note also the figure labeled "Learning Style." The I score is indicated on the horizontal line and the S score on the vertical. To chart your position, draw lines at a 90° angle through each position. The point of intersection is your placement. E.g:

The meaning of your scores will be explained in the section "Interpreting Tests."

2. Flexibility Scale. Turn to page 4, where you recorded your time for Part 1. At the end of the five paragraphs is another time score for Part 2.

1. Transform each score into seconds.
2. Score 1 is your base rate of reading when thoroughness is required. Indicate it on the Diagnostic Chart under *Speed* (Sp).
3. Score 2 is your "selective reading" or skimming rate. Determine your Flexibility Ratio (FR) as follows:

$$\frac{Score\ 1}{Score\ 2} = FR;\ \frac{20}{40} = .50$$

In general, the higher the ratio, the greater the flexibility. For example, with a base rate or Score 1 of 20 and a skimming rate or Score 2 of 60, the resulting FR of .33 reflects less flexibility than the .50 in the example.

4. Indicate your ratio on the Diagnostic Chart (FR). See Key on this page for answers.

3. Context Test. This is a measure of your ability to use the story content to determine the meanings of words. Use Key (this page) to determine the number of items you have answered correctly. Indicate your score on the Diagnostic Chart.

4. Reading Test. This is a measure of your reading ability on difficult material under timed conditions.

There are two scores, *Rate of Reading,* expressed as the average number of words read per minute, and *Comprehension.* See Key on this page.

KEY

(Page 2)

1. A straight line drawn through the sentence is just as correct as short lines through each letter, and can be accomplished more quickly.
2. Three
3. Feb.
4. (Current President)
5. Freezing
6. There are 52 weeks in a year.
7. 7:20
8. The word is "sentence."
9. 14 or "twice seven"

I-S Scale
(Page 3)

1. Yes 2. No 3. Yes 4. Yes 5. No 6. Yes 7. a 8. Yes 9. Yes 10. a 11. Yes 12. Yes 13. Yes 14. Yes 15. Yes 16. Yes 17. No 18. Yes 19. No 20. Yes

Total (Impulsivity Score) _____

21. b 22. No 23. No 24. No 25. No 26. No 27. No 28. a 29. Yes 30. No 31. No 32. No 33. No 34. Yes 35. No 36. No 37. No 38. a 39. No 40. No

Total (Stability Score) _____

Flexibility Scale

Part 1 (Page 4)

twenty

Part 2 (Page 5)

1. 4 2. 1 3. 1 4. 4 5. 2

Context Test
(Page 6)

1. b 2. c 3. a 4. b 5. b 6. c 7. a 8. c 9. c 10. a 11. b 12. d 13. b 14. b 15. a 16. b 17. c 18. b 19. b 20. c 21. a 22. d 23. d 24. c 25. a 26. c 27. c 28. a 29. a 30. b 31. d

Total (Vocabulary Score) _____

Reading Test
(Page 8)

1. d 2. c 3. b 4. d 5. d 6. c 7. a 8. c 9. b 10. d 11. a 12. c 13. c 14. c 15. d

Total (Comprehension Score) _____

Rate Chart
(Page 7)

min: sec	wpm	min: sec	wmp
0:30	2000	0:50	1200
0:40	1500	1:00	1000

Rate Chart (Cont.)
(*Page 7*)

min: sec	wpm	min: sec	wpm
1:10	856	4:40	214
1:20	750	4:50	207
1:30	666	5:00	200
1:40	600	5:10	193
1:50	545	5:20	187
2:00	500	5:30	182
2:10	461	5:40	176
2:20	428	5:50	171
2:30	400	6:00	166
2:40	375	6:10	162
2:50	353	6:20	158
3:00	333	6:30	154
3:10	316	6:40	151
3:20	300	6:50	147
3:30	286	7:00	143
3:40	273	7:10	139
3:50	261	7:20	136
4:00	250	7:30	133
4:10	240	7:40	130
4:20	231	7:50	127
4:30	222	8:00	125

Interpreting the Tests

Your test results are not entirely self-explanatory. There are two ways in which they can be interpreted, each way yielding unique information. The first method might be called *interpretation by single scores;* the second method is generally called *profile analysis:* it treats the profile or pattern of scores.

Single-Score Interpretation

Learning Style. The *I-S Scale* yields two scores which research has shown to be related to the manner in which students learn. The distribution of scores on the first twenty items, the *I Scale,* is shown in the graph. People who score high (a rank of 80 or above) tend to be friendly, changeable, quick thinking and quick acting to the point of being *impulsive.* The higher the score, the greater the tendency toward impulsivity.

People who score low (a rank of 20 or below) tend to be reserved, conservative, conscientious, and steady to the point of being *constricted* in their thinking. Once again, the lower the score, the greater the tendency toward constriction in thinking.

Items 21 to 40 constitute the S Scale. People who score high (a rank of 80 or above) tend to be relatively free of upsetting worries and tend to stand up well in stressful situations such as examinations. Those who score low (20 or below) tend to worry a good deal, even when things are going well.

Predictions about learning style may be made most safely when both the I and the S scores are treated

simultaneously. The two ways of looking at personality are unrelated, i.e., an extreme score on one dimension tells us nothing about what the other score will be. Therefore, the two scales can be placed at right angles to each other. Now, one can determine in which quadrant he places I (high in I and S), II (low in I and high in S), III (low in both I and S), or IV (high in I and low in S). *The following descriptions apply only to people who are extreme on both scales.*

I. This person's impulsivity is illustrated by his difficulty in focusing on one idea. Thus, his themes tend to be rich in ideas but poor in structure. Inadequate attention to details leads to difficulty in understanding examination questions: important words are missed; the reader leaps to conclusions too easily. Memory for foreign language and for formulae tends to be poor.

II. Constricted thinking is illustrated by the sparse content of themes. One idea may be spelled out at length, but in a pedestrian way. A less common problem of the constricted thinker is a tendency to focus only on details so that the important generalizations are missed. Reading also tends to be slow with undue attention to single words, and inadequate comprehension of thematic ideas.

III. The worries of this individual make concentration difficult. There is also a tendency for blaming his troubles on others, especially his instructors. Thus, problems with interpersonal relations commonly intensify a poor academic adjustment.

IV. When tension is added to impulsivity, the result is often a disorganized, dependent person who is unable to tolerate stress. Examination panic is common among such individuals. Both attention to and memory for details are seriously deficient. On the positive side, this person tends to produce original ideas easily.

Flexibility Scale: Speed. Efficient reading depends partly upon efficient control of the eyes and upon the effective operation of a part of the brain called the visual reception area. The ability to see small differences in visual forms rapidly and accurately we shall call perceptual speed. Some people have difficulty with this task because of poor vision. Others have trouble with muscle control so that the eyes "jump" from one line to another involuntarily and often without the reader's awareness. The mature reader has many rates of reading. He shifts upward or downward, reads intensively or selectively, depending upon his purpose. The counting of the Δ's requires intensive searching whereas the skimming test rewards a thinking reader. A low ratio indicates a slowness to shift rates when the purpose changes. A high ratio is desirable.

Inflexibility may result from a fixed habit of word-by-word reading, from unfamiliarity with efficient techniques, and/or from failure to develop skill in such techniques.

Context Vocabulary. Well-read people report that their vocabularies are increased significantly simply by reading. A sizeable proportion of these people seldom use a dictionary. They learn new words simply by observing the way in which the words are used from one context or passage to another. This ability to *infer* meanings from the context results from sensitivity to the clues to meaning, from relatively rapid reading, and from extensive reading.

Reading Test. The material in this text is similar to that read in college. The two scores, rate and comprehension, place a premium on rapid *thinking* and the discovery of the organization of ideas. Organized ideas are more easily remembered than are those which occur in a serial order. The reader is required not only to understand the essay but to remember its points long enough to take the test.

DIAGNOSTIC CHART

	Learning Style		Flexibility		Reading Skill			
	I	S	Sp	FR	Voc.	Comp.	Rate	
90-	15	16	35	.47	27	11	324	-90
80-	14	14	40	.38	25	10	286	-80
70-	12	13	45	.32	24	9	261	-70
60-	11	12	50	.28	22	8	240	-60
50-	10	11	55	.25	21	7	231	-50
40-	9	9	60	.23	19	6	222	-40
30-	8	8	65	.21	17		207	-30
20-	7	6	70	.19	15	5	193	-20
10-	6	5	90	.16	12	4	167	-10

LEARNING STYLE

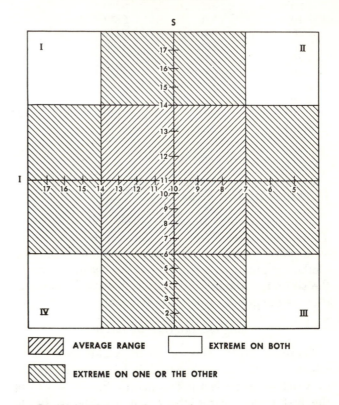

VZZZ AVERAGE RANGE □ EXTREME ON BOTH

XXXX EXTREME ON ONE OR THE OTHER

Interpretation by Profile Analysis

Single scores sometimes take on new meaning when they are examined in the light of other scores. For example, low comprehension may indicate careless reading if it is accompanied by a high rate. But if the vocabulary score is low also, poor comprehension may indicate a deficiency in scholastic aptitude.

Experience with combinations of scores such as these has led to the discovery of certain common problems. These problems have been investigated with respect to their causes, their relationship to achievement, appropriate corrective procedures, and the like. Read the following charts and descriptions keeping your own profile in mind.

pendently.) This reader tends to pay unnecessarily close attention to details. He is conscientious to the extent that he is unable to handle the volume of work required of a college student. Furthermore, important ideas become lost in the maze of details. The problem requires the development of skill in selective reading, the courage to dismiss the trivial.

Profile A

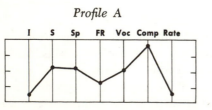

Low scores indicate constriction (I) and slow reading (Rate). Comprehension tends to be high and flexibility somewhat low. (The other scores seem to vary inde-

Profile B

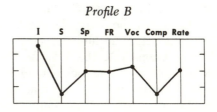

An extreme impulsivity (I) combined with tension (S) leads to inability to focus on ideas, mind-wandering, and poor comprehension. A slow rate intensifies the problem: an active mind, not required to apprehend ideas rapidly, will find other things to keep it busy. An increase in rate of reading tends to reduce the problem.

Profile C

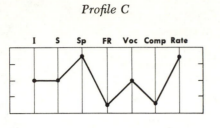

Unusual perceptual speed (Sp), rigidly adhered to (FR), results in a high rate and low comprehension.

This individual tends to be careless, particularly on those materials requiring intensive reading (the physical and biological sciences, directions, examination questions). Comprehension is increased by the formulation of specific questions to be answered and by practice in determining the structure of extended passages.

Other Problems. The above profiles illustrate common difficulties of students. Less common ones will be discussed within the text along with procedures designed to help you improve your strengths.

Your efforts to this point have been aimed toward understanding the present status of your skills. It is time, now, for the next step: learning how to learn.

Part Two concerns the crux of your academic life, successful learning. Academic achievement is crucial for a very simple reason: if you cannot pass courses, you cannot stay in college.

This is not to imply that passing courses is equivalent to becoming educated. You will do a good deal of learning which will never be measured, both academic and social learning. Bull sessions, extracurricular activities, "belonging to" a prep school or college, learning to know other young adults, their beliefs, their hopes, their personality characteristics, in order better to know yourself—this kind of learning is also part of becoming educated.

During the first year, you must prove yourself; you must demonstrate the ability to ingest and digest great masses of information. Not surprisingly, many potentially capable students fail to make the grade—or grades—for reasons which will be made clear later. For a large proportion of students, this section will make the difference between failing or passing, between a low C and a high B, between studying twenty hours a week for C's and D's and studying ten hours a week for B's and A's. In short, this section is designed to help you become a "professional learner" by providing you with a systematic learning procedure.

LESSON 1

Read this essay to become acquainted with the outward appearance of Survey Q4R,[1] a learning system. You will be asked questions about its outward appearance and about its inner parts and how they work. Read rapidly, *but carefully*.

II

How to Learn

How to Be Brilliant with Limited Resources

Most people think that the straight-A man is brilliant and that the straight-E man is stupid. It's not necessarily true. While there aren't many straight-A men who are stupid, there is a sizeable number of straight-E ones who are brilliant, or potentially so. Achievement in college is only partly a matter of capacity. It is, to a large extent, a matter of method. The situation is different from that in high school.

High schools have a wide range of talent. Thus the brightest may sometimes loaf and do well. But colleges *select* their students in such a way that the range of talent is restricted. They take great care to admit only those whom they feel sure will succeed. As a result, a

[1] Adapted from a study procedure first described by Francis P. Robinson in *Effective Study*, New York: Harper & Brothers, 1946.

freshman class is relatively homogeneous or similar with respect to ability. Differences in achievement now depend largely upon learning skill, upon knowing how to learn.

There is strong evidence that learning occurs by lawful means. That is, the mind's operation during the learning process follows certain rules. By cooperating with his brain, the student can direct it to a large extent, just as one would drive a car. For example, if it were necessary to memorize a number like 12,481,-632, he would look first for a pattern in the numbers, since the mind prefers a pattern to a disorganized list. In this case, there is a pattern, 1-2-4-8-16-32, each number being double the previous one, and there will be no difficulty remembering the individual numbers.

Of course, all patterns are not so obvious as this one. The pattern or organization of a chapter, for example, is not apparent from the title. It is necessary to look over the whole chapter to discover its pattern or the way in which its main ideas are related, just as it is necessary to see all the digits, 12481632, in order to discover the principle by which they are organized. The "looking over" is called a survey.

The survey helps the students to avoid "missing the forest for the trees." It helps him to see the whole picture before becoming involved with the parts of which it is composed. In that way, the parts take on extra meaning. They can be remembered easily. For example, what part is missing here? 12—81632. Obviously the four is missing. When the principle is known, the part or detail can be reproduced.

The second step in the learning procedure is best illustrated by observing the typical student's attack on a chapter. First he determines the length. "Hm-m. 30 pages." Then he starts with page one and reads, page by page, occasionally turning to the end to see how many pages remain. Finally finished, he sighs and closes the book. Now ask him, "What was it about?" He'll say, "Oh—let's see. About 30 pages."

If he had started by saying, "I wonder how many pictures there are," he would be able to report the number. If he had asked, "What conditions made it possible for Napoleon to rise to power?" he would be able to report that, too. Unfortunately, students seldom know what they're to learn, thus they learn very little. Moral: raise questions. How to raise the right questions will be discussed later.

The next step is obvious. *Read* to answer the question: read selectively, judiciously, rapidly. Whatever answers your question is important. Whatever is tangential to the question is less important or unimportant.

Now that you have found the answer, you are ready for the most important step. Underline? *No! Learn it!* Underlining is a sophisticated method of self-decep-

tion. You think you will return to those sentences and learn them. But when the exam comes, you may look at a question and exclaim, "Oh, I know that. I underlined it. It's on page 435—at the top of the page—what was it now?" No answer.

Get up your courage. It's not so hard. Go ahead and *learn it* by *Reciting*, in your own words.

Next, *"Rite."* Reduce both the question and the answer to a very few cue words. Reduce further by using abbreviations. Thus, the recitation and notes on a section entitled *Causes of Economic Depressions* come out:

Recitation	"Rite"
What are the causes of depressions?	Cau. dep.?
1. Inflation or cheap money	1. ch. mon.
2. Over-speculation, i.e., buying more on margin than one can cover by present assets, if necessary	2. Ov-spec. (marg.)
3. Corporations sell more stock than their assets warrant (called "watered stock")	3. Wat. st.

The last step reduces any need for cramming. It anticipates the rapid forgetting so characteristic of academic learning. As soon as the chapter is finished, close your book, pick up your notes, and *Review.* Ask the question and try to answer from memory. A second review is necessary at the end of several chapters. Reasons for it will be discussed later.

There it is. Survey — Question — Read — Recite — "Rite" — Review. By following this procedure you may be able to duplicate Linda's feat. She was about to leave school after five weeks because her grade report showed three D's and one E. She followed these steps and finished the semester with four B's. Mark was afraid that academic probation, caused by E's in Psychology and Naval Science, would keep him from pitching on the university team. He used SQ4R and ended the season with a batting average of .073, a won-lost record of 0-7, an earned run average of 8.70, a B in Naval Science, and an A in Psychology.

Stop!

Record time_____Min. _____Sec.

Determine rate by referring to the Rate Chart, page 133.

About the Comprehension Test. It is not a simple task to determine one's understanding of written material. You took a "short answer" test of comprehension in the diagnostic section of this book. Comprehension, as defined by that test, means both understanding of materials and *short-term memory*. That is, it is necessary that you be able to remember the details of the story in order to achieve an adequate comprehension score. As you will learn later, materials which are *well* understood tend to be remembered well.

To reduce the importance of short-term memory in the comprehension tests, a new kind of test has been developed and studied scientifically. It presents key sentences from the essay with one or two words left out. If the *idea* of the paragraph from which the sentence comes has been *understood,* the reader will be able to fill the blank with a word which makes sense.

Therefore, when reading the essays, *expend your effort in following the ideas* rather than in memorizing details. For all essays, a score of 70% is considered practicable. A perfect score will indicate overly-perfectionistic reading. A score lower than 70% indicates inadequate effort to understand.

EXERCISES

COMPREHENSION

While there aren't many straight (1) _____ men who are stupid, there is a sizeable number of straight (2) _____ ones who are brilliant, or potentially so. Achievement in college is only partly a matter of (3) _____. . . . There is strong evidence that learning occurs by (4) _____ means. . . . The "looking over" is called a (5) _____. Whatever answers your question is (6) _____. . . . The last step reduces any need for cramming. It anticipates the rapid (7) _____ so characteristic of academic learning.

Now check your answers against the Key, page 133.

APPLICATION

(The exercises appearing under this heading will provide a more complete understanding of the material discussed in the essay.)

SQ4R Estimate

Below are listed nine worthwhile activities. Consider each carefully and decide which step of the study procedure it illustrates. Write your estimate on the line at the right: *Survey–Question–Read–Recite–"Rite"–Review*. (A score of 5 is average; 7 is very good; 9 is superior.)

1. Stand near the sidelines at a freshman mixer to look over the talent. _____
2. Spend two minutes at the end of a lecture looking through notes you have taken. _____
3. Two nights before a test, spend a half hour predicting what will be on the test. _____
4. After reading over the questions on an exam, jot down the first ideas that come to mind on each question. _____
5. Look at the English equivalent of a French word on a word card, turn it over and try to repeat both words. _____
6. Listen to the instructor's explanation of an obscure point in the text. _____
7. Ask your roommate to hear you name the principal parts of the circulatory system. _____
8. Read the course descriptions in a college catalogue before making up your schedule. _____
9. Read over all the questions before starting a test to locate the easy and difficult items. _____

Check your estimate against the Key, page 133.

READING

The Proof of the Method

The Survey Q4R study method, about which you have just read, is a logical, step-by-step procedure for reading and learning an assignment. You will undoubtedly agree that it appears to be a sound, systematic, and efficient method. In other words, it looks good on paper. But you're probably also asking yourself, "Does it really work?" This is, of course, an important question, for just as "the proof of the pudding is in the eating," so is the proof of any study technique to be found in the degree to which it produces the desired results in a real situation.

How well does SQ4R work? A partial answer to this question is provided by the results of experiments in which various parts of the method were tested in actual reading situations. For example, one study revealed that students who surveyed an assignment before reading it read the material 24 per cent faster than students who read without first surveying. Of even greater importance was the finding that students who were given a list of questions to read *before* reading the assignment did a better job on tests taken immediately after completing the assignment than did students who had no previous questions. The test in this case consisted of new items as well as items included in the original list of questions. These same students, incidentally, showed an even greater superiority when they were retested two weeks later, a fact which provides strong evidence for the long-term value of formulating questions *before* reading an assignment.

Similar experiments have been carried out in order to determine the effectiveness of taking "cue notes" during reading. These studies indicated that the first two or three times this technique was tried the results were only slightly superior to those achieved by students who merely read without taking cue notes. After about a month's practice, however, the people in the note-taking group proved to be several times more effective than their non-note taking colleagues in their ability to comprehend, organize, *and remember* the assigned material. It seems clear, then, that it requires some practice in order to make the kind of note-taking involved in SQ4R really work, but the greatly improved performance resulting from skillful note-taking is certainly worth the few weeks' practice required.

The many studies of forgetting over a period of time have consistently produced the same discouraging results: one day after reading an assignment the average student has forgotten 40 or 50 per cent of what he had originally learned; two weeks later he has forgotten about 80 per cent of the material! This information helps to explain (but not to solve) the problem that so many of us have of forgetting much of the material we thought we knew after reading an assignment. The figures quoted above become even more discouraging when we remember that the average student may remember about 75 per cent of the chapter immediately after completing it. If he then forgets 80 per cent of this over a two-week period, simple arithmetic reveals the unhappy fact that his comprehension of an assignment two weeks after reading it will be approximately 15 per cent! No wonder it is so often necessary to "learn everything over again" a few days before the mid-term exam!

Experiments to ascertain the effectiveness of the recitation and review steps of SQ4R have provided rather striking support for their value in preventing the amount of forgetting that normally occurs. For example, students who followed a single reading of the assignment with an *immediate* recitation-review forgot only 20 per cent of the material in a two-week period, while those who read the assignment once with *no* recitation forgot 80 per cent. Even more important in the long run is the finding that students who follow a single reading with no recitation or review remember as little as 15 per cent after a two-month period, while those who review immediately after reading, and once every week or so thereafter, remember about 85 per cent. When we consider that these weekly reviews involve only about 10 minutes each, it becomes quite clear that the kind of review involved in SQ4R not only cuts forgetting to a minimum, but also that it is extremely efficient in terms of the amount of time required. The biggest time saving, of course, comes just before an exam. It obviously takes less time and effort to relearn 15 per cent of the material covered by an exam than it does to relearn 85 per cent!

It must be remembered that the encouraging results reported above were observed when only certain parts of the SQ4R procedure were used. Even more happy results along the same line are achieved when the whole method is employed. The most conclusive evidence for the effectiveness of SQ4R is not to be found in controlled experiments, however, but rather in the reports of hundreds of "D" students who became "B" and "A" students—and who did it with less expenditure of time—after they learned how to "SQ4R their way" through their assignments.

Still not convinced? Learn how to SQ4R by going through the next five lessons, and you will be!

LESSON 2

Survey

The style of this essay is simple, "breezy," fast-moving—so much so that you can easily miss the important ideas. Note well the title, and let it direct your attention while you read. Any point concerning *why* we survey and *how* it should be done is important.

Why Survey? And How?

You enter a half-filled bus. You face the rear. In doing so your eyes sweep the seats on your right. Then they jump the aisle, sweep the left. Three empty seats. Two on the right. One on the left. College boy next to one on left. Old man next to one on right. Attractive coed alone on right behind old man. You've now selected your seat. You sit on the left, if female, on the right behind the old man, if male. Good trip ahead you think, as you sink happily into your seat.

You have just seated yourself in a restaurant with your new date. You are a male. She is a female. You're glad that's the way it is. The waitress approaches with a pleasant smile and a friendly "good evening." She leaves two menus and departs. Slowly, almost casually, you reach for and pick up your menu. Then you open it smoothly. Now your eyes race over it. On the left— sandwiches, drinks, desserts. On the right—appetizers and dinners. You fasten your gaze on the right. Ignoring the food offerings, your eyes race down the column of figures preceded by dollar signs. Sliding rapidly past the 3 and 2 dollar items, they jolt to a stop in the one dollar range. Four choices between a dollar and a dollar-ninety-five. You settle for $1.25 knowing you have seven one dollar bills in your wallet. Even if she goes as high as $3.50, you're safe. You smile and relax.

If you have ever been in these or similar situations, you are already acquainted with surveying. Sizing up the situation or looking the place over before settling down are common occurrences. We do it every day.

With a little imagination you can think of many other examples. Just to cite a few more to start your brain circuits reverberating, consider the following situations.

You're job-hunting. You pick up the want ads. Your eyes pass quickly over the death notices, personals, automotive, and real estate. They settle on the employment or help wanted columns. Now they go slower but not too slow. They're looking for certain words—COLLEGE STUDENTS—SUMMER JOBS— PART-TIME HELP. Only then will they really drop into low gear.

It's 8:00 o'clock on a Sunday evening. You're in the lounge or at home in your living room. You have no TV guide so you begin to flip the dials on the TV set. Each channel is allowed a brief showing. Now you know what's on each channel and you select your program.

The pilot who is off-course surveys the terrain below for outstanding landmarks. The newcomer at the fishing site finds out who is catching the most and where he's doing it. The high school student who is about to graduate writes to colleges for catalogues or visits campuses for a quick look. All of these are situations utilizing the survey technique. Why do we do it? What do we look for? How do we find what we are looking for? How do we know when we have found it? How can we do this in reading?

We survey because we have a purpose or goal in mind. Because we are human and have some degree of intelligence, we seek short cuts to our goals. The related words, the different, the outstanding, or the unusual catch our eyes. These dominate the scene, while the irrelevant, unimportant, or insignificant fade into the background or get lost at the periphery. It's easy to tell which way to go at a fork in the road or a choice-point in a chapter if a signpost is present.

What we must learn to do is to use the signposts found in our reading. A child lost in a strange city has little use for street signs. He doesn't know where he wants to go even if he could read them. Therefore, he pays no attention to them even though he meets one at every corner. The college student who reads only to be able to say that he completed his assignment also has no need for signposts. Consequently he, too, blithely passes them by even though they leap out at him throughout the book.

Let's assume that, for once, you are going to read an assignment not because you are told to do so, but because you wish to understand it and remember it. After all, there just might be some value in knowing what you've read after you've taken all that time to do it.

The first step is to find the signposts and the second is to use them. Consider the common textbook and its clever author. His first signpost greets you even before you open the book. It's the title. The author boldly tells you, in several places, what the book is about— on the cover, on the backbinding, on the flap. The publishers, not wishing to give him full authority, also add their bit. They write a brief over-view on the book jacket or insist that the author or someone else write a preface. Sometimes they do both. The author also shows you his main topics in a table of contents, gives you an idea of the extent of his knowledge by providing you with an index, and occasionally even includes a bibliography, in case you want to check up on him by reading his source books. Sometimes he hides juicy tidbits under the cleverly camouflaged guise of the appendices.

These signposts provide the initial clue regarding his later style of presentation. Each chapter has a title. Each chapter also has some main points to be developed. These points are brazenly displayed by the author in bold type, usually occupying a central position on the page. Sometimes he labels them with Roman numerals or capital letters. Under these main headings are found subheadings. The author who really cares about college students and wants them to be his friends also writes a brief introduction and a summary. These, then, are the major signposts to guide you in your reading.

Take a 30-page chapter in any text written in the above fashion. Read the title and reflect briefly on it. Then read the introduction, main heads, and summary. This takes 3 to 5 minutes—6 if you really think about the title. This constitutes your survey. Of course, if you *really* want to strike off the shackles of passivity, you might pause reverently before the charts, tables, or pictures which cost so much to include and so frequently go unnoticed. In any case, you now have a better than rough idea of what's in the chapter. You know where you're going and what you'll meet on the way. You will be ready to respond to main ideas and won't easily get lost in details. Your past experience, already alerted, will come off the side-rails and join your present train of thought. Having discovered the author's outline, you will have a concise, ready-made framework on which to tie important details. And last but not least, you will have stumbled upon a veritable lode of source material from which to formulate important questions to be answered. We'll say more about this in the next chapter.

But, you ask, how about authors who don't like students, who write selections which don't have main heads and a summary? What's to be done about their writings? The procedure should be modified as follows: (a) Read the first and last paragraphs. (b) Then read the first sentence of every third paragraph. By attacking an essay in this style, you will learn where the author is leading you before traveling there blindly. Now it is possible to appreciate the conceptual path which he follows. Each step, each turn takes on extra importance because you can relate it to your destination.

Does all this sound like too much trouble? Do you think the procedure will be a waste of your time? If you answer yes to one or both of these questions, you are mistaken. *Every* efficient reader *always* surveys his reading regardless of its nature. He sometimes finds out that it isn't worthy of his careful consideration or perhaps shouldn't be read at all. It is just as valuable to know what *not* to read as it is to know what to read. Since this is true, it might be worthwhile to spend a little of your time learning how to do it. You too can win friends and influence instructors.

Alas, the cat is out of the bag. Instructors beware! The student is about to become a professional learner.

EXERCISES

COMPREHENSION

The first step is to find the signposts and the second is to use them. The first signpost is the (1) _____. The author who really cares about college students and wants them to be his friends also writes a brief introduction and a (2) _____. . . . Take a 30-page chapter . . . written in the above fashion. Read the title and reflect briefly on it. Then read the (3) _____, (4) _____, and (5) _____. For selec-

tions which don't have main heads and summaries, the procedure should be modified as follows: (a) read the (6) _____ and (7) _____ paragraphs. (b) Then read the first sentence of every third paragraph.

For answers, see Key, page 133.

APPLICATION

1. Surveying a Book

The next exercise presents the contents of a book jacket for your inspection. Your task: read the information contained on the front cover and front flap of the book jacket.

When you finish you should know:
1. What sort of theory the author presents;
2. What the theory will try to explain; and
3. What problem he was working on which led to the theory.

Now, review these three questions. *Hold them in mind while you read.*

What are the three questions?

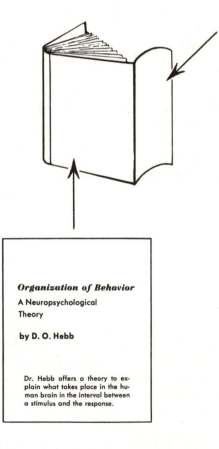

Organization of Behavior
A Neuropsychological Theory

by D. O. Hebb

Dr. Hebb offers a theory to explain what takes place in the human brain in the interval between a stimulus and the response.

In *Organization of Behavior*, Dr. Hebb combines present-day knowledge of psychology and physiology into a new theory of thought and emotion—an attempt to explain what goes on in the human brain between the arrival of an excitation at a sensory projection area and its departure from the motor area of the cortex.

Dr. Hebb started his work originally in an attempt to understand the peculiar lack of effect which many major brain operations had on intelligence and behavior. To account for this lack of effect (as well as for the great effects from apparently similar operations) he developed a hypothesis about learning, perception, and attention. Unexpectedly, the hypothesis was obviously relevant also to problems of motivation, emotion, and mental illness, as well as to the original problem. Thus it led directly to a comprehensive theory of behavior.

In the first five chapters, Dr. Hebb discusses the problems involved in studying behavior, and explains the theory he developed to solve these problems. From Chapter 6 on, the theory is applied to learning, volition, emotion, hunger and similar factors in behavior. Dr. Hebb explains the nature of consciousness in physiological terms and integrates the theory of learning and perception with pleasure, pain, and neurosis.

Anyone interested in learning, emotion, motivation, perception, physiological psychology, or comparative psychology will find in *Organization of Behavior* discussions that are pertinent, sometimes controversial, always refreshing and interesting.

ABOUT THE BOOK   Reprinted with permission from dust jacket of D. O. Hebb: *Organization of Behavior*, Copyright 1949, John Wiley & Sons, Inc.

Now show the results of your survey by filling in the blanks:

1. Dr. _____ has written a _____ psychological theory.

2. He explains what happens in the brain in the interval between a stimulus and the _____ to it.

3. He was trying to understand the lack of effect on intelligence of many major brain _____.

2. Surveying a Chapter

Most of a student's surveying is done on chapters in a textbook. Reproduced below are (1) the parts of a chapter which a skilled student would notice when surveying, and (2) parts which an unskilled student would notice.

Read carefully and decide what parts the skilled student would notice. Circle the numbers opposite those parts.

Chapter 3

ANXIETY

⎬ 1

This chapter concerns one of the most important hurdles of school children, anxiety. Its nature, particularly the way in which it differs from fear and its common symptoms, will be discussed. The bulk of the chapter will concern causes of anxiety with reference to the teacher's role.

⎬ 2

THE NATURE OF ANXIETY

⎬ 3

Differentiation from Fear.

⎬ 4

We all know fear. The bully on the street, the first day in school, numerous speeches before unknown audiences, important examinations, all were fear-arousing experiences. . . .

⎬ 5

Symptoms of Anxiety.

⎬ 6

CAUSES OF ANXIETY

⎬ 7

Before discussing the causes of anxiety, it must be understood that anxiety is largely learned, probably during the very early childhood years. Secondly, some children are more susceptible to anxiety learnings than are others. . . .

⎬ 8

The Genetic Component.

Neurotic Parents.

Unstable Environment.

Physical Limitations to the Learning of Skills.

⎬ 9

SUMMARY

We have considered the nature of anxiety, especially with respect to its difference from fear and its symptoms. Causes of anxiety were shown to be related to the environment and to the individual's abilities. Finally, the teacher's functions of providing security and of teaching skills important to the learner were suggested as enabling him to act as therapist for the anxious child.

⌐10
⌐11
}12

For answers, see Key, page 133.

READING

What Causes Learning Problems?

Most of us are overwhelmed by our own complexity. We insist that no two people are alike, and conclude, therefore, that the diagnosis of learning problems among college students must be a very complex task. Since the premise is faulty, so is the conclusion. Students are alike in many ways, particularly those who have academic difficulty.

Among the thousands of students who have passed through the learning clinic of the University of Michigan in the past few years, a small number of problems have occurred repeatedly. They have to do first, with learning, and second, with demonstrating what is learned, i.e., taking tests. Test-taking is a complex skill worthy of extensive consideration. It will be treated in Lesson 7.

Problems having to do with learning are of two kinds: (1) knowing *what* to learn, and (2) knowing *how* to learn it.

Why should it be difficult to know what to learn? Most courses include textbooks, lectures, outside readings, and lab manuals. There is plenty of material to be learned, so where's the problem? It is already apparent. There is too much to learn, more than any normal student can hope to master. In a vain attempt to know what to study, a student asks his instructor how to prepare for a forthcoming exam. The instructor, feeling beneficent before this poor, eager, struggling freshman, holds his chin, looks serious, and says, "I'm glad you asked that. Now listen carefully. I want you to learn only the important ideas. Don't bother with the details." With a gladdened heart, the neophyte thanks the master, and, walking away, says to himself, "Ah-h, just the important things. B-but, wait a minute. What's important?" He finds out what's important when he takes the examination.

There is a more satisfactory answer, of course. The study method described in the last lesson includes a procedure for determining what is important *before* you take an exam.

Knowing how to learn the material selected by that procedure is more difficult. Two kinds of problems arise here, those related to the learning procedure and those related to forgetting. Some students, like Linda in "The Disorganized Coed,"[1] spend as much as ten hours a day in study, reading and rereading and re-rereading, never knowing when to stop. They don't know what they know, and, therefore, are obliged to keep studying. Others memorize piece by piece, line by line, until they are able to quote pages. But successful rote learning is no guarantee of understanding, as is shown by Carl, "The Solid C Pre-Medical Student."[2] Both Linda and Carl succeeded after learning how to learn.

Failure to remember is caused by a number of conditions:

1. Failure to Learn Initially. Many students who complain of brain failure are unaware that the learning never took place to begin with. Most susceptible is the "underliner," the half-sophisticated student who selects the right ideas and underlines them, expecting to learn them before the exam. When E Day comes, he reads the question, closes his eyes, and smiling to himself, says "Oh, I remember that. It was on page 437, near the top. Now what was it?" And nothing happens. He is termed half-sophisticated because he is just wise enough to deceive himself into thinking, "I'll learn that later." Beware of that statement. If it's worth learning, it's worth learning *now*.

2. Not Organizing for Recall. The gifted student is most likely to trip over the problem of disorganized, incomplete learning. He is unused to study. One rapid reading has always been enough for his sticky brain. But lack of thoroughness in learning causes trouble on exams. Parts of answers are left out without the writer realizing it. Since the original learning was disorganized, he is unaware of the gaps in his answer.

Both the underliner and the skimmer will profit from the *active* learning required by recitation and note-taking.

3. No Review. Forgetting occurs so quickly that systematic review is imperative. The problem is most apparent among college students because their work load is so great. The phenomenon called "retroactive

[1] Lesson 3.
[2] Lesson 4.

inhibition" is the culprit here. Every time a new fact is learned, it tends to interfere with recall of previously learned facts. It looks as though the more a college student learns, the less he knows.

Problems of examination-writing are discussed in detail later. For the present, we should note that close to twenty per cent of the credit lost on examinations results from misreading questions. Furthermore, over fifty per cent of college students report that they suffer "sometimes" or "often" from "clutching"—exam panic. The simplest antidote for this kind of brain failure is to know the material, and *to know that you know it*. We'll say more about that later.

Two special problems are worthy of mention:

1. There is growing concern regarding a phenomenon termed a "special language disability." It is as though the person so afflicted fails to function normally in the language area of the brain. Such an explanation is unnecessary. The student has two deficiencies, probably causally interrelated.
   a. The first deficiency is in day-to-day memory for "nonsense" material, that is, for data that is not inherently sensible. Insofar as spelling fails to follow rules, he is unable to spell. Since learning a foreign language consists of attaching new sounds to old concepts, it is essentially nonsense learning, and is therefore difficult.
   b. The second deficiency is in "auditory memory." Moments after hearing a phrase, he is unable to recall it. This part of the problem makes writing from dictation particularly difficult. Both deficiencies appear to be related to level of tension or anxiety. While a reduction of tension results in improved learning, other techniques, discussed later, are helpful also.
2. The second special problem is that of the "rebel," or "head-banger." He brings with him to college a strong need to overpower persons in authority. Behaviors stemming from this need usually result in failure, itself a victory over the initial authority, parents. The rebel will be discussed at length in a later selection.

LESSON 3

Questions: Einstein, Darwin, and Paul Revere's Horse

While discussing study techniques with a small group of college freshmen in their dormitory lounge one evening, an instructor remarked that our curiosity is aroused by a riddle or an unanswered question—we want to know the answer.

"Take Einstein, for example," the instructor continued. "His many accomplishments resulted from studies designed to answer questions in his mind—questions not fully answered by existing theories. The same curiosity about the unknown led to the important work of Darwin, Newton, Galileo, and countless others."

"That may be true sometimes," replied one, "but what if the question is about something unimportant? About some things I couldn't care less!"

In answer, the instructor asked how many of them knew the name of Paul Revere's horse. Silence. Commenting that it didn't make much difference anyway, he then proceeded with the discussion. Fifteen minutes later, after presenting a number of suggestions concerning efficient study methods, he asked if there were any questions. Twenty-two people had the same question: "What's the horse's name?"

Was this bit of information important to them? Hardly. Neither is the punch line of a joke, but if you've ever heard anyone begin to tell a joke and then forget the punch line, you know how frustrating it can be. A riddle you can't easily solve may be just as bothersome, and the same is usually true of an unfinished mystery story, an unsolved puzzle, or the broadcast of a football game when your radio goes dead at the beginning of the fourth quarter.

Why is it that situations like this tend to bother us enough so that we actively seek the answer or solution—even when it may not be really important to us? Why is it that we *have* to know? Primarily because of curiosity—because of that slightly irritating and dissatisfying state of mind aroused by an unanswered question.

The point in bringing this up here, of course, is that you can capitalize on this phenomenon, this natural desire to know the answers. Simply direct your studying toward the answering of questions. Even an electronic brain doesn't produce information until some kind of question is fed into it.

Perhaps students aren't *exactly* electronic brains, and there are probably only a few of you who will ever be Einsteins or Darwins. Nevertheless, studies *have* shown that students who read an assignment in order to answer questions based on it understand the material better—*and remember it longer*—than do equally capable students who read and reread the same assignment without the aid of questions.

(If you read about the end of that football game in the sports section of the Sunday newspaper the chances are that you had certain questions you wanted answered, that you read the reporter's written account of the game quickly, and that you remembered the answers you were seeking!) Questions not only arouse a degree of curiosity (and thus direct reading toward an *active* seeking of answers), but they also help in the evaluation of specific details. Those details which help to answer important questions are obviously more important than those which do not, and greater attention should be given to them.

Sources of Questions

Many students respond to the above suggestions by asking: "Even if the idea of using questions as study guides is as good as it sounds, *where do I get the questions?*" One of the answers to this query is that the process of surveying a chapter before reading it should suggest a number of questions to you, especially if you realize that most textbooks are set up in such a way as to draw your attention to the more important ideas presented. Titles, subheadings, listings, italicized words, charts, and summary paragraphs may all suggest helpful questions, particularly if they contain words and ideas that are unfamiliar—and thus curiosity arousing. Besides these cues within the chapter, there are at least four other important and helpful sources of questions for you to tap. (1) Some textbooks include a set of review questions at the end of each chapter—you can use them most effectively by referring to them *before* reading the chapter. (2) Some instructors are kind enough to supply their students with question sheets. Don't use them for bookmarks or paper airplanes—even if *you* don't think they're important, they should indicate pretty clearly what the *instructor* considers important! And finally, it is often possible to add to your list (3) questions suggested by your lecture notes, and (4) questions raised during class discussions.

How to Ask Questions

Once you have a fairly good idea concerning the various sources of questions available to you, a few procedures and principles should be kept in mind to insure the best possible results from the questioning process:

1. Remember that questions asked *before* reading are more helpful for efficient learning than are those asked *after* reading.
2. The chapter title can be effectively used as a means of getting you "warmed up" so that you are thinking about the material to be studied. For example, the question, "What do I already know about this topic?" should help you to place the new material in the comfortably familiar setting of previous learning and experience. The new and unfamiliar is much more easily learned and understood if it is related in some way to that which is already known.
3. Main heads, the chapter subheadings usually set in darker or larger type, are the signs indicating the most important topics in a chapter, and

can be quickly changed from statements into questions. For example, the main head, "THORNDIKE'S LAW OF EFFECT" becomes, "What *is* the Law of Effect?" You will get better results (and direct your attention to more of the important details) if you read a main head deeply enough to come up with more than one question based on it. The heading above, for instance, will yield at least two more pertinent questions: "What led to the formulation of Thorndike's law?" and "How is the law helpful in life situations?"
4. Unfamiliar terms—often italicized—should suggest such questions as "What does this word mean?" and "How is it related to the main topic?"
5. Don't stop asking questions as soon as you begin to read. Some questions may have to be changed—or others added—if you discover during your reading that your original questions didn't encompass *all* the important ideas.
6. When you ask a question, try to *guess* the answer to it before you read to find the answer. This encourages you to think a little more actively about the material, and involves you more closely with it. This idea is really more important than it may sound at first, for we know that retention of learned material is better when the learning process is connected with some emotional reaction, however slight. If your guess is correct, you will discover this as you read, and you will react emotionally by being pleased or satisfied, and you will consequently remember the answer longer. (Thorndike's Law of Effect, by the way.) If your guess is way off base, you will discover this also, and the resulting displeasure or dissatisfaction will tend to fix the *correct* answer in your mind more solidly than would be the case if you merely observed the answer indifferently, and then moved on.

Finally, it should be stated that the use of questions can be equally effective with material that is not conveniently divided into sections, with main heads, summary, and so on. A freshman coed, resentfully struggling through a book of essays in an English course, got stuck completely when she ran up against an essay about a certain civil war general and his part in an important battle. Having developed a dislike for essays in general, and an even greater dislike for anything smacking of history, she decided to try the "questions method" to see if it would help at all in steering her through her unpleasant task. But she could think of only one question: "Why in the world would anyone think something like this was important enough to write about?" The result? She grudgingly admitted that she not only discovered the answer, but also that she actually found herself *enjoying the essay as she read it!*

Oh yes—one thing more. If you are by any chance interested in knowing the name of Paul's sturdy steed, you'll want to read the following paragraph:

There are a few who have maintained that Paul's horse was named "Ida." This is undoubtedly an apocryphal version, however, which is preserved by those who understandably regard "Ida Revere" as a unique and entertaining name for a horse. A more reliable source indicates that at one time Paul Revere owned a horse named "Sheherezade," and called "Sherry" for short. The question will probably remain unanswered, unfortunately, since Mr. Revere was obliged to borrow a horse from a farmer for his celebrated ride, and no available records refer to this famous steed by name. It should be noted that the original question was sufficiently perplexing to motivate the authors of this book to consult a number of sources before reluctantly concluding that no clear-cut answer seems possible.

EXERCISES

COMPREHENSION

While discussing study techniques . . . , an instructor remarked that our (1) _____ is aroused by a riddle or an unanswered (2) _____. . . . The point in bringing this up here, of course, is that you can capitalize on this desire to know the (3) _____. . . . Nevertheless, studies have shown that students who read an assignment in order to answer questions . . . understand the material better and remember it (4) _____. . . . Some textbooks include a set of review questions at the (5) _____ of each chapter—you can use them most effectively by referring to them (6) _____ reading the chapter. . . . When you ask a question, try to (7) _____ the answer to it before you read.

For answers, see Key, page 133.

APPLICATION

Using Main Heads for Questions

Write, in the spaces provided, two questions which might be raised by the following main head:

I. HITLER'S RISE TO POWER

_____?

_____?

The kinds of questions most commonly suggested by such a main head would fall in the "who-when-why-how" category. Therefore, you probably thought of such questions as:

1. Who was Hitler?
2. When did he rise to power?
3. How did he gain power?

These questions are valid ones, and should be helpful. It must be noted, however, that other, less obvious (but perhaps more important) questions may also be necessary in order to direct your attention toward more significant ideas presented by the author. For example, a professor writing some items for an exam might think of such questions as:

1. What conditions (social, political, or economic) enabled Hitler to gain control of the government?
2. What generalizations for our own time can we make—in other words, are there conditions which in *any* society would threaten democratic procedures?

Questions like these will not only encourage a more active thinking process while you read, but may also assist you in anticipating more accurately questions which will appear on the next exam.

Now read the next main head. Again ask two questions, but make one of these a "depth" question of the second type described above.

II. THE CIVIL WAR

_____?

_____?

Your "surface" question here might have been:

1. When was the Civil War?
2. Who fought in it?

Some possibilities for the "depth" question are:

1. What conditions (social, political, economic, etc.) led to the war?
2. Of what significance was this war in our history?
3. What were the immediate and long-term results of the war?

Now ask one surface and one depth question about each of the following main heads.

III. CAUSES OF ANXIETY

_____?

_____?

IV. THE RECEPTION OF DARWIN'S "MISSING LINKS"

_____?

_____?

V. MOTIVATION
   A. *Physical Drives*

_____?

_____?

(Note that depth questions may be suggested by the *relationship* of main heads and subheads; for example: "In what way does an understanding of physical drives aid in understanding motivation?" or, "In what ways are physical drives related to motivation?")

READING

The Disorganized Coed

Desire to succeed in college is a necessary, but not by itself sufficient, condition for success. Even though an entering student has had a brilliant high school record, even though his scholastic aptitude tests indicate a strong potential for success, these usually sound predictors, coupled with strong motivation, may not be enough. Linda had all of these and yet she nearly left college after the first five weeks.

In high school, Linda had won in a walk. She had achieved an A minus record without a struggle. She was popular, sophisticated, a natural leader; in short, she had the world on a string. But there was much talk of difficulty in getting accepted by the college of one's choice. It was necessary to take college entrance examinations and to do well on them. The high school record was not enough to insure acceptance. When she took the examinations, she became panicky. She was unable to think clearly and seemed to "block" on many questions. When the time came for an interview at a select women's college where she had applied, she received a shock. First, the director of admissions gave her a flat no. They could not accept her. Next, he advised her against attending college at all! With test scores like hers, chances of success were very slim. Rage and disappointment beset her by turns. For the first time in her life her ability had been seriously questioned. On the advice of her parents, she took the examinations again and did much better. Her scores this time more nearly agreed with the promise she had shown in high school. She applied to another outstanding institution and this time she was accepted.

Nevertheless, the seed of doubt had been sown. She seriously wondered whether she would succeed. Determined to do her best, she began by trying to master her notes and textbooks. She set aside Monday night for studying French, Tuesday for English, Wednesday for zoology, Thursday for chemistry, and Fri-

day for a general review. But that didn't seem to work. By the time she came to read over the zoology and chemistry notes, they were cold: they no longer made sense. The French dictations came on Monday and Friday, so Monday night she found out what she should have known Monday morning. Even worse, French vocabulary studied on Monday seemed to be forgotten by Friday, even though she read over the vocabulary list as many as fifteen times on Monday night. But chemistry was the worst demoralizer. She read it over and over, afraid to stop, never knowing when she had learned what she ought to know. When the hour exams came up, she was in such a state of panic that she was hardly able to read the questions. Some of them sounded vaguely familiar, but she was completely unable to formulate adequate answers.

She was much more confident in English. She had always been able to write well. True, her spelling was erratic and her sentences sometimes ran out of syntax, but her ideas were good. Nearly always she had been able to score well, mainly on the basis of the bright and amusing ideas which came to her. Thus, her first themes were dashed off rapidly, and she wasn't too surprised to find them scored as C's, with one marked D+. She would do better; a little more care perhaps. But at the end of five weeks, she had to face the truth. Her ideas were fuzzy; she was unable to give them any depth. Her sentence structure and spelling were now beginning to plague her.

Grades were sent out at the end of five weeks. Linda expected the worst and her expectancy was fulfilled. She received three D's, and an E in chemistry.

Her housemother found her in tears, miserable, confused, wretched, too scared to go home and too lost to go on. When asked whether she had looked for help at the Learning Clinic, she replied that she had tried to find it but got lost in the building.

Diagnosis of the problem was not difficult. Linda was a perfect example of the disorganized coed. The disorganization had congealed into a self-defeating cycle. Her long hours of fruitless study had convinced her that she was unable to succeed. Thus, defeat in examinations was certain, and her grades further reinforced her lack of confidence.

The skills counselor explained her difficulties to her as follows:

1. Preparations must be made prior to the recitation, preferably a full day before in order to make use of the reminiscence effect.
2. Study must be selective; attention must be focused differentially: the most important ideas should receive the most attention, the less important ideas, less attention.
3. Learning must be assessed: to know what you know, you must self-test by reciting.
4. Reviews must be spaced and systematic.

5. French and spelling require specialized learning techniques.

6. The total approach to study is Survey Q4R.

The counselor then helped her to organize her time so that her preparations preceded lectures, recitations, and labs. He instructed her in systematic study procedures for each course. He then assured her that she could succeed, and predicted that her quizzes in the following week would prove it.

She reported back in ten days. She had taken a laboratory quiz in chemistry and a dictation test in French. The results: chemistry—A; French—A.

Were there further problems? No, she informed the counselor. Everything would be fine. Not wishing to question her optimism, the counselor simply wished her continued success and asked that she drop in sometime.

She appeared once more, at the beginning of a new semester, and proudly presented her grade report for the preceding term. She had continued receiving A's and had raised her grades from three D's and an E to four B's.

Linda's story actually occurred. Her dramatic success seems almost too sudden to be true. Nevertheless, that's the way it happened. It provides strong evidence for the importance of system in learning. Linda had all the necessary ingredients for success in college except one: she had not learned how to learn.

LESSON 4

The First R: Reading

You have formulated the question. Now, how do you find the answer? It seems obvious and simple: just read the section following the main head. But is it really as simple as that? Observation of the reading sets used by successful and unsuccessful students suggests that methods of reading tend to be quite different for the two groups.

One way to cover the section is to start at the beginning and read word by word, line by line, paragraph by paragraph, "squeezing every bit of meaning" out of each word and sentence, "rereading two or three times if necessary." The parts in quotes are taken from statements of failing students when asked how they read an assignment. This is not the way to read.

The key to effective reading at this stage of Survey Q4R is *selectivity*, differentiating the important from the less important and the unimportant. Whatever answers the question is important; whatever helps to answer the question (perhaps by explaining a term) is less important; whatever fails to answer the question is unimportant.

When reading to answer questions, more often than not we find that the text includes a core of meaning, described in a few words, one or more minor points, and some relatively unrelated ideas. Not all the material will be immediately relevant.

As an extreme example of the selectivity required because of irrelevant material, consider the adult's rate of reading a telephone book. The small book at hand contains nearly 200,000 words. If it takes him thirty seconds to look up a number, he is "reading" at a rate of 400,000 words per minute. Or more to the point, consider the chemistry text which includes a good deal of historical material. If history is irrelevant to your immediate purpose of following the derivation of a chemical formula, the historical material will be ignored. We read selectively because it is the most efficient way to find answers to questions.

To select wisely, you must first know, in rough, the points made in the section. To do that, first skim through, reading a few words here and there. Then you can focus on the parts which bear on the question. You will also be able to arrange the ideas in order of importance. For example, a discussion of the causes of depressions includes *overspeculation* as one cause. If the term is defined on that page, your mental notes will include *overspeculation* as a subhead under Causes, and the definition as a subhead under *overspeculation*, e.g.,

Causes: 1. Overspeculation—Def.:
Buying more on margin than . . .

Here is an example of good reading to answer a question. The numbers indicate, in sequence, the parts of the paragraph on which the reader is focusing:

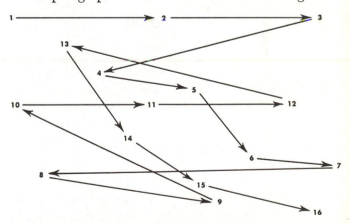

In the example, the reader first became oriented to the section (1,2,3), by determining the number of reasons discussed, skipped to (4), the signal phrase, "The first reason . . . ," noted the first reason (5), skipped to (6), another signal phrase, "Another reason . . ." and read the point (7,8). Then he skipped to (9), the final reason, which he did not need to read since he had anticipated it. Now he moves back to read the "first reason" more carefully (10, 11, 12), and finishes by a skimming review (13, 14, 15, 16).

This is an example of selective reading at its best. Don't hurry it. Skill will develop gradually as you work through the materials in this text.

Perhaps the most important idea implicit in this selection is the following: *selective reading is, in reality, selective thinking.*

EXERCISES

COMPREHENSION

One way to cover the section is to read word by word . . . "squeezing every bit of (1) _____" out. . . . The parts in quotes are taken from statements of (2) _____ students when asked how they read. . . . The key to effective reading at this stage of Survey Q4R is (3) _____. We read selectively because it is the most (4) _____ way to find answers. . . . You must first know . . . the points made. Therefore, one must first (5) _____ through. . . . The final reason . . . he did not need to read since he had (6) _____ it. Now he . . . finishes by a (7) _____ review. . . . Selective reading is, in reality (8) _____ (9) _____.

For answers, see Key, page 133.

APPLICATION

Reading Selectively

1. Write in the space provided, the question raised by the title. Then check your question against the recommended one* at the foot of the page. Do this now.

THE EFFECT OF SLEEP ON FORGETTING

_____?

Next, skim the following paragraph. Then, go through it sentence by sentence to determine whether each sentence is IMPORTANT (answers the question) or UNIMPORTANT (fails to answer the question) *with reference to the recommended question.* Indicate your choice by writing I or U in the parentheses.

Two subjects memorized lists of nonsense syllables before a period of (a) normal daily activity and of (b) sleep (1____). Both subjects were college students

* Key: 1. What effect does sleep have on forgetting?

(2____). Retention was tested after one, two, four, and eight hours of either waking activity or sleep (3____). Under these conditions different lists of nonsense syllables were learned and recalled, but they were all of comparable difficulty (4____). Each duration of sleep yielded better retention than a comparable duration of waking, a finding verified by later research (5____).[1]

See Key, page 134, for answers.

2. For this selection, write down two questions suggested by the title. Then check your questions against those recommended.*

THE BEGINNING OF COEDUCATION IN COLLEGES

_____?

_____?

Next, skim the following paragraphs. Then go through them, *keeping in mind the two recommended questions.* This time, write in the parentheses I, LI (less important), or U. Base your decision on whether the sentence answers or helps to answer *either* question.

A radical break with academic tradition and one in which the United States was a pioneer was the provision of higher education for women, an opportunity that was quickly grasped (1____). One hastens to say that it was not an offer made by men but mainly an achievement by the women themselves (2____). The Middle West opened the first door (3____).

The way for coeducation was prepared by the academies; and the normal schools were coeducational (4____). It is, therefore, surprising that the first coeducational colleges were severely attacked (5____). This was the penalty inflicted upon Oberlin College, which began as a coeducational school in 1833, admitted women to its degree course in 1838, and graduated four women bachelors of arts in 1842 (6____). Antioch was opened in 1853 as a coeducational college under Horace Mann (7____). But it was not mainly the independent colleges but the State Universities and land-grant colleges that most generously opened their doors to women students (8____).[2]

See Key, page 134, for answers.

* Key: 2. When did coeducation begin?
    Which colleges admitted women first?
    (*Use these questions in the next part of the exercise.*)

[1] Adapted from *Psychology*, Norman T. Munn, Houghton Mifflin Company, 1951.
[2] *A History of American Education*, H. G. Good. Copyright 1956 by The Macmillan Company. Used by permission of The Macmillan Company.

3. The following article is in textbook form. You're on your own. First, *Survey, Question, Read,* then answer the questions on the check test.

FUNCTIONS AND PROCESSES OF ECONOMIC SYSTEMS

The General Nature of an Economic System

1   *Need for an Economic System.* In a society
2 where each person supplies for himself all of his
3 wants, there is no need for an economic system. A
4 Robinson Crusoe could gather his own food, build
5 his own shelter, and provide his own recreation, in
6 short, fulfill his economic needs, without depend-
7 ence on any other individuals. But in a complex
8 society, where occupations are divided into many
9 categories, such as food suppliers, builders, etc.,
10 each individual performs, by and large, in only one
11 or in just a few capacities. He therefore becomes
12 dependent upon many others for the basic neces-
13 sities of life. When such a situation occurs, there
14 is need for a system to *regulate the activities* and
15 *provide order,* insuring that the many parts will
16 function harmoniously and adequately.

17 *Kinds of Economic Systems.* The occupational
18 structure and the relationship of these activities
19 to one another are often the same from one so-
20 ciety to another. However, responsibility for han-
21 dling three important tasks of economic systems
22 tends to vary greatly from one system to another.
23 These tasks are the responsibility for production,
24 the control of natural resources, and the division
25 of the total product. Because of this variance,
26 many different types of economic systems have
27 been developed. Generally speaking, they consist
28 of two types, *the managed economy* and *the free
29 economy.* These terms refer to the extent to which
30 the functions of the economic system, the respon-
31 sibility for production, control of resources, and
32 division of produce, are assumed by private in-
33 dividuals upon their own initiative (free economy)
34 or by a central agency such as government (man-
35 aged economy).

Tasks of the Economic System

36 *The efficient production of goods* is the first re-
37 sponsibility of the economic system. In order to
38 produce goods there must be *enterprise,* the wil-
39 lingness to take the initiative and provide the
40 leadership required for production. In a com-
41 pletely managed economy, the central agency
42 both initiates productive activity and maintains
43 the leadership of the enterprise. In a free economy
44 it is left to private citizens to decide to undertake

45 production, to raise the necessary capital, and to
46 guide the actual production. In a capitalist so-
47 ciety, for example, wealth takes the initiative and
48 hires labor to carry out the program which those
49 with wealth supervise.

50 In addition to enterprise, the system entails one
51 or more solutions for the problem of *incentive.*
52 Many different motivations may prompt individ-
53 uals to engage in production. Some of the more
54 obvious of these are fear (as with slave labor),
55 patriotism, social approval, advancement of the
56 arts and crafts, and, of course, personal profit. A
57 capitalistic system relies largely on income as a
58 motivating force, the profit motive for the enter-
59 priser and the wage motive for the worker.

60 *Guiding the use of natural resources* is the sec-
61 ond basic function of an economic system. This
62 involves the allocation of the resources among the
63 various projects which require it, the utilization
64 of these resources in most suitable locations and
65 with suitable tools (including the matter of work-
66 ers and their skills and aptitudes), and the move-
67 ment and distribution of these resources. In the
68 last-mentioned category, the system is concerned
69 both with speed and proper destination.

70 *Distribution* of the end and total products is a
71 third function of the economic system. There are,
72 of course, many different ways in which the goods
73 of production can be allocated and distributed,
74 but it is only in a managed economy that this
75 function is separate from the first two functions
76 we have discussed. When production and use of
77 resources rests upon private initiative and incen-
78 tive, the nature of distribution will be an out-
79 growth of these factors. When an economy is
80 based on a price system, as, for instance, capi-
81 talism in America, costs and profits regulate dis-
82 tribution of goods.

Check Test	*Line*

1. The purposes of an economic system are two:

    a. _____   14

    b. _____   15

2. Name the types of economic systems.

    a. _____   28

    b. _____ 28, 29

3. What are the tasks of an economic system?

    a. _____   **36**

    b. _____   **60**

    c. _____   **70**

READING

The Solid-C Pre-Medical Student

You probably know someone like Dave. Every high school has its quota of "brains." Dave was the prototype. He always acted worried before an exam, you'll remember, and everyone thought it was an act—after all, he *always* ended up with an A.

Dave was good at just about everything. It goes without saying that he was valedictorian. He had solid A's in high school. He could memorize anything: a full page of a Hamlet soliloquy, propositions in geometry, all the formulas for trig, the presidential succession—and definitions. If the text had definitions, Dave knew them. He could say them word for word, including all the ifs, ands, buts, examples, and page numbers.

In a way, he was a social success too; a little dull, maybe *too* serious, but the man you always chose for president. He was an officer in every organization he ever joined. You could depend on him. "Good old Dave—conscientious, consistent; he always got the job done."

Dave's father was a physician, a minor deity in the eyes of his son. Naturally, then, Dave had to attend med school and, perhaps, one day take over the older man's practice.

The neophyte healer had no trouble getting accepted in a pre-med program. He rushed into collegiate life determined to succeed. If necessary, he'd study day and night to earn the B average required for entrance into med school.

And he did study day and night. He pored over his books and lecture notes, finding a corner in his compartmentalized brain for every detail. As mid-semester exams approached, Dave began his usual worrying. He comforted himself with the memory that he had always felt that way before exams, but his fear persisted. He knew there was good reason for it: *he just didn't seem to understand the work.* Chemistry was the most puzzling, but the other subjects gave him the same trouble.

He took the exams and wasn't surprised to find that his grades were all C's. Oh well, it was early in the year. Perhaps next time. But next time it was the same: chemistry, C; math, C; zoology, C; English, C. Now he began to worry in earnest. After all, a B average was necessary for acceptance into the medical curriculum.

On the advice of his academic counselor, Dave visited the Learning Clinic. He told the skills counselor the nature of his problem and he answered many questions:

Counselor: "How much time do you devote to study?"
Dave: "At least six hours every day."
Counselor: "Doesn't leave much time for living, does it?"
Dave: "No, but that's not important. I've just got to get into med school!"
Counselor: "Do you underline when you study the text?"
Dave: "Oh yes; I work systematically. I work through an assignment line by line. Then I underline with red pencil everything that I think I should memorize."
Counselor: "How much underlining would there be on an average page?"
Dave: "That varies with the subject. In history, about half of each page; in chemistry, about four-fifths."

(The cautious, conscientious characteristics of Dave are obvious. The counselor now makes a prediction and checks on it.)

Counselor: "How do you take notes in lecture?"
Dave: "Well, that's a problem. In chemistry, for instance, the lecturer writes on the board a lot. Writing as fast as I can, I get down just about everything."
Counselor: "Does it make sense to you afterward?"
Dave: "No! That's the trouble. I get home and read my notes and they don't mean anything. The best I can do is to memorize them. But that doesn't pay off on exams."
Counselor: "You mean you're getting a lot of details that don't hang together. I wonder if that isn't the case in the textbook study too. You're learning all the pieces, but they don't seem to have any larger meaning."
Dave: "That puts it very well."

The following corrective steps were recommended:
1. Prepare for a lecture by reading anything related to it. This is crucially important. Such preparation results in awareness of the relative importance of ideas, logical sequences, materials to be found in the text and therefore requiring no notes.
2. Use Survey Q4R on the reading in order to be sure to see the large picture *before* reading the details.
3. During the lecture, *listen* to what the lecturer says. Don't miss a word. His ideas will make sense if you follow all the steps in sequence.
4. Look at the organization of the lecture by thinking back over the early parts several times.
5. Take notes *in your own words,* and only after deciding that this bit of material might be easily forgotten.
6. Stay seated for three minutes beyond the end of the lecture, and review all the notes. Organize them now in some logical sequence. Fill in missing parts that seem important now in light of the total lecture. (The lecture material is still fresh, partly because you have understood it.)
7. Review your notes that same evening.

In his usual conscientious way, Dave put the plan into action. He reported back in two weeks. In the meantime, he had garnered two A's. There was still a problem in solid geometry. How could that be handled? The importance of surveying the text in order to discern the pattern of problems being handled was pointed out. Dave began to see the relationship between today's work and that which had preceded it.

It should now be clear that Dave had been moving from tree to tree without ever realizing he was in a forest. His problem of "molecular" learning probably resulted from a style of thinking which placed undue value on isolated facts, and from his previous academic success achieved solely by memorizing.

Dave's final grades in the second semester departed from his earlier record: chemistry, A; math, A; zoology, A; English, B.

LESSON 5

R 2 and R 3: Recite and "Rite"

Let's follow three college students into the library in order to see how they proceed through an assignment. These students have learned how to survey and ask questions, and we discover with pleasure that all three of them use the techniques before reading their assignments. But then what happens? The first of our subjects (an eager and conscientious freshman) begins to take notes, furiously jotting down ideas in the margin of his text and on a pad of paper. We note that the writing is almost continuous, and that many of the ideas are important ones. The second student, also a freshman, is just as eager and conscientious as the first, but more methodical, for in this case the note-taking is in the form of a highly structured outline. There are numerous main topics and subtopics, primary and secondary points, listings, definitions, and frequent direct quotes from the text—just to make sure that the main ideas are recorded *in the author's exact words*. Our third subject? Well, he's a sophomore, perhaps a bit more confident than his less experienced colleagues, and instead of taking notes, he very carefully underlines the information which he considers important. And *is* it important? Yes—when we look more closely we find that he has underlined quantities of material, and that most of it is directly related to the questions he raised during his survey.

It has long been thought that taking voluminous notes, making thorough and well-organized outlines, and underlining important ideas and information are all sound study techniques. If this were true, we might predict that the three students we have just observed would be very successful ones. This is not necessarily so, however, since these procedures do not make the most efficient use of our learning machine, the human brain. At best, these three students will have to spend many more hours rereading, relearning, and reviewing the material before the next exam in order to pass it. At worst, they may well fail in spite of all their conscientious effort.

Why? Because none of the methods described above assures real learning of the material. Neither do they make possible an efficient review later on. The person who takes reams of notes while reading will still have before him the task of organizing and learning them before the exam. Those who carefully outline every chapter will, to be sure, have things fairly well organized, but outlining tends to become a rather mechanical transferring of material from book to note paper without any actual learning occurring during the process. Furthermore, both kinds of note-taking are tedious and time-consuming, so much so that we will probably give them up altogether in favor of the popular underlining method adopted by our sophomore. This technique is popular because it doesn't take much time, and because it is an extremely effective means of deceiving ourselves into believing that we have learned what we have underlined. It is true that many students become very skillful in underlining the important information in a chapter, but this does not mean they have learned it; they have merely recognized it, and it still remains there on the page, neatly marked for closer attention during that all-night cramming session just before the next exam.

What should be done, then, to make sure that we not only recognize important material in a text, but also that we learn and remember it? Actually, the answer to this question is relatively simple: when an important point or idea is discovered while reading, resist the temptation to pick up a pencil for underlining or careful note-taking. When you've found an answer to one of your questions, STOP—and *recite* the answer in your own words. Pretend you're taking an exam, and see how well you could do with the question you're working on without referring to the text. You don't have to write the answer, nor is it necessary to disturb your roommate with an oral recitation. Just *think it through* in the words you would use if you had to answer the same question in an examination. Since you have just read the answer in the text, this should not be too difficult, but if necessary, look back to the book for any points that are still a bit hazy. Then try again. This time you should be able to recite the information with no trouble, and when you can do this, you have done more than *recognize* the information—you have *learned* it!

As you will discover in the next lesson, material that

is learned tends to be forgotten quite rapidly unless it is reviewed briefly, but regularly, later on. Students who underline and outline often state that these procedures help them to review before an exam. What they fail to realize is that underlining and outlining actually tend to *postpone* learning, as we have seen, and that what they call reviewing is really an attempt to learn great quantities of information that could have been learned much more easily and effectively at an earlier time. We wish to emphasize here that note-taking *can* be a helpful aid to reviewing—but only if it is done properly.

Effective review notes consist of questions and answers. They are also brief. Notes for an average chapter in most texts, for example, should require no more than one side of a sheet of paper. Such brevity is possible because good notes consist not of the whole answer to each question, but only of as many key words or phrases as are necessary to help recall the whole answer during subsequent review sessions. Such key words are called cues.

If you think a few cue words are insufficient, just stop for a moment to consider how frequently a short phrase is enough to set off a whole train of thought. For example, *Your senior year in high school.*

Were you thinking about your senior year one minute ago? Probably not, but undoubtedly you could talk or write about it for five minutes, or even a half hour, if you had to—and you wouldn't need an outline or a set of notes to help you! The cue, *Your senior*

year in high school, would be quite enough to set off a whole series of memories that have been stored away in your brain for some time. This capacity for filing away great quantities of information in such a way that only a word or short phrase is necessary to bring it all out whenever needed is one of the amazing powers of the human brain. Why not make use of this capacity when confronted with the task of learning your history, psychology, or physics assignment? *Read* to find the answers to your questions; learn the answers by *reciting;* and then *write* the cues, the words or short phrases that serve as keys to the complete answers.

And now an important word of caution. The student who is really an efficient learner will resist the temptation to select his key words and phrases from the textbook. He knows that his notes will be much more helpful to him if they consist of cues selected from *his own recitation* of the information he wants to learn. In this way, there will be a more meaningful connection between cues and the complete answers, for both will be in the student's own words. This will make the reviewing procedure, discussed in the next lesson, much easier and more effective.

Before concluding, it might be well to review the "recite and rite" procedure described above. When you have completed the survey of an assignment, some tentative questions may have occurred to you. Whether they have or not, return to the first paragraph and formulate your first specific question.

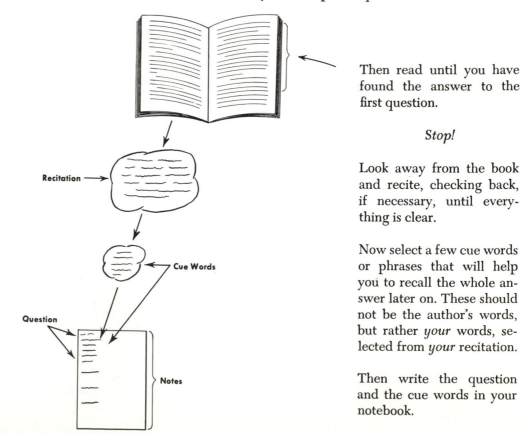

Then read until you have found the answer to the first question.

Stop!

Look away from the book and recite, checking back, if necessary, until everything is clear.

Now select a few cue words or phrases that will help you to recall the whole answer later on. These should not be the author's words, but rather *your* words, selected from *your* recitation.

Then write the question and the cue words in your notebook.

Now go on to the next section or question, and repeat the process until the assignment is completed.

This procedure may take a little extra time until you get used to it, but with a little practice you will find that it is actually quite quick and easy. The important thing, however, is that it will insure thorough learning, make reviews simple and effective, and make quite unnecessary more than an hour or two of review before the next exam. And perhaps best of all, the grade you earn on that next exam will prove to you that you are capable of doing college work.

EXERCISES

COMPREHENSION

The first student . . . begins to take notes. . . . The writing is almost (1) _____. A sophomore . . . very carefully (2) _____ the information which he considers important. . . . Most of it is directly related to the (3) _____. These procedures do not make the most (4) _____ use of . . . the brain. . . . None of the methods described above assures (5) _____ the material. . . . We are likely to give up note-taking in favor of (6) _____. What should be done to make sure that we not only recognize important material but that we learn and (7) _____ it? When you've found an answer, STOP—and (8) _____. . . . Underlining tends to (9) _____ learning. . . . Good notes consist of (10) _____ words. The cue . . . sets off a series of (11) _____ stored away in the brain.

For answers, see Key, page 134.

APPLICATION

Survey, Question, Read, Recite, and "Rite"

The following exercise will assist you in assessing the extent to which you have learned to apply the first 5 steps of SQ4R. There are 3 parts to this exercise. Pay particular attention to the order of the tasks which will be assigned for each part. *Do not read the directions for any part until you have completed the tasks assigned for the previous part.*

Directions: Part I

Survey, in 60 seconds, the short selection on pages 33 and 34 by reading the *title*, the *first* and *last* paragraphs, and the *main headings*. After your survey, turn to page 34 and complete Check Task 1 for Part I. Do your survey *now*.

Directions: Part II

Look at the first main heading. Turn it into a *question*. Fix this question firmly in mind, then *read* to find the answer. As soon as you find the answer, *recite* it in words which will be meaningful to you. If you can recite the answer before completing the reading of the first section, read the remainder of the section rapidly to be sure you have the complete answer. When you finish the section following this first main heading turn to Check Task 2, page 34.

Directions: Part III

Now that you have surveyed, asked a question, found the answer, and recited in your own words, write the question and your answer in abbreviated form on page 35. Then return to the article (page 33), raise a question based on the second main heading, read, recite, and write brief notes for this section. Record these notes on page 35 with the others.

THE CONCEPT OF RACE

The Meaning of "Racial Differences"

1 It is obvious even to the casual observer that
2 differences exist between certain groups of people,
3 differences which the anthropologist calls "racial."
4 By racial, he means differences which are hered-
5 itary and beyond the control of the individual.
6 The Negro's dark skin and wooly hair have noth-
7 ing to do with the country in which he lives, the
8 food he eats, or the school he attends.

9 At first glance it seems easy to identify a mem-
10 ber of the Negro race, or to tell a Chinese from
11 an Italian. You might therefore assume that the
12 scientist can give you a simple guide for deter-
13 mining racial affiliations. While it is true that a
14 number of inherited physical characteristics are
15 used to classify individuals into the major group-
16 ings of *Caucasoid, Mongoloid,* and *Negroid,* there
17 are several reasons why this division is far from
18 complete and accurate.

Problems in Classification by Race

19 *Gaps in Historical Evidence about Causes of*
20 *Racial Differences.* The early history of mankind
21 is known to some extent by the findings of arche-
22 ologists, from the discovery of bones and artifacts,
23 from which inferences about prehistoric man are
24 drawn. The evidence, however, is scanty, and
25 even the question of whether all men spring from
26 a single *homo sapiens* ancestor is not yet an-

27 swered. Scientists do not know whether the char-
28 acteristics we call racial were originally caused
29 by the adaptation of men to a particular environ-
30 ment (over, of course, a very long period of time),
31 or are due to a mutation of genes in the original
32 stock. Questions such as how these characteristics
33 came about and whether they have always existed
34 in their present form may be crucial for reaching
35 proper conclusions about the meaning of race.

36 *Overlapping Traits among Racial Groups.* A
37 second difficulty is found in the fact that racial
38 traits overlap, that is, are found to greater or lesser
39 degree among all groups. For example, while
40 Mongoloids are generally thought of as shorter
41 in stature than Caucasians, many individuals of
42 Mongoloid classification are, in fact, taller than
43 many individuals classified as Caucasian. The
44 use of traits in classifying is a technique relying
45 on *averages,* and while this often enables the
46 investigator to draw a general picture of a race,
47 it may lead to trouble in categorizing any par-
48 ticular person.

49 *Inbreeding.* A third major problem is that of
50 the inbreeding of races. It is possible, even likely,
51 that at one time in man's history the major races
52 were much more isolated than at present, and had
53 little opportunity for contact with one another.
54 Under such circumstances, the racial stock would
55 remain pure. But with intermarriage, character-
56 istics of each race are blended in the offspring, and
57 isolating racial factors becomes an impossible
58 task. Today there are almost no groups in exist-
59 ence in the world that are known to be pure, in
60 the sense that the stock has been unaltered by
61 intermarriage.

62 *Unclassified Peoples.* Still another factor to be
63 considered is the fact that there are at least three
64 groups of people who do not conveniently fit into
65 any one of the three major classifications. The
66 *Ainu* of Japan, the *Australian natives,* the *Poly-*
67 *nesians*—each has, as a group, certain racial char-
68 acteristics, but in each case these appear to be
69 combinations of some of the predominant traits
70 of two or more racial groups. This may be due to
71 some very early contact between the original
72 group and some other racially pure group; for
73 example, in the case of the Ainu, probably an
74 original Mongoloid group with a Caucasian group
75 —but again, the lack of historical evidence makes
76 such theories purely speculative.

77 Thus while we see that there are racial dif-
78 ferences, that is, hereditary differences between
79 certain groups of peoples, the effectiveness of the
80 concept of "race" is influenced by our lack of com-
81 plete historical knowledge, the overlapping of

82 traits, the inbreeding of racial stocks, and the in-
83 completeness of the categories.

Check Task 1 for Part I

If you surveyed the article correctly, you should be able to answer the following questions. They constitute an acceptable minimum of information which you should now have acquired. Record your answers on this page. Do not look back at the article.

1. What is the general topic dealt with in the article?

2. What two aspects of the general topic are discussed?

3. How many problems of classification are discussed?

4. What are some of the problems of classification?

Were you able to write something in the blanks following each of the above questions? Compare your answers with the ones listed here. The answer to question one is contained in the title. Your answer might have been: the concept of race, meaning of race, races of men. The two aspects of the general topic are the two main headings: The Meaning of "Racial Differences" and Problems in Classification by Race. Four problems of classification were mentioned. You could have learned this either by observing the subheadings given under Problems of Classification or from the summary paragraph. The four problems are: (1) lack of historical knowledge, (2) overlapping of traits, (3) the inbreeding of racial stocks, (4) the incompleteness of the categories. You might not have been able to list all four but you should have remembered at least two.

Now turn back to page 33 and read Directions: Part II.

Check Task 2 for Part II

Let us now check your recitation procedure. The most obvious questions suggested by this main head are:

What is the meaning of "Racial Differences"?
or What is meant by "Racial Differences"?

With either of these questions firmly in mind, you

should have recognized this sentence (lines 4, 5) in paragraph one as the probable answer:

"By racial, he means differences which are hereditary and beyond the control of the individual."

Your recitation should include both the question you asked and the answer you formulated. Since individual variation in recitation must necessarily occur, we cannot precisely specify what words you would have used. The description which follows gives a pattern which your recitation may have followed when you stopped reading after the indicated sentence. The parentheses are used to indicate actions or immediate verbal paraphrasing.

"Let's see. What is meant by Racial Differences? (rereading the sentence slowly) By racial, he means—who's he?—(look up one line)—oh, the anthropologist—By racial, anthropologists mean differences—(differences in people)—which are hereditary—(exist at birth)—and (which are) beyond the control of the individual—(the person can't do anything about them). (I wonder what kind of differences these would be. Physical?)

Then you would have read the remainder of the section noting the mention of skin color, hair, and later inherited physical characteristics. Now having completed the section, you look away from the article, ask your question again, and recite the final answer. "What is meant by racial differences? According to anthropologists, racial differences are those physical differences which we inherit at birth and over which we have no control."

Return to page 33, Part III.

Check Task 3 for Part III

Notes on the Article

Title of the article: _____

Question one: _____
Answer(s):

Question two: _____
Answer(s):

Now look below for a comparison of sample notes based on this article.

Sample Notes for Part III

THE CONCEPT OF RACE

I. Race Differences? Anthro.—inherited, physic. char., can't control.

II. Probs. classify by race?
   A. lack hist. knowl.
   B. trait overlap
   C. inbreeding
   D. incomplete categories—(some groups don't fit)

You should practice reducing your notes to cue words or phrases. Cues will work *if* you understand the material before attempting to put it in your notes. The answer for the second question could be placed in one line but sometimes it is better to list answers as we did above. *Only* the information necessary to answer the question should be included. Sometimes, a term or phrase may answer a question but have a vague or ambiguous meaning. Part D above might be of this nature, thus an explanatory note might be included in your notes.

READING

Taking Lecture Notes

Many experts on college teaching say that the lecture system is outmoded, that teaching by television is here to stay. But either way, lecture hall or television lounge, some students will lose out. Whether a lecture is presented via the podium or the TV tube, the listener has only *one chance* to get the message. Since one can't "regress" as in reading, the only recourse is to learn how to listen. Intelligent listening leads to intelligible notes.

Students have two major complaints concerning their part in the learning-by-lecture process. The first complaint: "They all talk too fast. While I'm writing down the *first* idea, the *second* one goes by me." This problem results from poor auditory memory. The words don't stay "in mind" long enough to apprehend the sentence. The second complaint: "I usually get everything written down—but it doesn't make much sense when I review it." This problem results from a mechanical note-taking process: the goal of the student is to take dictation, not to understand the point being made. Thus, he ends up with a series of words, all of equal value, the major ideas undifferentiated from minor ideas and illustrations.

To do the job well, let's begin by looking at two major differences between a textbook presentation and a lecture. First, the lecturer usually presents fewer ideas in an hour than does the text. (One result is fewer lecture notes than text notes. A half-page in your notebook is enough for the usual lecture). Since the lecturer can observe his audience, he knows when an idea is giving trouble and multiplies examples. A lighter concept load in the lecture allows time for integrating the last idea with those preceding it so that a structure develops. Second, the listener can't survey a lecture, *at first,* so he must make use of clues other than main heads and italics to select the important ideas.

Here are several kinds of clues to what is important:

1. *Foreshadowing*
   "There are two common points of view . . ."
   The lecturer signals his intention to present two points of view.
2. *Repetition*
   "Once more you observe the North underrating the fighting spirit of the rebels."
   Apparently the North's tendency to underrate the South is important since another example is being given.
3. *Issues*
   "Some psychologists state that S-R psychology is too mechanistic, therefore, invalid. But others . . ."
   The phrase "some psychologists," indicates disagreement among the group and, therefore, an important point.
4. *Consensus*
   "All geneticists now agree that . . ."
   If all members of a group agree with a point, the point is important to the field of inquiry.
5. *General-specific relationships*
   "The wealth of Cuba derives from its export trade."
   It is very likely that the lecturer will now discuss products that are exported. The student will indent for this point.
6. *Demonstrations and examples*
   "To illustrate, suppose we combine . . ."
   If time is taken for a demonstration or an example, we may assume that the point being illustrated is important.

Perhaps the foregoing presentation seems to belabor the obvious. If so, you will have no difficulty in labeling the italicized clues in the following lecture.[*]

> *Clues:*
> 1. Foreshadowing   4. Consensus
> 2. Repetition   5. General-specific
> 3. Issues   6. Examples

"It is *generally agreed* that a deficient vocabulary impedes efficient reading (a. ____). *One investigator* reports that 90 per cent of the variation in reading comprehension within a group can be attributed

[*] Smith, Donald E. P. *Help Yourself to Efficient Reading,* Ann Arbor, Michigan: University of Michigan Extension Service, 1953, pp. 10-11. Quoted by permission.

to differences in vocabulary and verbal reasoning (b. ____). *Let's consider* some vocabulary improvement techniques (c. ____).

. . . But most of these direct methods are time consuming and unproductive. *On the other hand,* wide reading by a person motivated to build vocabulary and sensitive to the power of words to stir emotions and to direct behavior is probably the most painless and efficient method (d. ____).

If a direct attack is necessary, *the following categories* of words are suggested as those which will be most easily remembered (e. ____):

A. *Curiosity words*—those which evoke the thought, "Isn't that strange! I just saw that word yesterday for the first time, and here it is again. I wonder what it means" (f. ____).

For answers, see Key, page 134.

Here are some final considerations: *The best preview for a lecture is a survey of the assigned reading.*

Put your reading notes and your lecture notes in the same notebook on facing pages. Whichever comes first, the reading or the lecture, the notes of the one (in the form of questions and answers) will enable you to avoid duplicating while taking notes on the other.

Review your lecture notes briefly before you leave the lecture hall. Retention is greatly facilitated by this immediate review. Three minutes spent in an immediate review is probably more effective than a twenty-minute review that same evening.

LESSON 6

Review: The Last Step to Mastery

Have you ever read an assignment, conscientiously studied the material in the chapter, taken careful notes on lectures related to the assignment, and felt that as a result you really understood the essentials of the unit you were studying—only to find that several weeks later (especially the week of an exam) you had forgotten almost all of what you had learned? Have you ever memorized a vocabulary list—or some rules of grammar—on a Friday, and then discovered in class on Monday that it was all Greek (or French—or Spanish—or German) to you? And have you had the experience of studying a diagram of the circulatory or nervous system—or a chemical reaction—so carefully that you could reproduce it blindfolded—only to feel when you *see* the same diagram on the lab exam the following week you might just as well *be* blindfolded?

Of course you have—unless you are quite different

from most of us! One of the many frustrating problems which students face almost daily in their college careers is that of forgetting material they once thought had been understood and learned thoroughly. This problem results from the fact that almost anything we learn—names of people, batting averages, dance steps, themes from symphonies, English history, German vocabulary, or chemical formulas—can be remembered over a period of time *only* if we *use* or *apply* these learned skills, concepts, and symbols with some frequency. We can remember some names easily because we use them often in our associations with the people we know. The symphonic themes become familiar if we enjoy music and listen to it often, and occasional attendance at week-end dances serves to keep our dance steps in pretty good form. But our opportunities to use what we have learned about history or chemistry or French grammar are in most instances relatively infrequent. (The *inclination* to use such information may occur even less frequently, but that's another matter.) Consequently we are apt to forget much of what we once knew in a matter of a few weeks—or even a few days. Thus, when exam time rolls around, we discover that adequate preparation for the exam means more than just refreshing our memories—it means *relearning* a substantial portion of the course material.

The solution to this problem is apparent: since learned material is likely to be forgotten if not used frequently, and since our chances to use what we learn in many academic courses are relatively slim, then the only way we can insure adequate retention of learned subject material over a period of time is to provide for frequent "use" of the material by means of *systematic reviews.*

And there's the rub! Most students feel a strong negative reaction to the idea of reviewing course material that has at one time been studied and learned thoroughly. And they ought to feel this way, for the word "review" is often incorrectly used as a label for "relearning." To many, the typical "review" involves long and tedious hours of seemingly endless repetition; it involves the enervating tension of last-minute cramming; it involves a loss of sleep and a severe curtailment of one's social life. And all too often the *results* of such drudgery are rather less than satisfactory! "Reviewing" is therefore most unpleasant, and is to be regarded as a necessary evil to which one resorts *only* during those semiannual rat races known as final exams!

At this point it should be stated that a good review does *not* involve the disagreeable grind described above. It requires a certain amount of effort, of course, but, even more important, it requires the development of reviewing *skill.* The proper type of review can be relatively easy, brief, and—most important—it can be *effective.*

How, then, should you go about performing the kind of review of which we are speaking? First, if you've been using the SQ4R method of studying you've won half the battle. For any chapter or unit that must be reviewed in preparation for an exam you will have a set of notes containing a number of questions, and after each of these questions there should be a few abbreviations for words and phrases—the reduced cues that remind you of the whole answer to the question. Using these brief notes, you can review the material effectively by (1) quickly looking over the questions in order to get the whole picture, (2) by translating the abbreviations into complete questions, and (3) by reciting the answers to these questions. If an answer has been forgotten, look at the notes for the answer. If you are able to recite an answer without the help of notes, then you *know* the material and your recitation constitutes *overlearning.* If you must use the notes, your recitation constitutes relearning. Overlearning and relearning are the principal methods of insuring retention.

The important point to remember is that your role in this type of review should be *active,* not passive. Instead of reading through your text or lecture notes again and again, *test yourself* constantly by reciting the answers to your questions. Merely understanding the material as you read over it does not necessarily mean that you have learned it, but if you can *give out* the information—as you must do on that next exam— then the chances are that you have learned it—and learned it well.

The *timing* of your reviews is almost as important as the method you use. Psychologists have found that most forgetting occurs within a day or two—or even an hour or two—after initial learning. In order to prevent this decay, an assignment must be reviewed *immediately* after it is finished. It shouldn't take more than five or ten minutes. Since it has also been found that *brief* and *frequent* reviews more effectively increase retention than do long and infrequent ones, you should review the material once more a week after the initial study period, using the same method described above. This time, use your notes from several chapters and a curious phenomenon will occur.

As you recite answers to questions covering a broad array of material, all within a half hour, you will suddenly develop new insights. You will discover cause-event sequences, similarities of happenings in different historical periods, or regularities (called laws) among the mass of apparent trivia in a science course. These insights, when offered in class discussion, cause instructors to label students "brilliant." (Thus, the title of an earlier lesson, "How to Be Brilliant with Limited Resources.")

You can see, therefore, that a good review does not mean long hours of tedious repetition for small dividends. It *does* mean using the right approach, and *scheduling* time properly so that those few brief—but crucial—weekly review sessions are not forgotten. The student who knows *how* and *when* to review, and who uses this knowledge to his advantage, has taken another important step toward becoming a professional learner.

EXERCISES

COMPREHENSION

One of the many frustrating problems . . . is that of (1) _____ material you once thought had been understood and learned. Almost anything we learn . . . can be remembered *only* if we (2) _____ it with some frequency. . . . Ordinarily, adequate preparation for the exams means . . . (3) _____ a portion of the course material. . . . The solution is to provide for "use" of the material by (4) _____ it. To many, "review" means . . . endless (5) _____. . . . A good review . . . requires a certain amount of effort and the development of reviewing

(6) _____. . . . For any chapter . . . you will have . . . notes containing a number of (7) _____. . . . Overlearning and relearning are the principal methods of insuring retention. . . . Instead of rereading your notes, (8) _____ yourself. . . . Almost as important as the method you use is the (9) _____ of your reviews. Review (10) _____ after finishing the assignment. Covering a broad array of material . . . you will develop new insights.

For answers, see Key, page 134.

APPLICATION

Reviewing Survey Q4R

In Lesson 7, you will take an examination on the first six lessons. Your notes for those lessons appear below in the familiar form: questions with answers. Spend the next ten minutes preparing for the examination. *Follow these steps:*

1. Cover up the answer to the first item in Lesson 1.
2. Read the question.
3. Try to answer the question briefly in *your words.*
4. Read the answer.
5. If correct, "cue reduce" the question and answer in note form.
6. If not correct, recite the answer in *your words,* then cue reduce.
7. When you finish the notes, *repeat the process once.*

No more review will be necessary!

NOTES ON LESSONS 1-6

Lesson 1: How to Be Brilliant with Limited Resources

What does college success largely depend upon?
    Knowing how to learn
Why?
    Narrow range of talent (colleges select the best); intelligence less important than in high school
How do you "use" the brain?
    Arrange conditions which the brain prefers:
    1. Survey to see pattern of the whole
    2. Raise questions to focus on the parts
    3. Read to answer questions
    4. Recite to learn
    5. Rite to record clues
    6. Review (twice) to remember

Lesson 2: Survey

What does survey mean?
    Sizing up a situation; looking a place over
Why survey in life situations?
    To answer questions, fulfill purposes

CUES

Coll. succ. dep?
    How lrn.
Why?
    All brite (coll. select)

How survey?
1. Use signposts (title, main heads, introduction, summary)
2. If none, read first and last paragraph, then the first sentence of every third paragraph

Lesson 3: Questions: Einstein, Darwin and Paul Revere's Horse

Why do unanswered questions bother us?
  Curiosity
Why are questions valuable?
1. Help select important ideas (they answer questions)
2. Understand material better
3. Remember it longer
Where do questions come from?
1. Title
2. Main heads
3. End of chapter questions
4. Technical terms

Lesson 4: The First R: Reading

How do you read an assignment?
  Be selective (emphasize important points)
How do you select important points?
  Important: if it answers a question
  Less Important: if it helps to answer a question
  Unimportant: if it fails to answer a question

Lesson 5: R2 and R3: Recite and "Rite"

Why should you recite?
  Recitation is required for learning
What's wrong with taking lengthy notes?
  They must be organized and learned later
What's wrong with underlining?
  It postpones learning
What are the characteristics of good notes?
1. They are answers to questions
2. They're brief (cues)

Lesson 6: Review: The Last Step to Mastery

Why is review necessary?
  It reduces forgetting
How?
  It provides for relearning and overlearning
How does one review?
1. Translate cue-word questions into complete ones
2. Cover the answer and try to recite it
3. Check your response against the notes
4. If correct, go on; if wrong, recite the right answer
When is review most effective?
  Immediately after learning (then space out others)

Now repeat the review. You are ready for an examination.

READING

Crutches, Cramming, and Creativity

The expert student, by definition, knows how to learn. He is able to specify with some degree of ac-
curacy the conditions necessary for his own learning. For example, he would expect to learn very little when suffering from a headache, from lack of sleep, or from "jangled nerves." But there are other conditions for learning over which he can exercise control.

For instance, he finds he must do something about course content which isn't logical. Sometimes, this doesn't seem to follow any rules: water boils at 212° F. In other cases, he must follow rules which he isn't expected to understand: $C = 2\pi r$. When material doesn't follow logical rules, it must be learned by rote, or "brute memory." Here the student provides a condition to aid memory: he uses a "memory crutch." The colors of the spectrum spell out the name, ROY G. BIV; when he studies the history of a nation, the student is concerned with the components:

P olitical
E conomic
R eligious
S ocial
I ntellectual
A rtistic

Other conditions relate to creative activity—the writing of themes, discovery of historical laws, and the solution of difficult problems in math.

Simple vs. Complex Learning

Both rote learning and the discovery of complex relationships require the association of ideas. We may think of the fact, "water boils at 212° F," as a simple association between two ideas, "water boiling" and "212° F." When the association is well established, each idea is capable of arousing the other. The discovery of complex relationships depends upon a web of such associations, some of the parts of which are more complex.

For example, having learned the specific events and conditions preceding each of several wars, we have taken the first step toward discovery of a complex idea, how wars are caused. Similarities and differences among the events and conditions from one war to another may reveal that some conditions always prevail, for example, a sudden change in the balance of power. In addition, one of several predisposing conditions may be necessary, such as imperialistic aims or economic threat.

Whereas simple associations can be developed by using a memory crutch or by simply repeating the two ideas (so that the first becomes capable of arousing the second), discovery of a complex idea requires more. It consists, first, of having a question in mind: "What causes wars?" Next, one must know a series of relevant simple associations ("conditions preceding each war") *plus* the recognition of similarities among the associations ("certain conditions are always present") *plus* identification of an order among the ideas ("a cause-effect relationship"). We may conclude, then, that a great deal of information must be kept in mind in order to do creative thinking. Now, how can it be done? How do we keep ideas "in mind"?

The Sentence as Complex Learning

The way in which we comprehend a sentence will serve as a simple example of complex learning. Each word, each phrase, and each clause must be recognized; then the relationships among the parts must be discovered; finally, the parts and relationships coalesce or come together to yield an idea. All of these events are controlled by a mind set, the automatic question, "What does the sentence mean?"

As you know, when we read very slowly, the first words are forgotten before we reach the end of the sentence. In that case, we don't understand what we've read. It seems necessary to have all the parts of the sentence in mind simultaneously in order to discover the idea. Increasing our speed of reading of that sentence usually solves the problem. (In a similar way, reading a chapter line by line usually results in little learning. By the time the last page is complete, the early pages are forgotten. Thus, we survey the chapter first in order to provide a rough framework to which the parts may adhere.)

In general, the better the parts of a sentence (e.g., its vocabulary) are known, the longer they will remain in mind despite slow reading. Stated in other terms, the more associations an idea has the longer it will remain in mind without rereading.

Thus, the discovery of a complex idea when studying a page depends upon the ability to deal with parts and relationships almost simultaneously. The availability of these parts is, in turn, dependent on the thoroughness with which they've been learned.

The Conditions for Learning

But what then about crutches, cramming, and creativity? A crutch (like "ROY G. BIV") is a conscious attempt to put meanings (i.e., associations) where there are none, for the purpose of facilitating recall. Associations which make sense can be aroused with only a fraction of the effort necessary to arouse nonsense materials. For example, if the nonsense syllable "dax" must be associated with the word, "saw," the learner might derive: *dax-ax-wood-cutting-saw*. Crutches are usually temporary, used until the direct association occurs.

Creative thinking is at the other extreme. It implies the development of something new by using information already available. The process by which it occurs seems to follow the example already given. Just as words considered together give rise to a larger idea, so do ideas, when associated in the same way, give rise to new ideas. The difference between understanding a sentence and creative thinking is primarily one of complexity.

When we read a sentence, the parts arouse the idea —as long as we maintain the set, "What do these words have in common?" i.e., what do they mean? When we try to discover regularities or laws in related events, those events arouse a larger idea, the law—

when we maintain the set, "*What do these events have in common?*"

The practical implication is this: to discover laws or rules in reading, to arrive at the insights demanded by "thought questions" on examinations, it is necessary to *arouse the relevant or "part" ideas simultaneously*. The greater the number of ideas aroused in a brief time, the greater the likelihood of arousing the relevant ones. Therefore, the student should review a *large quantity of well-learned* content in a brief time. The second review in Survey Q4R is designed to increase the likelihood that new ideas will occur. It does so by producing insights which, under ordinary conditions, only occur to the unusual person.

And that brings us to cramming, best defined as that activity in which naive students engage the night before exams. But that definition implies a criticism of the activity. "After all, it is a review of a large quantity of content in a brief time—just what you've stated above to be the requirement for brilliance." But we've left out the crucial phrase: *of well-learned content*.

Let's see what happens when we cram. We cover a number of items, many of them unrelated to one another, in a brief time. Thus we develop weak associations among them such that, when one item is aroused by an examination question, one or more unrelated ideas may appear in mind. We can't depend upon the correct item appearing. Strong associations, you remember, result from frequent use, that is from recitation and review.

Summary

We have given a simplified description of conditions which facilitate rote learning and creative thinking. Simple associations can be developed by repetition and/or by buttressing them with meaning. Discovery of complex ideas requires thorough learning of the parts so that they may be kept in mind long enough for mental manipulation. We may conclude that the "memory crutch" is sometimes necessary and that cramming can easily lead to confused thinking on examinations. On the other hand, Survey Q4R is found to provide the conditions necessary for complex thinking.

SUMMARY OF SQ4R

1. *Survey*
   Determine the structure, organization, or plan of the chapter. Details will be remembered because of their relationship to the total picture.
   a. *Think about the title*. Guess what will be included in the chapter.

   b. *Read the introduction*. Here the main ideas are presented, the "forest" which must be seen before the details, the "trees" make organized sense.
   c. *Read the summary*. Here is the relationship among the main ideas.
   d. *Read the main heads* (boldface type). Here are the main ideas. Determine where in the sequence of ideas each one fits.

2. *Question*
   Having in mind a question results in (1) a spontaneous attempt to answer it with information already at hand; (2) frustration until the question is answered; (3) a criterion against which the details can be inspected to determine relevance and importance; (4) a focal point for crystallizing a series of ideas (the answer).
   a. Use the questions at the beginning or end of the chapter.
   b. Formulate questions by changing main heads and subheads to questions.
   Example: *Causes of Depression*. What are the causes of depression? What conditions are usually present before a depression occurs?

3. *Read*
   Read to answer the question. Move quickly. Sort out ideas and evaluate them. If content does not relate to the question, give it only a passing glance. *Read selectively*.

4. *Recite*
   Answer the question—in your own words, not the author's.

5. *"Rite"*
   a. Write the question (one sheet of paper is to contain *all* the notes for this chapter—so keep it brief).
   b. Write the answer using only key words, listings, etc., that are needed to recall the whole idea.

Follow the above plan for each section of the chapter.

6. *Review*
   Increase retention and cut cramming time by 90% by means of immediate *and* delayed review. To do this:
   a. Read your written question(s).
   b. Try to recite the answer. If you can't, look at your notes. Five to ten minutes will suffice for a chapter.
   c. Review again after one week.

Important: Give the method a fair trial. It may be slow and difficult for the first tries (like golf, tennis, getting used to institutional meals). As skill is developed, study time is halved, learning is less painful. Modifications of the plan may be necessary for some subjects, but the main outline, *Survey Q4R*, remains one of the most efficient for learning.

LESSON 7

The Techniques of Test-Taking

One of the inevitabilities of college life is the examination. Probably no other regular occurrence in academia causes such an outpouring of vital juices. Tears, sweat, and adrenalin result in loss of weight, hysteria, outbreaks of allergies and, at the very least, the gnashing of teeth. And afterwards, surrounded by the debris of battle—chewed pencils, gum wrappers, discarded "blue books"—we ask ourselves, "Is it all worth it?"

Of course it is! One might as well ask the same question of the pianist after his first concert in Town Hall, or of the surgeon after his first operation, or of the engineer after his first creation is completed. The examination is your opportunity to demonstrate your new knowledge and to reap the rewards, even though they are no more than letter symbols of achievement.

But just as you would not walk on to the concert stage without having mastered your music, you cannot expect to walk on the stage of academia without having mastered your subject.

There are two requirements for success. The first is knowing the content; the second, demonstrating that knowledge. The first requirement has been the concern of the preceding chapters. Systematic use of the learning steps will not only insure learning, it will also eliminate one of the most important causes of exam panic: the uncertainty concerning one's preparation. That is, it is necessary not only to know the course—but *to know that you know it*. The self-testing provided by recitation and review is a rehearsal of the final act. It provides proof of preparation and a shield against panic.

Demonstrating one's knowledge is another problem. Here the slip twixt the cup and the lip can bring disaster. According to students, their primary difficulties are "clutching" (exam panic) and having too many answers occur to them *after* they turn in their examination papers.

You need not resort to tranquillizers to conquer panic. Rather, follow these steps:

1. Use SQ4R.
2. Carry your notebook to the exam *but don't open it*. It provides a feeling of security (because you *could* check a question if you really had to—before the test, of course), and your ability to avoid looking in it increases your feeling of confidence.

3. Panic is contagious. Stay away from the source of contagion—other students. Don't answer questions; if you do, those answers may become temporarily unavailable when you need them. Their probability of occurrence once may be high enough to bring them out on the exam; but to occur twice on demand, the answers may need to be much better known.

4. Admit to yourself that you will not know *all* the answers. Instead of saying, over and over, "I'm afraid I won't know it," say "Some of it I won't know—and some of it I will." Thus, when you read the first question and don't know the answer, you will respond, not with the conclusion that you know nothing, not by clutching, but by saying, "That's one I don't know." Verbal magic? Perhaps. But it's effective.

Now let's look to the second problem of which students complain, having the answers occur to them after the examination.

1. Don't lump all your studying into one or two great, grinding sessions just before the exam. Distribute your review periods rather evenly through the preceding week or so (an hour a day for three days will probably be *more* than enough if you've been using SQ4R). Then stop studying two days before zero hour. Continual reviewing of the same material during the hours preceding the exam is an effective way to *prevent* its arousal when you want it. Leave your learning alone. The brain remains active, sorting and reworking after you close the book. Give it time to work for you. The child will never cross the street alone if mother always insists on holding his hand.

2. Continue your daily habits as usual. Too much sleep or too little, changes in eating habits, attending a movie (because you're told it's a good thing to do before an exam) when you abhor movies—any of these may modify your physiological functioning so that you are "not yourself" during the examination.

3. For the most efficient use of your knowledge, the following procedures should be followed:

THE ESSAY EXAM

a. *Set up a time schedule*. If six questions are to be answered in sixty minutes, allow yourself only seven minutes for each. When the time is up for one question, stop writing and begin the next one. There will be 15 to 18 minutes remaining when the last question is completed. The six incomplete answers, by the way, will usually receive more credit than three complete ones.

b. *Read through the questions once.* Answers will come to mind immediately for some questions. Write down key words, listings, etc. *now* when they're fresh in mind. Otherwise, those ideas may be blocked (or be unavailable) when the time comes to write the later questions.

c. *Do the easy questions first.*

d. *Before attempting to answer a question, put it in your own words.* Now compare your version with the original. Do they mean the same thing? If they don't, you've misread the question. You'll be surprised how often they don't agree.

e. *Outline the answer before writing.* Whether the teacher realizes it or not, he is greatly influenced by the compactness, completeness, and clarity of an organized answer. To begin writing in the hope that the right answer will somehow turn up is time consuming and usually futile. To know a little and to present that little well is, by and large, superior to knowing much and presenting it poorly—when judged by the grade received. Simplify the reading task of the instructor by numbering supporting ideas wherever appropriate.

f. *Take time to write an introduction and summary.* The introduction will consist of the main point to be made; the summary is simply a paraphrasing of the introduction. A neat bundle with a beginning and ending is very satisfying to the reader.

g. *Take time at the end to reread the paper.* When writing in haste we tend to:
   (1) Misspell words
   (2) Omit words and parts of words
   (3) Omit parts of questions
   (4) Miswrite dates and figures (1343 written as 1953; $.50 as $50., etc.)

h. *Qualify answers when in doubt.* It is better to say "Toward the end of the 19th century" than to say "In 1894" when you can't remember whether it's 1884 or 1894. In many cases, the approximate time is all that is wanted; unfortunately 1894, though approximate, may be incorrect, and will usually be marked accordingly. When possible, avoid *very* definite statements. A qualified statement connotes an appreciation of the tentative nature of our knowledge.

THE OBJECTIVE OR SHORT ANSWER EXAM

a. *Read through once, answering the obvious questions.* For the more difficult, write your *first reaction* in the margin and *circle the number* (to in-

sure finding the item later). As you go through the questions, later items will be found useful in answering early ones. First reactions tend to be the correct ones.

b. *Don't think too hard about the choices.* You can make a case for almost any choice if you try. These are recognition type questions. The answers should be apparent.

c. *Don't be a "head banger."* If you think your instructor wants you to choose *c*, then choose it. Don't say, "Well, *b* is just as good and I can prove it to him." An exam is not an appropriate battle ground for working out your authority problems.

d. *Be daring.* Research shows that the cautious person is penalized by answering only those questions of which he is very sure. Unless there is a sizable penalty for wrong answers, it's best to guess. Seldom will your guesses be blind. Rather, they tend to be based on partial information, some of it unverbalized.

e. In multiple choice items, the alternative which differs most in length from the others tends to be correct. The test maker requires qualifying words like *usually* and *sometimes* to make choices correct and others like *always* and *never* to make choices incorrect. Therefore, the correct one tends to be either longer or shorter than the others.

Learn this lesson well. Successful grades require *knowing it* and *showing it*.

EXERCISES

COMPREHENSION

The examination is your opportunity to demonstrate your new (1) _____. . . . You cannot expect to walk on the stage of academia without having (2) _____ your subject. . . . Systematic use of the learning steps will not only insure learning, it will eliminate one of the most important causes of exam panic: the (3) _____ concerning one's preparation. The self-testing provided by recitation and (4) _____ is a rehearsal of the final act. . . . Your notebook . . . provides a feeling of (5) _____. . . . Don't lump all your studying . . . before the exam. (6) _____ your review periods. On the essay exam, first set up a (7) _____. Research shows that the (8) _____ person is penalized. Successful grades require (9) _____ it and (10) _____ it.

APPLICATION

1. Starting the Essay Examination

The steps below are those to be carried out as soon as the examination starts. Indicate the *correct order* of the steps by writing in a number for each, from 1 to 4:

a. Outline an answer. _____
b. Determine how much time should be allotted for each. _____
c. Survey the items and do some marginal cue jotting. _____
d. Determine how many questions are to be answered. _____

2. The Essay Question

Read the following answers to an essay question. Determine what makes them differ in quality.

Question: Name and illustrate the four general classifications of animals by mode of existence or habitat.

Answer A.
1. Marine animals living in the sea.
2. Fresh-water animals living in streams and lakes.
3. Terrestial animals living on land.
4. Parasites, living on or in other animals.

Marine animals live in the sea. One kind is planktun. It's very small and floats. Another kind is the whale which is very large. Fresh water has mosquito eggs, frogs, cray fish and many other small animals. Terrestrial animals live on land. Dogs and cats, moles and birds are included. Fleas, lice and tape worms are parasites because they live on or in other animals. Some perasites have hyperparasites.

Answer B. Classification of animals by habitat:

1. *Marine*—Millions of animals, all sizes from the microscopic plankton to the enormous whale, inhabit the sea. Generally, marine animals are unable to survive in fresh water.
2. *Fresh water*—Lakes and streams contain such varieties as mosquito eggs floating on the surface, frogs living in the vegetation, and crayfish crawling along the bottom in their constant search for food.
3. *Terrestrial*—The vast numbers of land animals are common knowledge. They include the sub-terrestrial earthworm and mole and the aerial kingdom, from birds to butterflies.
4. *Parasites*—Animals play host to innumerable parasites. Fleas, lice, and tapeworms are generally known by the discomfort they cause. Less well known are the microscopic parasites whose hosts are hyperparasites preying upon parasites.

Both answers are completely correct. One received a C+ and the other, A. Following are some of the qualitative factors which make a quantitive difference:

a. Misspelling of technical words.
b. Tautologies—needlessly saying the same thing in different words (e.g., "visible to the eye").
c. Use of inexact language rather than more exact scientific terminology.
d. Circular definitions (e.g., "He's unemployed because he's out of work.")

Find at least one example of each of the following characteristics in Answer A.

a. Misspelling:
b. Tautology:
c. Inexact language:
d. Circular definition:

3. Taking a Test

a. Achievement in college is only partly a matter of _____.
b. Review anticipates the problem of _____.
c. The study method is called _____ (*abbreviation*).
d. The first signpost or help in a survey is the _____.
e. Others are the introduction, _____, and _____.
f. State three reasons why questions are useful during study.

g. Name four sources of questions.

h. When reading an assignment, one should be _____.

i. The important ideas can be differentiated from

the unimportant by determining whether or not

they _____ a _____.

j. Recitation is superior to underlining because recitation insures _____ and underlining _____ learning.

k. Name two characteristics of good notes.

READING

Grades: Standing vs. Standards

It's surprising how little students know about the nature of grading practices, especially so in view of the fact that their academic future depends on the grade-point average. Of course, there are well-worn stories about grading in the lore of every college: "Professor Doe has a simple way of grading term papers: he throws them down the stairs; the heaviest one, the one that goes the farthest, gets an A." Or there is the elderly professor who encouraged his students to study old final exams. When the class began to write the final, one student observed, "Professor, these are exactly the same questions you asked last year!" "Oh, that's all right," said the professor, "this year I've changed the answers." But such stories only dimly reflect the grading process.

There are two primary purposes for grading: (1) to determine the *standing* or rank of the class members within the group; and (2) to determine whether or not class members have reached the *standard,* a criterion of excellence, consisting of a proportion of the course content.

Standing

Let's first consider the grade as an index of standing within the group. Most instructors seem to feel that one's academic achievement benefits from competition. If they are not interested in providing a competitive situation, if they are interested only in knowing what proportion of the course content a student knows, there would be no reason for assigning ranks or grades. Thus, instructors use grades to motivate (i.e., to challenge or frighten students into learning).

Grading on the Curve. One result of the emphasis on grades to indicate standing is the practice known as "grading on the curve." The curve in question is a "normal distribution curve," depicted in the figure.

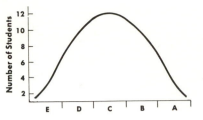

Instructors who use the curve in a rigid manner assume that a small number, perhaps 5-10%, should receive A's and an equal number should receive E's while most of the class should receive an average grade of C. Most instructors do not use the curve rigidly, however. Instead, they study the spread of scores and assign grades at natural breaks in the distribution. For instance, the bar graph illustrates the distribution of grades on a German test.

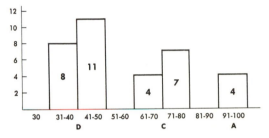

The instructor was disappointed with the results, i.e., he felt that the class didn't do as well as previous classes might have. Therefore, most of the students received D's and C's. No one received scores below 30, from 51 to 60, or from 81-90.

Cumulative Grades and the "Relaxation Factor." There is a curious phenomenon which occurs when scores on several hour tests are added to determine the final grade. Some of the students who receive a high grade on the first hour test relax and slip down on succeeding tests. Some students who receive a low grade on the first test rise higher on succeeding tests. However, the relaxation factor influences the distribution more than the low grade—fear factor. In other words, more students slip backward than move forward. The over-all effect, when scores are added together, is that the class *cumulative* average goes lower on each test. Thus, the student who earns a score good enough for an average grade on the first test—and *maintains that level of achievement*—will find his final cumulative grade is above average.

The moral to be derived: consistent achievement pays off in better grades.

Standards

What proportion of the essentials in a content area does a student know? Does he know enough French to be allowed to bypass the elementary course? Does he know enough law to protect adequately the rights of his clients? These kinds of questions are answered by tests designed to measure absolute knowledge. Such tests are ordinarily less subject to the whims and idiosyncrasies of one man than are course examinations. They are used as predictors of success in undergraduate courses, in graduate school, in occupations, and as a protection for the public in the case of the professions.

Many instructors feel that grades on their course exams reflect standards rather than standing. And this is sometimes true. An experienced teacher can do a rather good job of estimating the quality of work of the present class as compared with the preceding one. However, they tend to be unaware of the dangers in this practice. One of the most important is the human frailty of remembering the good and forgetting the bad. Thus, one hears references to "the good old days" when "young men and women came to college to learn." The remark implies that today's learners are inferior to those of the past, a generalization with no basis in fact. As a result of this human failing, measures designed to reflect standards ordinarily consist of short-answer items which can be objectively scored (true-false, multiple choice, matching, and filling in blanks).

The student is best advised not to concern himself overly much with the idiosyncrasies of a grader. Whether the grade one achieves reflects standing or standards, there is no adequate substitute for knowledge in achieving it.

LESSON 8

Concentration: A Large White Bear and Other Distractions

Before you start reading this selection, pause for ten seconds. During this time try *not* to think of a "large, white bear." Remember, do not let yourself think of the large, white bear at all.

(Pause for ten seconds)

If you succeeded, you're an unusual person. Very few people can avoid thinking of a "large, white bear" under these circumstances. Even sitting like Rodin's "Thinker" and using your "will power" is of no avail.

But let us suppose for a moment that, just as that ten seconds began, your wastebasket had blazed into flames. You certainly would not have been thinking of large, white bears in that case!

Now the scene shifts. You are at your desk, diligently reading the textbook in your toughest course. Suddenly in the middle of the paragraph you catch yourself thinking about a hamburger, the date coming up on the week end, a cup of coffee, or that attractive student in your ten o'clock history lecture. "That's enough of that!" you tell yourself somewhat angrily. With firm resolve you straighten up and begin to read about ". . . theoretical considerations relative to the integration of economic processes . . ." and it happens again. The words blur and become meaningless, and once more your thoughts have wandered to more pleasant contemplations.

You cannot concentrate on the book. Your will power seems to have lost its will—or its power. What can you do to fend off the human side of yourself—besides starting a fire?

We might begin working on this problem by asking: what are you doing when you're not concentrating on something? You're concentrating on something else, of course. As long as you are awake, you are concentrating on one thing or another. However, by concentration we usually mean *sustained attention,* focused in one direction with no distractions. When we say we "can't concentrate," we really mean we have difficulty keeping our attention directed toward physics, philosophy, or French. We're concentrating, all right—on the many mental detours and side roads into which various distractions lead us.

And how do these distractions arise? The prime movers of errant thoughts are *needs*. Man is motivated to act because of needs. Whichever one is dominant at a given time will determine what he pays attention to.

In the chart below are indicated three needs that Student M has one night at 9:30. In this case, the need to study is low on the totem pole, and no matter how ferociously Student M tears into his textbook, he will not get very far. What can be done about it? Obviously, he can either reduce the need for money and food, or he can increase the need to study—or better yet, do both.

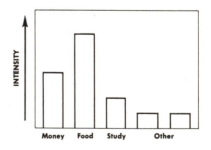

Reducing the hunger drive is easy. All one has to do is eat. But before biting into that cheeseburger, let's see if eating can somehow be turned into an advantage in doing a better job of studying. It can be done by resolving to study for a certain period of time—20 or 30 minutes or an hour—and then taking the cheeseburger break at the end of that time as a reward. Thus, you have turned a need and its reduction into an incentive, something to work toward.

Handling the need for money, or love, or friendship is harder. If your book is open but you are thinking about writing home for money or seeing a special friend, you can reduce the needs involved mainly in two ways. First you can write the letter home, or see the object of your need right away. Second, you can jot down notes on a piece of paper: "Write home tomorrow noon," "Make a telephone call at 10:30 P.M." From then on, the paper will remember for you, leaving your learning machine free from that distraction. Not until 10:30 P.M. or tomorrow noon will you be further distracted by those needs.

Speaking of distractions, what can be done about the student in the next room who has a stereophonic hi-fi set and impaired hearing? While soft, mild music can sometimes aid concentration, particularly if it cuts out disturbing noises, loud, cacophonous music is a hindrance to concentration. The only thing that can be done to combat any external distraction, whether it be music, pin-up girl, boyfriend's picture, or an exciting novel, is to be far away from it. Arrange your study spot so potentially distracting needs will not be triggered off by some sight, sound, or smell. It is sound practice to have a cubbyhole somewhere which is used for nothing but studying. If that isn't always feasible, then at least have your desk facing the wall and send your roommate to a movie!

Now let's consider how the need to study can be increased. When we are not interested in a book, our need for studying is low, and we are likely to have difficulty concentrating. Our interest may be low because of many things, among them being:

1. lack of previous knowledge of the field,
2. lack of purpose or direction (no questions to be answered),
3. poorly written books,
4. inadequate reading or studying skills.

Strange as it may seem, any or all of these problems can be resolved, and our interest heightened, by following SQ4R. While SQ4R cannot give us a substantial background knowledge in a new subject-matter field (general introductory texts or outline books can do this), it does provide a rough background and an organization of the major points being made. Again, while SQ4R is certainly not going to provide anyone with a long-term life goal, it does

provide powerfully motivating short-term goals, i.e., questions that *must* be answered.

Even with poorly written, dull books, SQ4R provides first aid. It helps us direct our attention toward determining the author's main points, no matter how well hidden with verbiage they may be. Once they are found, questions can be asked, and the rest of the 4 R's follow along.

It cannot be stressed too strongly—even though it has been the major theme of this book so far—that SQ4R is the most successful method yet devised to increase learning ability. Once you have learned the SQ4R skill by employing it many times in studying interesting, well-organized texts, you will find it possible to tackle the toughest assignments and make sense out of them.

Other techniques, of course, will help concentration. You will do better in a straight chair at a desk in a cool garret room than you will in an easy chair in front of a roaring fire. Taking advantage of your clear, sharp periods during the day, organizing your work efficiently, and putting yourself under the pressure of time limits can be done by using a time schedule. How this can be accomplished so well that you even have one day each week completely free of study is discussed at the end of this chapter.

After this, when you have retreated to your distraction-free desk and find your "mind wandering," follow it to find out where it goes. In other words, determine what needs are stronger than the need to study. Reduce the extraneous needs in the ways suggested, and increase the need to study by using SQ4R. Hereafter, concentration will be your tool. Then, like a photographer, you will be able to focus just on the subject at hand.

EXERCISES

COMPREHENSION

What are you doing when you're not (1) _____ on something? However, by concentration we usually mean (2) _____ (3) _____. . . . The prime movers of errant thoughts are (4) _____. . . . Whichever one is (5) _____ at a given time will determine what he pays (6) _____ to. . . . Thus, you have turned a need . . . into an (7) _____.

. . . When we are not interested in a book, our need for studying is (8) _____. . . . SQ4R . . . does provide powerfully motivating (9) _____-_____ goals. . . . Other techniques will help concentration. Determine what needs are (10) _____ than the need to study.

READING

This Week I've Got to Get Organized

"Time is money," a wise old philosopher once said. The two seem to have much in common. For example, many students who are new to the learning game find that time slips away as easily as money from an undiscovered hole in a pocket. Therefore, explore some methods of getting the largest dividends from your time investment.

In any college crowd, the successful student stands out. He is the one who has read and learned the lesson *before* the class period, and who has the assigned homework done on time. He is seldom faced with the problem of feverishly concocting a paper just before the deadline. Often he is the one who holds important campus positions and has the necessary time to enjoy other extracurricular activities.

How does he do it? How does he find time for all his school work and for other activities too? He has learned by trial-and-success to organize his time effectively. There is another old saying: If you want something done, give it to a busy man. People find themselves able to produce a great deal when they have much to do. Of course, under pressure of time we often work more efficiently. It is also true that *too much* pressure blows a fuse, as it were, in our "learning machine." We become subject to panic and then to disorganization. Fortunately, the intelligent, productive use of pressure can be learned.

What happens when we are under moderate pressure, as, for instance, when a term paper is due shortly? First, we are usually more *motivated* as the due date becomes imminent and are thus able to sit down and begin the task. Sometimes we are able to *organize* our work more efficiently, although usually a better paper results if the ideas are not crowded together just before the deadline. Moderate pressure, then, often leads to conditions which prevent time-wasting distractions from detouring us.

It is usually surprising, if not downright shocking, to discover how much "time-frittering" we do. To estimate your spend-thrift rating, keep a running account of what you do during a typical day. For a rough check, recall how much studying you did yesterday. Now what did you do with the rest of the time? There is probably a substantial amount of time not present and accounted for.

To determine where the money is going, young couples set up a budget. If some of the income might be spent more wisely, appropriate uses are included in the budget. To find out where your time is going, and where it should be going, you can set up a "budget" also. By following the steps below, you can *organize* your time along the lines followed by successful students. Setting definite times to study specific courses provides time pressures helpful in *motivating* you. Not only will your work be done on time, but you should have one study-free day each week.

Before starting the steps below you may wish to look over the sample time schedule following this article. It can serve as a guide as you make out one for yourself.

1. Tear out one of the blank Study Schedules from the back of the book. Your schedule will be set up on an hourly basis, from 7 A.M. until 10 P.M., six days a week.

2. Put your class schedule and any other permanent activity for this semester in the appropriate blank in ink (indicated on the sample by capital letters). All the rest of the schedule should be filled in using a pencil, perhaps colored ones, to facilitate changes later.

3. Now schedule your meals. Breakfast, as well as washing and dressing, should be completed so you are ready to begin work at eight. Incidentally, breakfast should not be missed since it provides energy for the day's work and diminishes that soggy, dragged-out, mid-afternoon feeling. Take a one-hour block for *lunch;* this period is used both for eating and for other forms of enjoyment—reading, chatting with friends, listening to records. *Dinner* is a two-hour block—as from 5 to 7 P.M.—during which time you can again relax from studying.

4. At this point write in the courses you are currently taking. There is a box for this entry at the bottom of the page. Alongside each course indicate the credit hours it carries. Multiply the credit hours by two to get a rough estimate of the number of hours to be reserved for homework each week. You can always change this later if you need more or less time in certain courses.

5. Now you can begin one of the last steps—logging in the times for studying. These guides should be helpful:

a. Pick out one specific time each day to work on your hardest course. This should be a period when you are as alert as possible and least likely to be disturbed. For instance, on the sample schedule English has been blocked in at 7 P.M. for this reason. Your second hardest course can be handled in the same way.

b. To fill in the rest of your study hours, it is necessary only to know who is supposed to do the talking in class. If the instructor does the talking, it's a *lecture* class. Set aside an hour as soon after the class as possible. (Note the English, history, and psychology study periods following classes on Monday, Wednesday, and Friday.) Spend the first 5 or 10 minutes reorganizing your class notes from the lecture. First, survey the entire lecture and notice whether you have left out any major ideas. If you have, add them to your notes. Now, cross out insignificant material. You can carry on using any other of the steps of SQ4R that are necessary so that you learn the important points brought out in the lecture.

If you do the talking, in other words, if it is a *discussion* or *recitation* section, then schedule a study period for that course as soon before the class as you can. (Note math recitation study periods just before class on Tuesday, Thursday, and Saturday.) This warm-up period will give you an opportunity to go through the material you have studied, and will enable you to participate more fully and effectively in class—a trait not overlooked by professors. This warm-up is particularly helpful in foreign language classes.

c. Studying over one hour in a particular course is usually not any more advisable than eating one kind of food for too long—you become satiated. Break up the routine by switching to dissimilar subjects. In some courses you may not be able to study for an hour before the subject matter begins to get confused. For instance, most students cannot study grammar or vocabulary in a foreign language more than fifteen or twenty minutes without the satiation setting in.

d. Reward yourself with a five or ten minute break each hour. Get up, stretch, walk around, get a drink of water, look through a magazine, get something to eat. You will work harder with a goal in mind, and will return to work with renewed vigor.

6. *Theme Writing.* A theme that is assigned on Monday to be turned in on Friday morning is too often written on Thursday night. Procrastination of this sort can put pressure on you, but in this case pressure causes a feeling of panic. There is a frantic attempt to think of something to write about, and the result is often a poorly organized paper.

It is much simpler to make pressure work for you rather than against you. You can enlist its aid by dividing the work into three operations: (1) On the day that the paper is assigned think through the topic, do some reading if necessary, and jot down an outline of what you want to say. (2) The next night, while reading through your outline, you will see it in a new light. Changes will probably present themselves. Then type a rough draft. (3) The next evening read through your draft and again make any changes that seem necessary—or even have your roommate read it to see whether it gets across. Then type the final copy. People switching to this procedure usually raise their grades substantially.

7. *Review.* Reviewing is the fourth R, and its importance has been stressed already. You can build a period for reviewing right into your schedule. *Each day* you might set aside a half hour or so in the evening to go over your notes from the lectures and homework of the day to determine whether you have learned the important ideas. At the *end of the week,* the same process can be followed—setting aside a half hour or so per class to go over the basic material of the week. Use your SQ4R notes as cues and see how much you remember.

8. Use your "free day" each week for what you want—you have earned it. You will also experience the pleasant feeling of having enough time to do everything you want to, and of knowing how to make time pressure work for you instead of against you.

9. When you have your schedule completed, there is only one step that remains. *Use it!* But use it as a guide, not as a straight jacket. Revise it when necessary. But *use it.*

SAMPLE STUDY SCHEDULE

	MONDAY	TUESDAY	WEDNESDAY	THURSDAY	FRIDAY	SATURDAY	SUNDAY
7	BREAKFAST	BREAKFAST	BREAKFAST	BREAKFAST	BREAKFAST	BREAKFAST	SLEEP
8	HISTORY LECTURE	Study Psych.	HISTORY LECTURE	Study Psych.	HISTORY LECTURE	BREAKFAST	SLEEP
9	Study History	Review Math	Study History	Review Math	Study History	Review Math	BREAKFAST
10	ENGLISH LECTURE	MATH REC.	Review Psych.	MATH REC.	ENGLISH LECTURE	MATH REC.	FREE
11	Study English	Study Geology	Review English	FREE	Study English	Free Study	FREE
12	LUNCH	LUNCH	LUNCH	LUNCH	LUNCH	LUNCH	DINNER
1	PSYCH. LECTURE	GEOLOGY LECTURE	PSYCH. REC.	GEOLOGY LECTURE	PSYCH. LECTURE	FREE	DINNER
2	Study Psych.	Study Geology	ENGLISH REC.	GEOLOGY LAB	Study Psych.	FREE	Review of week
3	FREE	Study Math			Review of day	FREE	
4	Study Geology	PHYSICAL EDUCATION	RECREATION	PHYSICAL EDUCATION	FREE	FREE	FREE
5	RELAXATION AND DINNER	RELAXATION AND DINNER	RELAXATION AND DINNER	RELAXATION AND DINNER	RELAXATION AND DINNER	RELAXATION AND DINNER	SUPPER
6							Study Psych.
7	Study English	Study English	Study English	Study English	RECREATION		Study English
8	Study Math	Study History	Study Math	Study History	RECREATION		Study History
9	Review of day	Review of day	Study Geology	Review of day	RECREATION		FREE

TEXT

_____

_____

_____

Courses	Hrs. Credit	Hrs. Study (2✕)
English	4	8
History	3	6
Math	3	6
Psychology	3	6
Geology	3*	4*

* 1 credit hour is for the 2 hour lab period and should not take outside study.

Every year thousands upon thousands of adults return to school to improve their reading. The large majority of them are successful career men and women, eager to polish up skills which are too primitive for the reading demands of a rocket age.

The basic ingredients of the courses designed for businessmen are the same as those found in college reading improvement courses. Part III, a core course for colleges, contains the ingredients for learning to read efficiently.

LESSON 9

Perception: The Foundation of Reading Ability

Most college students are good readers. Admission policies tend to screen out many applicants who are unskilled in this tool subject. But some ineffective readers get past the screening. Their lack of skill is often incorrectly attributed to poor instruction or to lack of purpose. It may well be caused by a chink in the foundation processes, the perceptual skills.

Effective reading is an outgrowth of a physical structure much like that of a building: the footings consist of the senses, those processes, like vision and hearing, which keep us in touch with the world, and which give us a foundation in reality. The superstructure, the uprights and crossbeams which organize our incoming sensations, are called perceptual skills. And, leaning on sensation and perception, like the outer shell of a building, are the conceptual processes, the thinking, relating, selecting, formulating parts of the structure. We have already said much about the conceptual side of reading and more will be covered in the next lesson. The perceptual processes, on the other hand, constitute the forgotten component of reading skill.

Perception: Four Factors . . . and a Fifth

To understand the meaning of perception, it is helpful to follow through the steps by which it may be studied. First, we must give a large series of tests to a group of people. These tests include, among others, the Greek letter test appearing in the front of this book. Next, we determine which tests are related to one another *more than* they are related to other tests in the series. That is, the people who score high in one test may also score high on two or three other tests, while their scores on the remaining ones may be medium or low. When certain tests appear to cling

III

How to Read

together or cluster in this way, we say that they identify a *factor,* some underlying process. Four perceptual factors account for most of the difference in perceptual skills within a group. Because of what they seem to measure, they may be named closure, speed, memory, and accuracy.

Perceptual Closure. Closure is the term used to indicate the neural events which take place when the following pictures are identified:

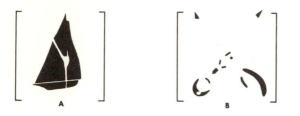

Picture A will be readily identified as a sailboat. Picture B is much more difficult and is seldom identified correctly as a pair of scissors. One must "close a gap," thereby completing the figure. People differ greatly in their ability to recognize whole pictures from a few parts.

Size of vocabulary is known to be related to the closure factor. It might be reasoned that the ability to guess the meaning of a new word by noting the surrounding ideas results in learning new vocabulary. When the paragraph is understood even though the meaning of an important word is unknown, the mind must have filled in a gap, a "conceptual gap."

If we now reason by analogy, we might expect that a person scoring high on this factor would be able to understand a sentence by reading only a few words in it. The other words would be filled in by the mind. Therefore, this person would probably be a rapid reader. And this actually is the case.

Perceptual Speed. A second highly important factor is speed in noting similarities and differences. In the following problem, the task is to find the figure on the right which is the same as the one on the left.

One must be able to shift rapidly back and forth and to notice small differences in order to do well. This skill is necessary for quick recognition of words. Interestingly, fluency of speech is also related to this factor. And, of course, the similarity of the speed factor to rate of reading is clear.

Perceptual Memory. Ability to reproduce from memory a pattern perceived visually is the best measure of this factor:

How visual memory relates to reading is difficult to say. Apparently, the pattern remains "in mind," long enough to be reproduced. Other things equal, one who does well on this factor might be expected to have no trouble in understanding *sentences.* Rereading of sentences would seldom be necessary since the first words, phrases, or ideas might be expected to stay "alive" until the sentence was completed.

Perceptual Accuracy. This factor is best measured by the speed test. Instead of scoring for the number of items answered correctly in one or two minutes, scoring is based on the percentage of correct answers. Some people double check their answers while others make a quick choice and leap onward.

The Fifth Factor. The fifth factor is not strictly perceptual but it seems to have a profound effect on perceptual skills. The fifth factor is *tension.* It has a strong negative effect on perceptual speed.

While the underlying neural events are not known, tension appears to affect reading as follows: As we "track" or follow the words across the line during reading, minute adjustments occur in the musculature controlling the direction of visual aim, i.e., where the eyes are pointing. Tension appears to disrupt that control *momentarily* and *without the reader's awareness.* As a result, the eye slips up, down or sideways, picking up extraneous letters or words. The reader, who thinks he is still aiming at a particular word, finds that it changes it's shape or that he is now reading on the line below. Thus, he must constantly refixate words, look at them over and over to be sure what they are.

Factor Combinations

Present evidence indicates that superior readers tend to be relatively high on all four perceptual factors and that inferior readers tend to be low. Since the factors are relatively unrelated, we should expect some people to be high in speed and closure and moderate to low in memory and accuracy. This seems to be the case for the disorganized reader. He reads rapidly but inaccurately. He seldom remembers the material long enough to do well on a comprehension test.

Others will be high on memory and accuracy and low on speed, on closure, or on both. The slow reader with good comprehension should be high on memory and accuracy and at least average in speed and closure. The slow reader with poor comprehension may be:

1. high in accuracy (for words), *and*
2. low in memory, *and/or*
3. low in speed, *and/or*
4. low in closure.

What can be done about these skills? Once more, from present evidence, it appears that there is a large constitutional component involved, particularly in the chemistry of the central nervous system. Insofar as practice can ameliorate deficits, the following procedures are most effective:

1. *Low accuracy:* develop a set or habit of accuracy by (1) formulating a question or purpose before reading and by (2) rereading to check correctness.
2. *Low memory:* determine the framework of the material by a survey, thus providing large ideas with which the details may be associated; review frequently.
3. *Low closure:* trying to read faster results in increased effort, i.e., increased muscular tension, with the result that closure improves; practice reading with words deleted to *force* the mind to bridge gaps.
4. *Low speed:* frequent timed readings in which you *anticipate* what is coming next; anticipation is the sensitizing of neural processes with the result that recognition occurs rapidly.

It will be noted that reading under time pressure appears to influence speed and closure. In addition, it forces concentration so that at least one cause of low accuracy, mind-wandering, is reduced.

There is little to be said concerning tension. If it is chronic, medication or psychotherapy or both may be necessary. In the meantime, perceptual errors due to tension can be reduced by using the finger or a stylus to follow the line, by covering preceding and succeeding lines by a 3 x 5 card with a long narrow slot cut out, and by practicing reading materials with large print and well-spaced words and lines.

Conclusion

The forgotten component of reading skill is perception. Herein lies the key to many of the individual differences in reading skill and to the special problems of those extremely low in one or more aspects of perception. Procedures designed to improve reading rate appear to influence perceptual skills also, either by improving those skills or by providing compensatory measures to offset the effects of faulty perception. For example, reading rapidly provides a feeling for the context so that only a few words in a line need to be recognized.

EXERCISES

COMPREHENSION

Lack of skill is incorrectly attributed to poor (1) _____ or to lack of (2) _____. The (3) _____ processes are the forgotten component of reading skill. The factors are named (4) _____, (5) _____, (6) _____, and (7) _____. The fifth factor is (8) _____. Anticipation is the sensitizing of neural processes so that recognition occurs (9) _____. The most effective kind of practice to improve skill appears to be reading under (10) _____ pressure.

APPLICATION

Rate Improvement

Read the following selection at your normal rate. Time yourself carefully, and determine your rate in words per minute by referring to the time-rate chart on page 135. Then do the comprehension test, and record both rate and comprehension scores in the spaces provided.

Efficient Vocabulary Building

A number of word-building techniques have been suggested. Diligent study of the dictionary is advocated by some. Others say look up all the new words one meets. Still others suggest the learning of certain common word roots, prefixes, and suffixes. The claim is sometimes made that the learning of fifty or one hundred of these parts assures mastery of 100,000 words or more. This claim is yet to be demonstrated.

It should be remembered that a word is simply a tag or label for an experience having meaning. Learning the label without having had the appropriate experience or meaning is lost effort. The word is often forgotten more quickly than it was learned.

All is not hopeless. Vicarious experience can often be substituted for direct experience. For example, college students seem to understand the meaning of "charlatan" when "a medical quack" is offered as an example of one genus and a "confidence man" as another.

But such a method is time consuming. Wide reading by a person motivated to build vocabulary and sensitive to the power of words to stir emotions and to direct behavior is probably the most painless and efficient method. Finding a word in several contexts will bring gradual understanding of the meaning.

Time_____min. _____sec. Rate_____wpm.

COMPREHENSION CHECK

1. Which of the following word-building techniques is *not* mentioned in the article? (a) direct study of the dictionary (b) putting new words and their definitions on cards (c) looking up all new words in a dictionary (d) learning common word roots and affixes.
2. It is said that mastery of 100,000 or more words is assured if we learn how many common parts of words? (a) 25 or 50 (b) 50 or 75 (c) 75 or 100 (d) 50 or 100.
3. The claim that knowing a few word parts results in mastery of thousands of words is (a) proved by evidence (b) proved to be untrue (c) an obvious over-estimation (d) yet to be demonstrated.
4. According to the article, learning a new word without an appropriate experience or meaning (a) is difficult (b) is impossible (c) is often necessary (d) requires special techniques.
5. The most efficient vocabulary-building technique is (a) wide reading (b) using new words in original sentences (c) memorizing common word roots and affixes (d) dictionary study.

% Comprehension_____

See Key, page 135, for answers.

Now read the following selection, *trying* to read faster. *Push* yourself a little, and see if you can't improve on your rate for Part A. Use the chart on page 135 for computing rate, and record rate and comprehension scores. Remember—*faster* this time!

Reading Rate and Simultaneous Body Movements

The story is told of an elderly gentleman who was visiting a reading center at an Eastern university. A technician was demonstrating a pacing device which forced attention and rapid reading by bringing a shade down the page at a predetermined rate. Asked whether he wished to try it, he said, "All right. Set it at 200 words a minute. That's my limit."

He struggled to keep ahead of the shade but managed to murmur to himself and to keep his thumbs twirling rhythmically as he read. He scored 70 per cent on a test of comprehension following the exercise. When the technician suggested setting the machine at 300 words a minute, he protested vigorously. "I couldn't possibly do it. Look how poorly I read that article." But he tried it.

As the shade moved past the first lines, he became tense, his head swayed as his eyes moved, and his thumbs twirled at 250 revolutions per minute—but no faster. Gradually the thumbs stopped moving, the head stopped swaying, and the murmuring ceased. Only the eyes continued to move. He had learned to read! His comprehension? A very respectable 90 per cent.

The story illustrates some of the habits which interfere with good reading. Others are gum chewing, head scratching, foot waving, pencil chewing, etc.

Time_____min. _____sec. Rate_____wpm.

COMPREHENSION CHECK

1. The gentleman was sure that he could read only (a) 250 words per minute (b) 300 wpm. (c) 200 wpm. (d) none of these.
2. When he was forced to increase his rate, his comprehension (a) improved (b) decreased (c) stayed the same.
3. The reading center mentioned might have been at (a) Northwestern University (b) Harvard University (c) University of Southern California (d) any of these.
4. Which of the following was *not* mentioned? (a) moving finger along line of print (b) twirling thumbs rhythmically (c) moving head back and forth (d) saying words to self while reading.
5. One conclusion we can draw from this selection is:
   (a) Increased rate is accompanied by better comprehension
   (b) One must speed up the movements of the whole body in order to increase reading rate
   (c) Our eyes should do the work while reading, since they can move so much faster than our head, fingers, etc.
   (d) Pacing devices bring about the biggest and quickest gains in reading rate.

% Comprehension_____

See Key, page 135, for answers.

You undoubtedly read faster the second selection, simply because you *tried* to. And, unless you overdid it, you probably had an adequate comprehension score. This is a helpful technique (consciously trying to read faster), and if you try doing it for ten or fifteen minutes every day, using easy material, you will soon find that your rate has increased considerably.

Certain other techniques can help you in the initial stages of trying to push yourself out of the word-by-word rut. They are listed below, and are designed to help develop an alert mental and physical set. If they appear childish or silly to you at first, don't let that fool you. They work!

Read the following paragraph. Really *push hard* on this one. Aim for a big jump in rate, *even though you think you'll miss some ideas. Don't* let yourself reread anything—missing the main idea will be no excuse. And before you start, get ready for maximum effort by:

1. Putting both feet flat on the floor.
2. Sitting up straight in your chair.
3. Holding the book with *both* hands at a comfortable angle—*not* flat on the table.

Feel uncomfortable? Good! A little irritated? Even better! You'll read faster now—and remember, *Push!*

Do We Dare *Skip* Words?

Common belief to the contrary, it is usually unnecessary to read every word. Experimentation will show that most material is fully understood by reading less than half the words. The remainder is reconstructed by a brain which thinks many times faster than the eyes can move.

The procedure depends partly on the habit of *anticipating* what the author will say. This is well illustrated by the ease with which familiar material is read. The second reading moves much faster than the first simply because we know what to expect; we've been over this road before. The same process operates to some extent in most of our reading. Anticipation becomes more accurate and memory more dependable if a preview of the materials is possible. This is accomplished by skimming through chapter or section headings, by reading the introduction and summary, and by utilizing any other available aids for getting a broad picture of the selection.

The result: the efficient reader moves over the page quickly until he is *jarred.* "This isn't what I expected," or "There's a new idea!" Now he will read carefully, perhaps even look back over an earlier section. Another way of stating the point is that the efficient reader is *selective;* he focuses on important points and skims over the familiar or unimportant, anticipating as he goes.

Time_____min. _____sec. Rate_____wpm.

COMPREHENSION CHECK

1. There is evidence that good understanding can usually result from reading only (a) 70-80% of the words (b) 40-50% (c) 20-30% (d) 60-70%.
2. According to the article, reading something the second time is easier because (a) we can skip many of the words (b) we know what to expect (c) we generally read it more carefully (d) we are jarred by important ideas.
3. Anticipation becomes more accurate if (a) we preview materials before reading (b) we read introductory and concluding paragraphs first (c) we utilize skimming as one of our study techniques (d) all of these.
4. The author believes that the most important characteristic of the efficient reader is that he (a) skims frequently (b) reads almost every word much of the time, but skips words when possible (c) reads only half the words in an assignment (d) reads selectively.
5. It also seems that the good reader (a) never reads every word (b) always reads every word (c) lets his brain fill in blanks left by skipped words (d) becomes actively and emotionally involved in his reading.

% Comprehension_____

See Key, page 135, for answers.

This should have been your best rate, considerably faster than in either the first or the second selections. But what about comprehension? If you were *really* pushing hard enough to "stretch" yourself, you probably missed some points and scored lower on the test. This often happens when we attempt to increase our rate, and is so discouraging that we usually give up the idea and revert to our initial snail's pace—with nothing having been accomplished.

It is important to recognize that increased rates of reading will almost inevitably be accompanied by lower comprehension—*temporarily.* When comprehension drops, however, *don't* slow down again; rather, hold rate constant at the new higher level until you get used to it, and good comprehension will be restored. Then push up to a still higher rate, hold it constant until comprehension catches up, and so on. The chart below illustrates the typical pattern of scores during a rate-improvement program. Note

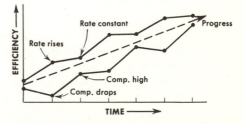

Fluctuations of rate and comprehension during reading improvement

that in spite of occasional drops in comprehension, the over-all trend is an *upward* one.

Continue practicing your rate of reading every day. In the back of this book are some articles appropriate for this purpose. Ten or fifteen minutes a day will result in some very substantial increases if you use all the techniques described above.

And remember—*Push!*

READING

Psycho-Technics

In many reading improvement courses, particularly those in which one of the primary objectives is the increase of reading rate, there are regularly scheduled practice sessions utilizing certain mechanical devices. These devices are designed, of course, to help students improve certain reading skills, and it is appropriate that they should be given some consideration at this point.

The Use of Mechanical Aids in Reading Programs

The most commonly used devices can be divided into two general categories: (1) those designed to increase reading rate by forcing the student, under pressure, to read each succeeding exercise a little faster than the preceding one; and (2) those designed to increase reading rate by improving eye span and eye movements.

In the first category are machines called pacers. When using these, the reader places a book on a platform, and then reads *ahead* of a shutter (or within a band of light) which gradually covers the page at a constant rate of speed. The rate at which the shutter or band of light moves is increased at the beginning of each practice session, until a satisfactory reading rate is achieved. Thus, in addition to the pressure toward increased rate exerted by the reader himself, pacing devices provide assistance through external pressure.

Reading films and tachistoscopes are included in the second category. When such films are used, a short article or story is projected on the screen, one or two paragraphs at a time, but with only one phrase or line of print in focus at a time. The rate at which the phrases or lines are illuminated or brought into focus increases with each successive film. Thus, the reader is not only forced to proceed at a predetermined rate, as with the pacers, but he must also utilize a regular pattern of eye movements in order to fixate properly on each phrase as it is presented.

The tachistoscope, as the name implies (tachisto = quick; scope = view), is a device which flashes images on a screen for a brief period, often less than a tenth of a second. Numbers, words, and phrases are used for tachistoscopic practice in reading classes, and the width of the projected image is gradually increased, so that, with practice, longer and longer numbers and words can be perceived at a small fraction of a second. The objective of this kind of exercise is to increase eye span (number of words perceived in one fixation), and thus, reading speed and efficiency.

The Effectiveness of Mechanical Aids

Opinion concerning the value of such devices is divided. Some insist that the large gains in reading rate achieved in many classes are due largely to the use of pacers and other similar aids, while others maintain that the devices are of little practical use. Since the improvement they encourage occurs in an *artificial* situation, it is not carried over, or transferred, into a more normal reading environment where no machines are used.

There is a body of research evidence which bears on this question. It may be briefly summarized: there is no significant difference in the amount of improvement in reading skills between classes trained *without* machines and those trained *with* machines. Such evidence neither confirms nor refutes the claims of those who insist that certain mechanical devices are of primary importance in any good reading program. It indicates, rather, that the really important factor may be *effort*, a sincere attempt to improve reading skills through guided and systematic practice. If this factor is operating, then gains in reading skills should be substantial—with or without mechanical assistance.

Then why bother to spend time using pacers, tachistoscopes, and other similar paraphernalia? There are two reasons. First, the studies summarized above are based on *average* improvement of large groups of students, and overlook the possibility that certain individuals might need the additional external pressure of a machine in order to achieve maximum gains. The second reason is that there is a certain psychological value in using a pacer or a tachistoscope. It is something interesting and different to do, it is something concrete to work with, and it, therefore, encourages *more* of that effort which is so important in developing really efficient reading skills.

It is clear, therefore, that you may find it helpful to do some work with a pacer or tachistoscope, particularly if you are having difficulty making any substantial gains in rate, or if you find your interest and desire to practice flagging now and then. These devices can be maximally helpful *only* if they are used properly, so you should keep the following suggestions clearly in mind when you become involved in "mechanized" practice sessions.

Pacing Devices

MATERIALS

For your initial work with pacers you should use stories and articles that are interesting and relatively easy. Since you will be concerned with level of comprehension as well as rate, some provision should be made for testing your understanding of each article you read. A number of articles appropriate for practice with pacers are included in the appendix of this book, and each one is accompanied by a comprehension test.

Later on you may be interested in practicing with textbooks and other more difficult material, but this should be postponed until you have made substantial gains with the easier materials.

RATE SETTINGS

Initial rate settings should correspond to your rate on the diagnostic reading test. After you have become familiar with the operation of the machine (one or two exercises will be enough for this), determine subsequent rates in the following way:

1. With each exercise set the machine from twenty to fifty words per minute faster than on the preceding exercise.
2. If you find at first that you are able to read faster than the rate at which the machine is set, it may be advisable to use intervals larger than fifty words per minute for a time. As soon as you reach a level at which you have to push to keep ahead of the machine, however, revert to the smaller increases.
3. *Always* select a rate greater than the preceding one. *Never* use a slower rate, or the same rate two times in succession. If on one exercise your comprehension is so poor that you hesitate to jump even twenty words per minute, then increase the rate by *ten* words per minute—but *increase* it!

PROVIDING FOR TRANSFER

It should be obvious that no amount of practice with any machine will be of any practical value unless it also helps you to read faster *without* mechanical assistance. Some provision must be made for insuring carry-over, or transfer, of increased rates developed with machine practice to normal reading situations. The easiest way to do this is to follow each machine-paced exercise to match as nearly as possible your machine rate by *putting pressure on yourself*. In this

way, you will avoid becoming dependent on the pacer for rapid reading rates.

PRACTICE SESSIONS

As in the development of many skills, you will find that satisfactory gains will occur more rapidly if you practice rather frequently—three or four times a week, for example. It is also important to keep these practice sessions brief. You will find, after a little practice, that you can do one exercise with a pacer and one without, including comprehension tests, in twenty or thirty minutes. If you do this much three or four times a week you should soon notice some very substantial improvement. If you are unable to practice more than twice a week, however, you may wish to do more at one sitting, but never practice longer than an hour. If you put real effort into your work with pacers you will begin to fatigue after an hour or so, and you will reach a point of diminishing returns. The best results will be achieved with frequent practice sessions of moderate length.

The Tachistoscope

TRADITIONAL USE

Many researchers have concerned themselves with the eye movement patterns of poor readers. They have discovered that slow or inaccurate readers have "poor" eye movements—they fixate many times on one line of print, reading one word at a time; they move their eyes erratically rather than rhythmically; and they often reread words and phrases instead of moving on at a steady pace. Since most good readers seem to have more efficient patterns of eye movements than poor readers, it was thought that training programs designed to improve eye movements would help poor readers to develop better reading skills. Consequently, various tachistoscopic devices, as we mentioned earlier, have been used in an attempt to improve eye movements, primarily by increasing eye span. In some training programs, students who at first could perceive no more than two or three digits exposed for a tenth of a second learned to recognize more than a dozen digits at an exposure time of one-fiftieth of a second! Still other students have learned to perceive longer and longer words, phrases, and even short sentences during similarly brief exposures.

LIMITATIONS

The object of the type of training described above was to enable students to perceive several words with one fixation, thus reducing the number of necessary fixations per line, and, as a result, increasing reading speed and comprehension. These programs do not achieve their ultimate objective very satisfactorily, however, primarily because of a problem mentioned earlier in connection with pacing devices. That problem is one of transfer. Learning how to read whole phrases in one brief fixation with a tachistoscope is quite different from doing the same thing in a normal reading situation; skills developed in one case do not easily transfer to the other. This is particularly true when numbers are used in the training sessions. This type of practice may develop excellent license-plate spotters for police departments, but it is only distantly related to the problem of reading ideas in a book or magazine! The same thing is true, to a lesser extent, when words and phrases are used, and there is no evidence that such training has any but a negligible effect on eye movements and reading skill. In fact, contrary to earlier belief, it now seems that poor eye movements do not *cause* poor reading, but rather that they are *results* of poor reading. Students who manage to improve their reading skills also demonstrate definite improvement in eye movement patterns, whether they were exposed to eye movement training or not.

EFFECTIVE USE IN RATE IMPROVEMENT

Even though tachistoscopes are of questionable value when used to improve eye movements, they *can* be used to good effect in another way. Like pacing devices, they are interesting to operate, and provide additional incentive for many students. They can be used for stimulating warm-up exercises to alert your mind for quick perception just before you start with your practice with a pacer. If you use words and phrases (not rows of digits) in five or ten-minute periods, you may find your work with subsequent exercises more rewarding.

Summary

Significant improvement in reading skills can be achieved in programs in which no mechanical aids are used. Such aids may be helpful for some students, however, particularly as motivating devices. When used properly during frequent, but relatively brief, practice sessions, pacers and tachistoscopes can help students achieve maximum gains.

LESSON 10

Comprehension: A New Strategy

Much instructional material designed to improve reading comprehension results only in "busy work." Commonly, exercises consist of a number of paragraphs with instructions to find the topic sentence or main idea. Following each are questions to determine whether or not the reader has understood the central meaning or main idea of the passage. Generally, such materials *test* comprehension; they do not *teach* it. Instead, as we shall see, they teach the learner how to outwit the examiner!

To illustrate, a question which tests understanding of the main idea of a passage usually includes four possible answers:

(1) one will be too broad,
(2) another will refer to a detail, thus, be too narrow,
(3) another will be irrelevant, and finally,
(4) one will be correct.

After experience with such material, the student becomes sensitive to the "too broad, too narrow, irrelevant" scheme. He is then able to select the correct choice *often without reading the paragraph.*

But, then, how *does* one improve his comprehension? To answer this question, we must refer to the processes which lead to understanding sentence ideas.

Sentence and Paragraph. The processes include (1) arousing the meaning of each word, and (2) simultaneous activation of all words. Out of the simultaneous activity of all words there develops a new network, the *sentence idea.*

By extrapolation, we might conclude that a paragraph idea derives from the simultaneous activity of all the sentence ideas. But even though sentence ideas will remain in mind longer than single word ideas, they will not remain active long enough to develop the new complex, the main idea of the paragraph. Therefore, a strategy different from speeded reading is necessary.

A New Strategy: Problem Solving

Adult readers are not generally aware of the number of steps they take when determining what a paragraph means. An analysis of their thought processes shows that they use a problem-solving procedure. The problem is this: what is this paragraph about? To solve the problem, they:

1. *Gather Evidence: Read the first sentence.*
   Example: Joe was so nervous that he spilled the bottle of ink all over the new rug.
2. *Hypothesize: The main idea of the paragraph is . . .*
   Name—Joe
   Said—spilled-ink-rug.
3. *Check: Read the next sentence to evaluate hypothesis.*
   When his uncle saw the mess, he flew into a rage and struck Joe.

Name—Uncle
Said—struck
Revise: Joe-spilled-ink-rug
        uncle-struck
Corrected hypothesis: Because Joe spilled ink on the
                        rug, his uncle struck him.

The key to the process is the hypothesis that the first sentence contains the main idea. By cue reducing that sentence, it can be carried in mind. Then, subsequent sentences can be compared with it to determine whether they add something new. If so, they are cue reduced and the new parts are added. If they add nothing new, the original hypothesis is retained.

The method reduces the need for extended activity of sentence ideas. But even more, it avoids the problem of determining a topic sentence in paragraphs of differing structures.

Paragraph Structures. Some paragraphs begin with a main idea or topic sentence. Subsequent sentences merely spell out the idea further. Such paragraphs can be depicted like this:

Others have the main idea or summary statement at the end:

Still others look like this:

In this case, no one sentence carries the main idea. Rather, it is implicit in the whole paragraph.

Another kind of paragraph has the main idea in the middle, with introductory sentences gradually leading to the topic sentence, which is then followed by further illustrative or explanatory statements:

Finally, topic sentences may appear at the outset, be explained and illustrated, and then restated or summarized at the end of the paragraph:

Such a variety of paragraph structure makes the search for a topic sentence a challenging enterprise and often a disappointing one. On the other hand, the paragraph analysis procedure described above will yield the main idea despite the structure of the paragraph.

The steps, once more, are as follows:

(1) gather evidence (read the first sentence),

(2) establish hypothesis (that the first sentence is the main idea),

(3) check (read the second sentence),

(4) revise if necessary (restate the hypothesis to include new ideas).

EXERCISES

COMPREHENSION

Much instructional material . . . is "busy work." Generally, such materials (1) _____ comprehension; they do not (2) _____ it. With practice on them, we learn to (3) _____ the examiner. . . . Of four possible answers, one is too (4) _____, one is too (5) _____, one is irrelevant, and the last is correct. Simultaneous activity of all the words in a sentence leads to a (6) _____ idea . . . *A New Strategy:* (7) _____. To solve the problem: what is this paragraph about? they gather (8) _____, establish a (9) _____, and then (10) _____ it.

APPLICATION

Paragraph Analysis

The following paragraphs are designed to give practice in the problem-solving strategy of paragraph analysis. Each paragraph is presented line by line, with blanks to be filled in and with the answer key near the right margin. Cover the key when you begin. As you fill each blank, uncover the next line of the key to check your correctness.

The first paragraphs are simple to enable you to learn the method. Later ones become quite difficult. (You will notice a step, "Guess," which was not included in the essay. It will give practice in anticipating the next ideas.)

1. Question: What is this paragraph about?

   "The ship's captain did not expect to be able to find the boy."

   1. Name? _____   *captain*

   2. Say? _____   *not able to find boy*

   3. Guess: This paragraph will be about the _____ of a ship   *captain*

      (either air or _____) who is looking for a _____.   *water, sea; boy*

   "Cross winds and currents cause drift, and a head is such a small object to spot in a vast area of rough water."

   4. Check? (Were you right?) _____   *yes*

   5. Guess: This paragraph will be about a ship's _____ looking   *captain*

      for a _____ in the _____. He must have fallen   *boy; water, ocean, sea*

      over_____.   *board*

   "As we learned later, the boy fell overboard a little after 7 A. M."*

   6. Check? _____   *yes*

   7. Repeat: captain—boy— _____   *overboard*

   Main Idea: A sea _____ is looking for a _____ who   *captain; boy*

   fell _____.   *overboard*

2. Question: What is this paragraph about?

   "General Lee was cheered by his troops as he moved majestically along the road toward his headquarters."

   1. Name? _____   *Lee*

   2. Say? _____   *was cheered*

   3. Guess: This paragraph will be about the feeling between Lee and

      his _____. They have probably just fought and _____   *troops, men; won*

      a battle.

   "When he finally reached his tent, officers and privates pressed toward him, trying to offer their help."

   4. Check? _____   *?*

   5. Guess: This paragraph will be about a time when Lee was about to

      _____ his men into battle.   *lead, take*

   "He told them over and over in a trembling voice to go home, put away their guns, plant their crops and obey the law of the victors."†

   6. Check? _____   *no*

   7. Repeat: troops—cheered Lee—go home—guns—obey _____   *law*

   _____ _____.   *of victors*

   Main Idea: Although defeated, Lee's _____ remain _____   *troops, men; loyal*
   to him.

* Adapted from Grant, Captain G. H. "Man Overboard." *Reader's Digest Advanced Reading Skill Builder,* Bk. 1, pp. 6-10. The Reader's Digest Association, Inc., 1958.
† Adapted from Dabney, Virginius. "Appomattox . . . Epic Surrender." *Reader's Digest Advanced Reading Skill Builder,* Bk. 3, p. 72. The Reader's Digest Association, Inc., 1958.

3. Question: What is this paragraph about?

"It was such a crowded scene with so many objects to attract attention that, at first, Nick stared about him, really without seeing anything at all."

1. N? _____   *Nick*

2. S? _____   *stared without seeing*

3. Guess: This paragraph will be about a man or boy named _____,   *Nick*

   in a place of some sort which is _____ with objects.   *crowded, filled*
   Apparently, he is a stranger here.

"By degrees, however, the place resolved itself into an almost unbelieveably bare and dirty room, with a couple of windows, only a tenth of which was glass, the remainder being stuffed with old school workbooks and assignment sheets."

4. Ck? (Is he a stranger?) _____   *yes (probably)*

5. G: This paragraph will be about a man or boy named _____,   *Nick*

   a stranger in a dirty _____. Since the windows are stuffed   *room*

   with school materials, it could be a _____ room.   *school*

"There were several long old rickety desks, cut and notched, and inked, and damaged in every possible way."

6. Ck? (schoolroom?) _____   *yes*

7. G: This paragraph will be about _____, a stranger in an   *Nick*

   old, dirty _____ room. Since he's new here, he may be   *school, class*

   a _____.   *pupil*

"There was a detached desk for the schoolmaster, Squeers, and another for Nick, his assistant."*

8. Ck? _____   *no*

Main Idea: This paragraph is about a dirty _____ room in   *school, class*

which a _____ named Nick is to be an _____   *man, boy; assistant*
schoolmaster.

4. "The period since the end of the Second World War is now widely recognized as the Age of Anxiety."

1. N? _____   *period W. W. II*

2. S? _____   *Age of Anxiety*

3. G: This paragraph will be about a time after _____ when   *W. W. II*

   people were very _____.   *anxious*

"It has been a time when men and women have been beset, as never before in history, by a host of fears and persistent doubts, uncertainty as to the future of the world, and worry of all sorts as to their individual destinies."

4. Ck? _____   *yes*

5. G: This paragraph will be about a time after _____ when   *W. W. II*

   people were very _____.   *anxious*

* Adapted from Dickens, Charles. *Nicholas Nickleby.*

"To list but a few of the specific anxieties which beset American men and women and young people today is to glimpse a world of chaos seemingly endless in dimensions."*

6. Ck? _____   *yes*

Main Idea: After _____, people were _____.   *W. W. II; anxious*

Note: This paragraph started with a main idea or *topic sentence*. The next sentences spelled out the idea a little further. When a paragraph is organized this way, you need only check each new sentence to decide whether it fits under the first idea.

5. "The political importance of the 18th Century London Coffee House must not be dismissed with only brief mention."
   1. (N? S?)

   2. G: This paragraph will be about the importance of the _____   *coffee*

   _____ in the _____ affairs of London during the   *houses; political*

   18th Century.

   "It might at that time have been justly called an important political institution."

   3. Ck? _____   *yes*
   4. G: Why was it important? Maybe with no radio and only a few

   newspapers, people exchanged their _____ in the coffee   *views, ideas,* or *opinions*
   house.

   "Public meetings, petitions, and the rest of the modern machinery for influencing government had not yet come into fashion."

   5. Ck? _____   *yes*

   6. G: The _____ _____ was important in _____   *coffee house; political*

   affairs because there were no other ways to _____ govern-   *influence*

   ment.

   "In such circumstances, the coffee houses were the chief organs through which public opinion vented itself."†

   7. Ck? _____   *yes*
   Main Idea: (Restate the last guess.)

6. "One wonders whether the recession was caused, at least partly, by the car-makers."
   1. N? _____   *recession*

   2. S? _____   *caused by*

   3. G: This paragraph will explain what _____ manufacturers   *car*

   have done to _____ a _____.   *cause; recession*

   "In defiance of all rational consumer interests—economy, safety, and beauty—they have tried to foist upon the majority of the public over-priced jukeboxes."

* Meserve, Harry C. *No Peace of Mind.* New York: Harcourt, Brace & World, Inc., 1958, pp. 4, 5.
† Adapted from Macaulay, T. B. *History of England.*

4. Ck? (Does it tell what car-makers have done to cause a recession?) _____   *yes*

5. G: This paragraph will explain *how* car-makers helped cause the recession by making the _____ of thinking that the _____ of the buyers like _____ which look like _____.   *mistake; majority*
cars; jukeboxes

   "Actually, only deprived and neurotic people want to buy such cars and only the wealthy can maintain them."

6. Ck? (Is this about *how* they made the mistake?) _____.   *no or ?*

   Is it the majority they were wrong about? That is, according to the author, were they right about what a minority wants? _____   *yes*

7. G: This paragraph will explain how _____ helped to _____ the _____ by making cars which appealed to a _____ of the buyers.   *car-makers*
cause; recession
minority

   "They assumed—as indicated by 200 horse-power engines, tail-fins and space-ship platforms—that the majority of the population is mentally ill."*

8. Ck? (According to the author, did they appeal to a minority?) _____
   _____   *yes*

   Main Idea: Car-makers helped _____ a _____ by assuming that the _____ of the people are _____.   *cause; recession*
majority; mentally ill

   Note: The author made his point, i.e., that the auto manufacturers appealed to a minority and then *drew a conclusion.* He suggests that car-makers assume most people are mentally ill. If we agree that a desire for power, tail-fins and space-ship-like platforms indicates mental illness, the conclusion may be correct.

7. "It is possible that the creative mind works most fruitfully during the hours of darkness." (N? S?)

   1. G: It will explain *why* the creative _____ works best at _____.   *mind*
night

   "It is undistracted by the exacting tempo of the day."

   2. Ck? _____   *yes*

   3. G: More reasons _____ the mind works _____ at night.
   "Furthermore,"   *why; better*

   4. Ck? _____   *yes*

   ". . . the imagination travels farthest when distance is no longer limited by the visible landscape but extends to the universes of stars in the dark corridors of space."

   5. G: More _____.
   "Finally,"   *reasons*

   6. Ck? _____   *yes*

* Adapted from Hayakawa, S. I. "Why the Edsel Laid an Egg: Motivational Research vs. the Reality Principle." *ETC: XV*, No. 3 (Spring, 1958), p. 219. Reprinted by permission of the author.

"... ideas that seem too ambitious by day look more plausible by night."*

Main Idea: The _____ mind _____ best at _____.

creative; works, functions; night

8. Main Idea?

"Dress is a very foolish thing." (N? S? G?)

"And yet it is a very foolish thing for a man not to be well dressed, according to his rank and way of life." (Ck, Correct, G)

"It is proof of a man's good sense that he is as well dressed as those whom he lives with." (Ck, G)

"The difference in this case between a man of sense and a fop [an over-dressed man] is that the fop values himself in terms of his clothes." (Ck, G)

"The man of sense laughs at dress even while he knows that he must not neglect it."† (Repeat)

Main Idea: _____

9. "An intelligent, persistent attack on the problems will be an antidote to anxiety. / Vast and complex as the problems are, we shall suffer less if our minds and energies are absorbed in a constructive approach to them than if we simply look at them and deplore their size and complexity. / There is real peace of mind in knowing that you are throwing all your strength into the effort to create human brotherhood, or preserve human liberty, or bring world order and sanity a little nearer. Once you have identified a problem and started to do something constructive about it, your anxiety is reduced.‡

* Adapted from Atkinson, Brooks. "We Who Work at Night." *Reader's Digest Advanced Reading Skill Builder*, Bk. 4, p. 57. The Reader's Digest Association, Inc., 1958.

† Adapted from Macaulay, T. B. *History of England*.

‡ Adapted from Meserve, H. C. *No Peace of Mind*. New York: Harcourt, Brace & World, Inc., 1958, pp. 157-58.

READING

Skimming

Students in rate-improvement classes often remark, after reading at a rate of 800 words per minute, that they didn't read the material at all. "I only skimmed it," they say, and the word "only" indicates very clearly that they feel they have cheated in some way —that skimming is a careless or haphazard means of covering printed material. The fact that their comprehension of skimmed articles is high is not convincing; to them, only careful, word-by-word reading is "good" reading.

Such an attitude is unfortunate, for it means that many students, in their efforts to read "well," only waste time by plodding slowly through material that could be understood as well—perhaps even *better*—if it were skimmed.

Skimming is our fastest rate of reading, and we all do it. We skim a phone book to find a phone number, the classified section of the newspaper to see if there are any jobs available, and the sports page to learn the scores of yesterday's games. We skim the table of contents to see whether it contains a chapter relevant to the paper we're writing, and if it does, we skim the chapter to find what ideas it presents which might be new and useful to us. How foolish it would be to read the whole newspaper to find the baseball scores, or the whole book to find one chapter or paragraph to use in writing the paper! And by the same token, it is just as unnecessary to read every word of our assignments in order to discover and understand the important facts and ideas they contain.

The kind of information we are supposed to get from an assignment will, as a rule, determine the kind of skimming we do. Single words, dates, and simple facts can be discovered quickly by letting our eyes run over the page at random—*if* we know what clues to look for (remember how to survey?). And once the over-all structure is apprehended, the author's main ideas and attitudes begin to take shape in our minds as we look over the first and last sentences of single paragraphs.

It is important to realize that during these various processes, we are not reading carelessly. Comprehension will be high, and retention good, because during effective skimming we are seeking answers to certain questions. "When was he born?" "Why did he criticize the Church?" "Where does the author present his conclusions?" "How does this point of view differ from Freud's?" "What evidence does he offer?" Questions like these *sensitize us to the answers*. We react more quickly and positively to phrases which answer our queries than to material which is less relevant.

This sensitizing phenomenon is similar to that noticed when we look for someone we know in a crowd of people. If we are just looking over the throng with no one particular in mind, we're apt to see a mass of undifferentiated faces, and may easily overlook acquaintances. But if we are looking for a specific person, his face will seem to stand out from the others, and will "pull" our eyes back to his location after they have once swept past him. This is because we have a mental image of the person we're seeking, and this image readies our brain for recognizing him. When the motor is warmed up, so to speak, it is all ready to react swiftly and surely.

The analogy should be obvious. Random and undirected scanning of a "crowd" of printed words or ideas will result only in a blurred, undifferentiated image. But when we are quickly skipping—or skimming—through a paragraph to find answers to specific questions, relevant words and phrases stand out from the rest of the material because we are anticipating them to some extent.

Thus, when looking for someone's birth date, numbers and words signifying years will seem to stand out. If certain conclusions are sought, then cue words like "first," "most important," "consequently," and "finally" will pop out and guide our eyes to the specific information we're seeking. Skimming *is* careless if it is done without thinking, without an active seeking of answers to questions. (But then, the same thing is true of word-by-word reading.) However, when skimming is preceded *and* accompanied by an alert and questioning attitude, it is often the most efficient means of reading an assignment.

Finally, as we have stated earlier, comprehension is frequently *better* as a result of skimming than it is after reading very slowly. This is because of the old forest vs. trees concept. Skimming to find the general structure or the main ideas helps to create a framework, within which smaller details make sense. Without the framework, details fail to hang together—they make little sense by themselves, and are more quickly

forgotten. Thus, even when skimming *by itself* is insufficient for complete comprehension (as is true for complex or highly detailed technical reading, for example), skimming is a necessary preface to more careful reading, for it will help you to sense the whole structure of the assignment. With the structure in mind, even the smallest details will be seen in relation to other details, and to larger ideas, and thus the details can be learned more easily and will be remembered longer.

LESSON 11

Vocabulary: Are Words Important?

Winston Churchill, distinguished in many areas, was perhaps best known during the war years for his powerful vocabulary and his eloquence of expression. But it is not necessary to point to Churchill to demonstrate that most people hold a large vocabulary in high esteem. The numerous books, magazine articles, newspaper features, and special classes which are related to vocabulary building all testify to that.

Everybody seems to want a larger vocabulary—but why? It has been estimated that 90% of our usual verbal or written language can be accounted for by 1000 words: Why then should we want to learn more and more words?

Words alone are meaningless. Their importance stems from our attaching meaning to them, so that they express ideas and are symbols for various objects, actions, feelings, and qualities. Many people had this vividly demonstrated to them as they walked through P. T. Barnum's museum and show. As they milled around seeing various exhibits, they came upon a large sign reading EGRESS with an arrow pointing toward a gateway. As the people pushed through the gate, they found themselves outside the building and had to purchase another admission to re-enter and see the rest of the show. They did not have a correct idea of what the word "egress" means.

Still, the question as to why words are important has yet to be answered. Before formulating an answer, it might be worthwhile to point out that people in many professions are concerned with the study of words and language function—semanticists, philosophers, linguists, philologists, learning theorists, anthropologists, communication engineers, and sociologists, to mention a few.

Words—or language, if you will—enable us to relate ourselves to others and to our environment in general. They help to "bind time," that is to look into the past and to project into the future, so that unlike other animals, we are not prisoners of the immediate present. Our very process of thinking is usually done using verbal symbols, and even the way we look at the world is linked to our language and its structure.

Words are rooted to the very core of human experience. A life without words is almost too depressing to contemplate. It is also obvious that the more words we know, the more experience we will have had and the richer our life is likely to be. The fact that words reflect experience is well known to the users and developers of mental tests who almost always include a vocabulary section in intelligence tests. The richness of a reading experience by one who has an extensive vocabulary can be easily self-demonstrated by noticing your own reactions to reading from a "Dick and Jane" children's book as compared to a play by Shaw or a speech by Churchill.

The learning of abstract words entails some special problems, however. One of the most serious is a loss in ease of communication. People find it harder to agree on the meaning of words like "democracy," "love," "intelligence," and "sinful." Even two people "in love" will attach different meanings to the word.

On the other side of the coin, however, abstract words (ideas) have great utility—they are a verbal shorthand. Just as "one picture is worth a thousand words," so may one word be worth a bevy of other words, sometimes even whole sentences. For instance, when we call a person "meticulous," we are suggesting to others that the individual is "neat, orderly, almost compulsive in wanting everything in the right place, checks things over several times to make certain they are correct, etc." The one word "meticulous"—which comes from Latin and means "full of little fears," incidentally—can give a whole series of impressions or information just in itself.

A more apparent example of the utility of words is the vocabulary requirement in academic courses. More than 70% of the content of an introductory course in botany, geology, physiology, and German, for example, consists of its nomenclature, the names for things. Of vital interest then is to discover the most effective way of increasing one's vocabulary.

Vocabulary Building

One method of vocabulary enlarging is so widely used and efficacious that it seems almost mysterious. It is the natural method of learning languages which enabled all of us to pick up a great portion of our vocabulary before we could ever read a dictionary. This process of learning new words still goes on for all of us, and the wider our experiences, the more extensive our vocabulary is likely to be.

Learning words in this day-by-day process seems almost like an osmotic process. It consists of learning what a word means by understanding the *context* in which it is used. Another way of saying the same thing is that the words surrounding a particular word give it a meaning, as the word "mother" in the sentence, "Mother was found in the bottle." Here the context lets us know that this is a different kind of mother from the one Whistler painted; it is a vinegar mother, the fungus found in vinegar.

Even though the process of learning words by context is a natural one, it can be sharpened and improved. Five context clues which you need to perfect (context even changes the pronunciation of "perfect") will be revealed in the exercises. How you can best use context to help your vocabulary building will be taken up shortly.

Another generally accepted way to expand a vocabulary is to take a short course in Greek or Latin. This notion is based on the claim that some 60% of English words have their ultimate roots in Greek and Latin. While there is some truth to the idea, only the most highly motivated will undertake the study necessary to reap any benefits. There is a way in which a sensitivity to Latin and Greek roots and affixes can be used. It will be discussed next.

The Direct Approach

Usually when we are curled up with a good book, we are motivated to find out the meaning of a strange word only when it makes us *curious* or when it *frustrates* us. Our curiosity is aroused when we cannot guess the meaning of the word and the word is of some importance to the meaning of the passage. Sometimes, a word will frustrate us if we have just heard a friend use it or we have just run across it a short while before. In college work, knowing and using the *technical* vocabulary of a course can make a great difference in understanding the material in the area— a fact which, needless to say, reflects itself in the grade garnered.

The direct approach to vocabulary building does not involve buying any special books. Nor does it involve running to a dictionary every time you come across a strange word—since you are human, you would probably not do so anyway. Even if you did take time out to rummage through the dictionary, you would interrupt your reading and probably forget the meaning within a few minutes.

When you come to an unfamiliar word, try to guess at its meaning using either *context clues* or *Greek-Latin root cues*. Generally, context will give you the best approximation of the meaning, but from time to time a definition of a word can be teased out if you can link it to its roots. Take the word "electroencephalo-gram" for instance—the first part looks like "*elec*tricity" and the last part is found in "tele*gram*." All that remains to piece the puzzle together is the middle part, "encephalo," which is also found in "encephalon" (the brain) and "encephalitis" (inflammation of the brain). Putting the parts together we come out with "an electrical gram (or record) of the brain."

At this point, do not look up the word in the dictionary. Put a light check mark near the word so that you can return to it later. If you decide that you want to add the word to your vocabulary, the best way to do it is to put the word and the sentence in which it was found on one side of a 3 × 5 card (see below). On the other side put down its definition and any other material you wish (such as part of speech, plural form, etc.), and then make up a sentence of your own using the word.

FRONT

tyro   (tié-row) or (tí ro)

Anyone could tell by the shy way he took her hand that he was a tyro at dating.

BACK

tyros (pl.)   noun

Definition and synonyms
Sentence of your own.

If you no longer want to be a tyro, novice, initiate, neophyte, or greenhorn in vocabulary know-how, all you have to do is carry the cards around with you and glance at the front side during spare moments to see if you remember what the word means. However, to make certain that you will never forget the word, use it three times in *speaking* or *writing* and it will always be yours.

But enough of talking about vocabulary. Let's do something about it!

EXERCISES

COMPREHENSION

The importance of words stems from our attaching (1) _____ to them. Our process of thinking is usually done using (2) _____ symbols. The word (3) _____, which means "full of little fears," can give a whole series of implications just in itself.

The wider our (4) _____, the more extensive our vocabulary is likely to be.

The natural method of learning the meaning of a word is by understanding the (5) _____ in which it is used.

We are motivated to find the meaning of a strange word when it makes us (6) _____ or (7) _____. In college work, knowing and using the (8) _____ vocabulary of a course can make a difference in understanding the material.

Generally, (9) _____ will give you the best approximation of the meaning of a word, but occasionally a (10) _____ of a word can be teased out if you can link it to its (11) _____.

APPLICATION

Functional Vocabulary Building

This exercise is designed to allow you to work through the direct method of vocabulary building. Read the passage below and do what is suggested.

Sharon had just slipped beneath the blankets when her roommate opened the door quietly. "Awake?" she asked.

"Barely. The evening hardly left me tingling with excitement."

"Blind dates are like that sometimes."

"This one topped all. Even if he had been *crass* it wouldn't have been so bad, but he was utterly *vapid*. What an evening!"

Choose the italicized word above which is least familiar to you and fill in the relevant information about it on the file card below.

FRONT

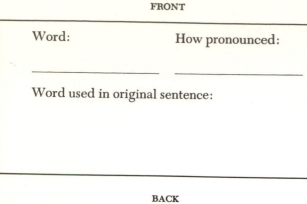

Word: How pronounced:

_____   _____

Word used in original sentence:

BACK

Part of speech, plural form, etc.:

Definition:

Your own sentence using the word:

crass—(Krass-rhymes with grass) adj. Dense, dull, obtuse, lacking refinement, coarse.

vapid—(văp′ ĭd—rhymes with rapid) adj. Inane, insipid, without life, spiritless, flat and without zest.

Remember: if you really want to retain this word, use it 3 times in speaking and/or writing.

Successive Approximation

To learn the technical vocabulary of a course, it is sometimes helpful, if not necessary, to get the full meaning of a word from several sources. This can be done by picking up clues in various ways and "zeroing in" on the concept. You can work through the stages of this successive approximation in the example below.

FIRST EXPOSURE

Psych Lecture
Prof. Zilk speaking:
    . . . "Now between the receptors and effectors is the neural network called the nervous system. This vast adjustor system transmits impulses from the source of stimulation to motor nerves, muscles, and glands usually via the central nervous system.

"The basic nervous unit which transmits the electrical impulse is the *neuron*. The neuron is a body cell which has a specialized function, and the neurons are linked together to provide extensive circuits throughout the body. I see time is up. We'll discuss the structure and functioning of the neuron next time."

FIRST APPROXIMATION

In the box below make a quick sketch of what a neuron might look like from the above lecture. Include

a few words which best summarize the first hazy approximation of this concept.

Your sketch and description might have appeared like this:

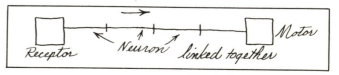

SECOND EXPOSURE

Talking with Instructor after Class:
    Student: "You said these neurons were linked together in a circuit. Are they sort of hooked together like electrical wires when you splice them?"
    Dr. Zilk: "No, actually two neurons do not touch each other at the junction or synapse. It is most likely that the impulse is able to jump a gap because of chemicals which are at the synapse."

SECOND APPROXIMATION

Sketch what you now know about the neuron and include any new concepts (words) which you have learned.

You might have done this:

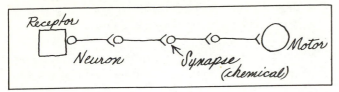

College Dictionary

neu•ron (nyoor on, noor —) n. a nerve cell (see illus.)

Diagram of a Neuron
A. Cell; B. Nucleus; C. Dendrite; D. Axis

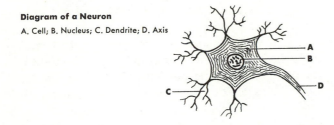

THIRD APPROXIMATION

Through sketch and concepts set forth what you now know about neurons.

This is a refinement, but the synapse is vague.

FOURTH EXPOSURE

Psychological Dictionary

neuron (nu ron): n. The single cell which is the fundamental unit of structure of *nerve tissue*. Each neuron consists of a central portion, the *Cell body*, from which extend two fibers, the *Dendrite* and the *Axon*. . . . *Excitation* starts at the dendrite and is transmitted to the ends of the axon. The meeting area of axon and dendrite is the *synapse*.

FOURTH APPROXIMATION

Put down your present concept of the word "neuron."

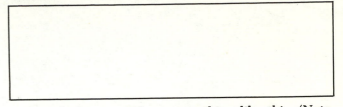

You might have put down something like this. (Note change from "axis" to "axon.")

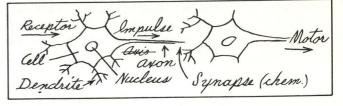

FIFTH EXPOSURE

Intr. Psych. Test

In higher animals the "synaptic type" of nervous system allows them to make specific responses to stimulation, e.g. withdrawing the hand from a hot stove. The basic nervous unit is the *neuron* (see Figure A) and it is made up of a cell body and appendages. Conduction of an impulse is usually in one direction only—from the dendrite, along the axon, to the end brush. At this junction the impulse can pass from the end brush to the dendrite end of the next neuron. Synapses may slow down impulses, block them, and shunt them into different channels also.

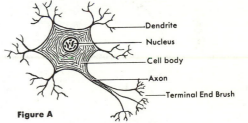

Figure A

FIFTH APPROXIMATION

By this time you have some understanding of the structure and the functioning of neurons. In the space below include everything you can remember about neurons.

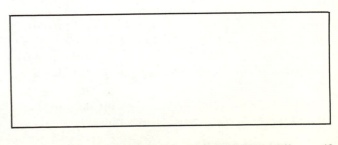

You might have done this:

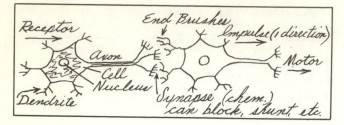

A Final Word

You perhaps will not usually spend as much time or follow the same method in teasing out the meaning of new terms, but you should become familiar enough with the meaning so that you can readily explain the concept when called for on an examination.

READING

Word Power as Concept Formation

Hundreds of thousands of words have been written about vocabulary development. They are read avidly by intelligent people, people who understand the importance of vocabulary to thinking and understanding. Much of what has been written promises short-cuts to mastery of new words. And what are the results of the promised short-cuts? Readers are disenchanted. *There is no short-cut* to vocabulary development. The reasons for this statement will be apparent from the following discussion of concept formation.

First, it should be understood that spoken words have no meaning in and of themselves. Words are *labels* for meaning; they stand for ideas derived from experience. Thus, experience is a prerequisite for vocabulary improvement. We first develop an idea, then learn its label. Let us consider several experiences:

Experience 1. Tommy rushes on to the lawn of the neighborhood's snootiest resident to retrieve his baseball. The lady steps out on the porch and says, with raised eyebrows, "Young man, have you no manners? Don't you know that you are trespassing? Obviously your parents are raising you to be a law-breaker." Tommy has no defense. He feels very small and embarrassed.

Experience 2. Tommy is fourteen. Hs asks Sondra, a fifteen year-old sophisticate, to a school dance. Sondra says, witheringly, "Me? Go to a dance with you? Run along little man; don't bother me." Reaction: *small and embarrassed.*

Experience 3. Tommy has taken his date to dinner at an expensive restaurant. He examines the menu and finds no prices listed. He says to the waiter, "Where are the prices?" The waiter looks down his nose at our hero and responds frigidly, "Our clientele don't choose dinners by the price." Reaction: *small and embarrassed.*

Now, Tommy is reading a novel.

The clerk said, "I'm sorry madam. We don't have charge accounts." She replied, superciliously, "Well, if you don't want my business, I'm sure there are other shops that do."

"What does *superciliously* mean? I know. That's when a person raises his eyebrows and looks down his nose at you so you feel small and embarrassed."

Tommy has developed, by means of repeated experiences, the concept for which the label stands. Each new experience aroused vestiges of the previous similar experiences. The similarities among those experiences were the facial expression, the tone of voice, and Tommy's emotional response. Gradually, the similarities began to stand out from the larger occasion, becoming a stable entity in its own right. This entity is the concept. Now, he needed only to hear the label, *supercilious,* to add a new word to his vocabulary.

Concepts develop when we experience a number of situations which have one thing in common. To state it in terms we've used when talking about the sentence idea: simultaneous activity of two or more ideas will result in the development of a new, higher level idea. The new complex (a concept) is capable of arousing the parts (separate experiences), and each part is capable of arousing the new idea.

By now it should be apparent why short-cut methods to vocabulary expansion are ineffective. The study of word lists with definitions is effective only insofar as concepts are already developed, waiting for the label to appear.

Direct experience is not necessary, fortunately. Indirect, vicarious experience, derived from movies, plays —and, especially, *reading*—will provide an adequate substitute for direct experience. Indeed, until new methods are developed, the most important key to a powerful vocabulary is *wide reading*.

LESSON 12

Critical Reading: How to Avoid the Pitfalls

Read the following two stories[1] quickly, pausing briefly after each one to think how you would categorize the men in each case.

[1] Hayakawa, S. I. *Language in Thought and Action*. New York: Harcourt, Brace, 1949, p. 47. Reprinted by permission of Harcourt, Brace & World, Inc.

A. He had apparently not shaved for several days, and his face and hands were covered with grime. His shoes were torn, and his coat, which was several sizes too small for him, was spotted with dried clay.

B. Although his face was bearded and neglected, his eyes were clear, and he looked straight ahead as he walked rapidly down the road. He looked very tall; perhaps the fact that his coat was too small for him emphasized that impression. He was carrying a book under his left arm, and a small terrier ran at his heels.

You probably discerned that, despite a great similarity in the stories, the impression of the man in each case was different. In A, you might have categorized the man as a "knight of the road" or less elegantly as a bum, tramp, hobo, or n'er-do-well. The gentleman is B was obviously to be respected, perhaps Abe Lincoln himself or an underpaid professor.

What was the essential difference between the stories? Story B carried roughly the same description as A but various bits of information were added: "eyes were clear," "looked straight ahead," "walked rapidly," and "carrying a book." Then, for the real clincher, a small dog, man's best friend, ran at his heels, suggesting that the man may have been down on his luck but his heart was golden. If the dog had been snapping at his leg, however, we might have wondered about his basic goodness again.

Let's say that these two somewhat conflicting accounts came from two different witnesses, as often happens in the courtroom. Which one would you believe? Why? It is difficult to pick one over the other, but there might be a tendency to choose B since it contains more information. What if witness C added one more item to Story B, that the man carried a revolver in his right hand. Now what would you think?

Fortunately, we usually do not have more than one account of an event, and are not confused by conflicting and inadequate accounts. Or *is* this fortunate? How do we know when we are reading something which is really accurate?

Let us begin our attempt to clarify this problem by posing one more question: Which writing is unbiased? To put it another way, when does a piece of writing not reflect the writer? How objective can one be when describing what he experiences? We shall return to these questions later. Right now, let's see how bias influences communication.

The first source of bias is the person who is doing the talking or the writing. If he has seen an accident and tells someone else about it, his report will be biased. It may be biased because he was driving the other car, or because one of the drivers was a woman, or because he didn't see all that happened. In any event, another witness will see things differently.

An accident is hardly a fair example, you might

respond. It takes people by surprise; they aren't expecting it. True. But the same thing can happen when people have their eyes glued to an event; after all, the fans do not always see things the same way as the umpire does.

And if it seems that distortions are large when one man describes an event to another man, such distortion is nothing compared to the alteration and butchering that takes place when a story is passed from one to another. If you need confirmation of this view, try the old parlor trick of giving one student, say, "Story B" to read and have him repeat it to the next person, who gives his account to the next person, and so on ad infinitum. Any similarity between the original story and the end result will be coincidental.

So far we have been talking about someone who actually sees something happening and distorts it without realizing it. In public speaking and writing such distortions are not always unconscious. Often the person purposefully wants you to think in a certain way. He denounces the opposition leader as a "bureaucrat" and a "stooge for Boss Jones" while his own man is a "statesman" and a "friend of the people." In its mild forms writing can be shaded and slanted very subtly and the majority of readers will accept it unquestioningly. At its most obvious extreme, such consciously slanted information is the propaganda of Goebbels, the Soviet Union, or the ultimate control exercised in the novel, *1984.*

How can anyone read critically enough to counteract the bias which is bound to enter what we hear and what we read? Several steps can be taken:

1. *Suspend judgment until you have read different accounts and analyses of the same event.* In an auto accident, the more witnesses that can be found, the more likely it is that the jury will get a substantiated account of what happened. If two of your best friends who have been going steady have a fight, it's best to get both sides of the argument. If the Democrats come up with a proposal on tariffs, see what the Republicans have to say, and vice versa. Is labor or management telling the truth? If you can, try to use several papers or magazines with differing slants to keep yourself informed. See what facts they agree on.

2. *What is the reputation of the author?* What makes him an expert? Who does he think he is anyway? We would generally place more confidence in the report of an independent medical researcher concerning the effect of smoking on cancer than we would on a report from a researcher in a laboratory subsidized by the cigarette companies (unless their report is not favorable; then it might be considered creditable).

Famous people often make pronouncements which

they are not qualified to make (Big League Hero): "I eat Bopsies because they're good for me." Most times, it is far from easy to evaluate how the author knows what he is talking about.

3. *Check the facts.* What is a fact? It is a statement capable of being verified. "There are houses on this street." "That blond freshman is from California." "The Battle of Hastings took place in 1066." Go through the article with a fine-tooth mind and see if the author really supports his case with facts. And if you have other sources, see if he has left out some important facts!

4. *Determine whether his "inferences" and "judgments" are warranted.* An *inference* is a statement of an unknown made on the basis of something that is known. "She was angry," could be inferred if she threw a vase of flowers at him. We are all like Sherlock Holmes, constantly making inferences from tones of voice, noises in our car, and even bedraggled, mudsplattered clothing.

Judgments are expressions of approval or disapproval. "This is a wonderful refrigerator," is a judgment based on the fact that it has run 24 years without any repairs. "You rat!" is a judgment expressing disapproval. We make judgments in terms of "good" and "bad" all the time.

If we can spot the difference between facts, inferences based on facts, and judgments which reveal feelings and attitudes about certain facts and inferences, then writing can be critically analyzed. For instance, everyone would recognize "Kissing spreads germs" as a fact (it can be proved or disproved). "Kissing is dangerous" would be a logical inference from the fact. An example of a judgment might be "kissing is fun." Most authors are either not aware of how inferences and judgments creep in to distort their writing, or they are aware of it and hope you will not be.

5. *Look for devices the author uses to bring about a certain feeling on your part.* Detecting these devices is as tricky as finding booby traps laid by an enemy—they are hard to detect unless one is consciously trying to do so. Even innocuous appearing phrases such as "sneaked in" are slanted and carry a different connotation from "entered quietly." Today the expression "socialized medicine" has an unfavorable cast, while "health insurance for all" sounds much more acceptable; but, again, getting down to the specifics of what each speaker really means is of most importance.

Here, as elsewhere, practice makes perfectly good sense. To develop your skill as a critical, incisive reader, you will have an opportunity to see how a crisis is discussed in a liberal and a conservative magazine. On your own, take any of the moderate weekly news magazines and try to penetrate their slanting devices. Try not to be taken in by the colorful prose. Instead, maintain a critical set: is it a fact? an inference? a judgment? who says so? why?

Before rushing out to garner the magazines from the local news butcher, there is one note of caution. Bias enters everything we read from another source—ourselves! Most of us read journals (and have friends) which are the most compatible with our point of view. And when we read something we don't agree with, there is a strong likelihood it will be altered and distorted. This tendency to change things to our own way of thinking might be illustrated by the conjugation of an irregular verb, an idea of Bertrand Russell's: "*I* insightfully penetrate the real truth in what I read; *you* have a tendency to alter what you read; *he* is hopelessly biased and distorts everything to his way of thinking."

Earlier, the question of which writing is unbiased was posed. As you may have guessed, anything written by humans has some bias in it, although some factual writing—like a telephone book—can be relatively unbiased.

EXERCISES

COMPREHENSION

There might be a tendency to choose Story B over A since B contains more (1) _____. How (2) _____ can one be when describing what he experiences? The first source of (3) _____ is the person who is doing the writing. He (4) _____ his report without realizing it. How can anyone read (5) _____ enough to counteract bias. A fact is a statement capable of being (6) _____. An (7) _____ is a statement of an unkown made on the basis of something known. (8) _____ are expressions of approval or disapproval. Even innocuous appearing phrases such as "sneaked in" are (9) _____. Bias enters everything we read from another source: (10) _____.

APPLICATION

Identifying Bias: Part I

The following excerpt is the opening paragraph of an article from a nationally circulated news magazine. When you have read the paragraph, try to answer these questions:

1. What would the author have me believe?
2. Why is an article such as this one written?
3. How much of the paragraph do I believe (or disbelieve) because of what was actually said, and how much because of previous prejudices of my own?

1   Caught in a flareback of history, desperate Dem-
2 ocrats tried with might and main to wriggle out
3 of the Harry Dexter White scandal. Their line was
4 different from the flat assertions of outrage ("Red
5 herring," "I do not intend to turn my back . . .")
6 that greeted the 1948 charges against White and
7 Alger Hiss. This time the fact of espionage was
8 more or less admitted. Harry Truman acknowl-
9 edged that White was disloyal, and even the
10 New Republic said: "There can be little doubt
11 that White was guilty of the actions described by
12 Miss Bentley," i.e., passed secrets to the Com-
13 munists and influenced U. S. policy according to
14 Communists' wishes. . . .

1. What would the author have me believe?

_____

2. Why is an article such as this one written?

_____

3. Name three facts presented in the paragraph:

_____

See Key, page 136, for answers.

How biased is the writing? Is it just the ordinary bias any human being is subject to when trying to convey an idea in words? Is there what might be called intentional bias? What words, phrases, structuring can give you clues about the bias of the article? Here are a few to start:

Loaded Words. These are words with high emotional value and considerable "surplus meaning." For instance, "caught" and "desperate" in line 1, and "wriggle" in line 2 convey a definite feeling (perhaps something like a trap—and the wriggle has a kind of wormish or snake-like quality). Other kinds of loaded words are useful because they have no standard meaning; for instance, *democratic,* or (see line 9) *disloyal.*

  a. "Their line was different from the flat assertions of outrage. . . ."
    Loaded word: _____

    Connotation: (what does it make you think of?)
    _____

The Unproved Premise. Naming the affair described as a "scandal" (line 3) thereby establishes that it *was* a scandal, and no further evidence is offered to support that premise. You may agree, but what will you use for proof?

  b. "Harry Truman acknowledged that White was disloyal. . . ."
    *Unproved premise:*_____

  c. ". . . and even the New Republic said. . . ."
    *Unproved premise:*_____

Linking. This handy device puts something new with something old and familiar, in the hope that you will associate the same thoughts and feelings to both. Alger Hiss was a national scandal; consequently, you probably have a negative reaction to the name Hiss (even if you are sophisticated enough to know that he was convicted of perjury and not of spying). Therefore, linking White's name to his should give you a negative feeling about White (lines 6, 7).

The Small Qualifier. Although "more or less" has been added to qualify the word "admitted" in line 8, the rest of the paragraph reads in such strong positive terms that the undiscerning reader may well glance over the words of qualification.

Over-generalization. The support for the statement that "espionage was more or less admitted," is the following two statements: (1) "Harry Truman acknowledged . . ." (lines 8, 9) and (2) ". . . even the New Republic said. . . ." It does *not* say why Truman and the New Republic should constitute the official representation of the subject of the article ("desperate Democrats"), nor does it specifically say anything further about espionage. Indeed, it seems to ask you to equate "disloyalty" with "espionage." In light of these points, do you think there is sufficient evidence to warrant the conclusion?

Opinion Glorified. Both Miss Bentley's "description" and the New Republic's comments on the case (lines 10, 12) are obviously matters of opinion. Both the *opinions* are assumed by the writer to be *fact.* Are you willing to make that assumption?

The Omnipotent Generality. This is also known as the Draw-Your-Own-Conclusion technique. When you read that White "influenced U. S. policy according to Communists' wishes," do you have an idea as to just *how* and *what* (or *whom*) he influenced? If you do, the idea came from some experience other than the reading of this article. And your idea is probably different to some degree, or perhaps to a great degree, from ideas formulated by other readers of the same paragraph. (Of course, generalization may be quite legitimately used in writing, but elaboration and clarification need to follow. When they are omitted, or occur three pages later, as in this article, the effect is very different.)

    Now here is paragraph two of the same article:

1   Despite this fact, said the Democrats, the Re-
2 publicans were not justified in repeating the charge
3 against White or in disclosing that Truman had

4 the facts on White months before White left
5 Government service. "I don't think the people
6 will eat warmed-over spy," said Democratic Na-
7 tional Chairman, Stephen Mitchell. It was
8 pointed out by other Fair Dealers that the "politi-
9 cal climate" of the years when White served the
10 Russians was very different from the climate to-
11 day. Somehow, this was supposed to be an excuse
12 for White and the people who protected him.

Name the clues to bias which might be represented
by each of the following:

d. "Despite the fact . . ."_____

e. "had the facts on"_____

If you read critically, you noticed that a very effective
new device has been employed in this paragraph. A
rather *weak* argument for the opposition has been
presented (lines 8-11) and then removed by the technique of *ridicule* (lines 11, 12). If you asked for evidence that "the Democrats" said "the Republicans were
not justified in repeating . . . or in disclosing . . ." you
received the following statement as evidence. "I don't
think the people will eat warmed-over spy." The apparent lack of relationship between the statements and
the evidence is called a *non-sequitur* (literally, a "non-
following" point in a logically reasoned argument).
Other arguments may be removed by *arbitrary dis-
missal* ("Of course no one believes . . . ") or by appeal to *group loyalty* ("All good Americans now think
that . . . "), etc.

Note. The original caption for this section of the
article was "The Climate of Treason." The remainder
of the section appears below:

"In fact, the political climate of the Roosevelt and first
Truman administration was the real weight of the case
against the Democratic leaders. Political climate is man-
made. The moral confusion that marked the Roosevelt
Administration made it possible for White & Co. to at-
tain great power. That this confusion still exists is evi-
denced by Truman's continued refusal to accept the meaning of the White Case.
"Nobody would accuse Roosevelt or Truman of disloyalty. What they were accused of was creating and
maintaining a political climate in which treason flourished."[1]

Identifying Bias: Part II

Now, how about the other side of the story? Here
is a selection from an article in another nationally
circulated magazine. Once again, you will want to
think about these questions:

1. What would the author have me believe?
2. Why is this article written?

[1] Excerpted from "The Climate of Treason." *Time Magazine,* November 23, 1953.

3. How much do I believe already because of my
own prejudices?

1 "The mistake in Attorney General Brownell's
2 attack on President Truman over the White case
3 did not lie in opening up the facts. Police work
4 and defense of security are regular chores for a
5 great power . . . Making it the chief issue in
6 American party alignment is something else . . .
7 Political controversies are important for the forces
8 they release rather than for the things they get
9 done. Little new was uncovered in the White
10 case. All of the names and most of the facts had
11 been familiar to the public for some years. What
12 Mr. Brownell did was to commit the Republican
13 Party to a personal attack on former President
14 Harry S. Truman and all his Democratic asso-
15 ciates for laxity, chiefly in the years 1945 and
16 1946. By so doing, Mr. Brownell increased the
17 power and prestige within the Republican Party
18 of the old isolationist forces which opposed de-
19 fense against the Nazi attack in 1939. They are
20 the same groups which later opposed the United
21 Nations and fought the Marshall Plan . . . The
22 real business of President Eisenhower's Adminis-
23 tration and of all America now is the defense of
24 freedom in 1954. The grand issue tendered by
25 Mr. Brownell is whether proper measures were
26 taken in 1945 and 1946 . . . [Mr. Eisenhower's]
27 party seems to be primarily concerned with
28 whether Harry White (who is dead) should have
29 been fired seven years ago."[2]

You probably have spotted some major differences
already between this article and the last one. It is
more cautiously worded, more rational in approach.
But is it less biased? Let's examine it more closely.
If you were on your toes, you spotted examples of the
following types of biased writing:

> loaded words
> unproved premise
> linking
> ridicule
> over-generalization

a. The phrase in line 1, "The mistake in Attorney
General Brownell's attack . . ." and in line 5,
"Making it the chief issue . . . " are examples

of _____.

b. The sentence in lines 16-19 (beginning "Mr.
Brownell increased . . . ") is an example of

_____.

[2] Berle, A. A., Jr. "The Folly of Demagogy." *The Reporter,*
December 22, 1953.

c. The sentence in lines 26-29 (beginning "Mr. Eisenhower's party . . . ") is an example of

_____.

d. The sentence in lines 7-9 ("Political controversies . . . ") might be an example of _____.

e. List at least two positively-loaded words or phrases (that make you feel at once that they are "right" and that there is no controversy about accepting them, even though you may not know exactly what they refer to in this context): _____

_____

f. List four words or phrases that are negatively loaded (that give you an immediate reaction of "badness" or distaste when you read them): _____

_____

In addition to these old acquaintances, two new techniques, the *dodge* and the *flank attack* have been added. A dodge is a perfectly good, valid, forceful point that actually has little to do with the matter at hand (or at least with the argument to be answered). Read again lines 9-11. You may admit this to be a good point, but does it successfully dispose of what the opposition has said? Can you identify the assumption behind this statement? (Perhaps something like this: Since the names and facts in this case were known before, *therefore* the value of further presentation at this time by the Republicans is negated.) Like most assumptions, it needs to be *made explicit* and then *carefully evaluated* before the statements which follow from it can be judged.

The *flank attack* is a thrust at an unguarded side of the enemy. In a sense, it changes the focus of the battle from the center of the line (the events culminating in the White case), which may be our least defensible position, to another point. Read again lines 11-16 and notice how deftly your attention is shifted to new ground, to a contention that Brownell's activities have had negative effects.

READING

Spelling Is Nonsense

For some unaccountable reason, the executive, the parent, the man in the street—sometimes even college professors—judge a man's intelligence by his ability to spell. Such a practice is grossly unjust. The relationship between spelling ability and brightness is so small as to be negligible. And when conditions for learning words are optimum, even this small relationship disappears.[1]

To press the point further, some children classified as imbeciles excel in spelling. The child need not know what the word imbecile means to be able to spell it!

One's intelligence indicates one's ability to deal with ideas, with meanings, in short, with things sensible. Now, no matter how sensible a man is, he won't be able to determine the spelling of *enough* unless he is told. True, some spelling words follow rules; the thinking man is able to spell *sleigh* by applying the crutch, "*i* before *e*, except after *c*, or pronounced as *a* as in *neighbor* and *weigh*." But then what should he do with *either, neither, height, deity, leisure, heir, weird*, and *seive*, not to mention *heigh-ho!*

Materials which are nonsensible are called nonsense materials, as noted earlier. If mastery of such materials does not yield to cold logic, how will it occur? Once more we return to the problem of rote learning, or brute memory. We must develop an association between the sound of a word and its picture. Such an association is difficult for some people to establish. Tension may result in obliterating traces, or attention to a word may be inadequate so that the spelling is not seen clearly or the sound not heard correctly to begin with.

One way to remedy this problem is to increase attention by increasing the strength of stimulation. Greater input = greater number of associations. The procedure is as follows:

1. Limit your words to be learned to two kinds:
    a. those which you understand. In general, the more meaning a word has, the easier it is to learn.
    b. those which appear to be your personal demons. Most people who consider themselves poor spellers consistently err on only 50 or 100 words. Find those words in your old theme papers.
2. Write the word in large script.

A discharge from blood vessels caused by injury:

hemorrhage

3. Trace the word with your index finger three times *saying the word* (*not* the letters) aloud as you

[1] Porter, Douglas. "Some Effects of Year Long Teaching Machine Instruction." No. 8 in *Automatic Teaching*, E. Galanter, ed. N. Y.: John Wiley & Sons, Inc. 1959.

trace. Begin tracing and saying simultaneously and finish both operations simultaneously. (Do this now with the word *hemorrhage*.)

4. Next, close your eyes and try to visualize the word in your "mind's eye." (Do this now. Some people are unable to visualize. If you are one of those, skip this step.)

5. Next, trace the word on the desk, saying it aloud as you trace it. (Do this now. If you are unable to see part of the word or to trace it, repeat steps 3 and 4.)

6. Now, write the word normally. (Do this now.)

7. Compare the word you have just written with that in large script. Find any errors?

8. If there is an error, repeat the whole procedure, paying particular attention to the trouble spot.

Now learning will be relatively complete, and retention will be high. You have provided multiple sensory input: vision, hearing, touch, muscular sensations (kinesthesis), all in the context of meaning.

Now try these:

A physician who specializes in vision:

ophthalmologist

Sleeping sickness:

encephalitis

A specialist in behavior:

psychologist

IV

Mastering the Content

LESSON 13

How Learning Styles and Subject Requirements Differ

A single learning procedure appropriate to all learners and to all subject matters would be ideal. Unfortunately, the differences among people and kinds of course content are too great for any known procedure to encompass. But the situation is far from hopeless. Some of the important differences in both people and content *are* known and it looks as though the Survey Q4R method can be modified to take those differences into account.

Subject Matter Differences

Perhaps the most obvious and most important difference in subject matter is that between the social sciences, on the one hand, and mathematics and the physical sciences, on the other. Introductory courses in mathematics require the student to learn a new artificial language, a language of symbols. A symbol is a representation of reality, something which *stands for* something else, as in "Let X stand for the distance traveled by A." Certain operations can be carried out with the symbols, for example, arithmetic operations such as adding and subtracting. In addition to the individual symbols, there are sets or groups of symbols, called equations, to indicate relationships among the symbols.

Once the student has learned the symbol language and the operations or "rules of the game," all of his conclusions (answers to problems) are predetermined and exact. Two people will arrive at the same answer. This rule does not apply to the social sciences. Most of the symbols of psychology, sociology, history, and economics are neither precise nor artificial. "Anxiety," "social mores," and "competition" are names for conditions which are difficult to define precisely. The symbol X can stand for any quantity, but "anxiety" refers to a vague, incompletely defined feeling state of an organism. Furthermore, while the rules of a mathematical system can be derived logically, the rules of the social sciences must be discovered. In psychology, for example, one must first discover the important feeling states of an organism, then give each a name, then determine the internal or external conditions which cause the feeling states, and, finally, discover the relationships among them. The work is highly subjective, and, therefore, subject to much disagreement, i.e., two people may arrive at different answers. For that reason, the course content is seldom precise or exact, and final answers are seldom found. The best that can be done in the social sciences, presently, is to predict behaviors or answers, and to include the margin of error in the prediction. (And, of course, the margin of error itself has a margin of error.)

Mathematics: Quantity + operation = exact answer

Psychology: Feeling state (± error) + conditions (± error) = behavior (± error)

Physical sciences like chemistry and physics are neither as exact as mathematics nor as inexact as the social sciences.[1] Introductory courses do, however, concentrate on the most clear-cut parts of the sciences. The symbols of chemistry relate to real materials, the operations have been discovered, and the results of sets of procedures are known. The margin of error is usually small.

Thus, both mathematics and the physical sciences may be treated as areas to be mastered with rote memory of symbols of greatest importance. To a large extent, relationships can be *deduced,* that is, figured out logically by using a set of simple assumptions or rules. The social sciences, however, require little rote memory. Primary emphasis is on understanding relationships, many of which must be *induced.* The learner begins with a series of events or behaviors and *discovers what they have in common.* For instance, a number of situations may arouse anxiety. One looks for the similar parts of those situations to determine an anxiety arousing condition. Of course, this is not the simple concept formation process which it appears to be since situations mean different things to different people.

It is apparent that some kinds of courses call primarily for rote learning and others for understanding. Methods such as those described for spelling are designed for the rote learning required in mathematics, physics, chemistry, and other courses in which the learning of symbols is important (including, of course, foreign languages). Survey Q4R is designed for courses in which understanding through inductive thinking is required, i.e., primarily in the social sciences.

Nevertheless, all courses are most easily mastered by the use of both kinds of techniques. One first surveys the new chapter in mathematics, determines its place in the course and the number and kind of new operations it discusses. Then, questions are raised and answered, noted and reviewed. Likewise, a series of concepts developed inductively in sociology must next be mastered. Tracing the word and its

[1] For example, Ohm's law is relatively correct only under certain limited conditions.

definition will build in those components requiring rote learning.

Learner Differences

Fully as important as differences in subject matter are those of learning styles. Extensive study of college students reveals systematic differences in the kinds of academic tasks handled best by people of differing "constitution."

Groups I and IV. Reference is made here to your placement on the chart of learning style in the front of this book. Individuals who are extreme in extraversion and impulsivity tend to profit more from a systematic study procedure than do those in Groups II and III. Group I and IV individuals tend to prefer the social sciences. They are "at home" with unsystematized knowledge and enjoy an opportunity for trading opinions. Their knowledge is held loosely, and new ideas are welcomed. They tend to be impatient with memoriter tasks, with working problems, and with knowledge which is fixed or static. They have a fertile and relatively undisciplined imagination, seldom having trouble thinking of ideas for themes or new approaches to old problems.

On the negative side, Groups I and IV have difficulty memorizing material. They tend to forget quickly, to remember irrelevancies, to see relationships which do not exist. They tend to confuse text statements with their own opinions. Their themes are often disorganized, main idea arousing main idea, ad infinitum, with no single idea being developed adequately. They learn less and less about more and more. Finally, the extreme extravert is subject to exam panic. He tends to be unable to handle stress: his emotion is easily aroused and then overwhelms him.

It is easy to see why externally imposed structures like those of Survey Q4R help the extravert. They provide a discipline to his thinking and a system to the task which he is unable to provide. With time and practice, he will adopt the system, make it a part of his habit structure, and transfer it to other problems such as a new job.

Groups II and III. At the other extreme are the highly systematic, perfectionistic, well-disciplined individuals who lean toward systematized learning, who memorize easily, and who tend to value things more than social interaction. The exact sciences provide the kind of definiteness which is consonant with their philosophy of living. Right is right and wrong is wrong: right and wrong are clearly not a matter of opinion. For these individuals, mathematics and the periodic table of chemistry are no problem. Even foreign language tends to be easy.

On the negative side once more, such people learn more and more about less and less. They have difficulty developing new ideas, and lean toward authority for the answers to their problems. "If it's not in a book, there is no answer." Anything new is highly suspect. Their themes tend to be well organized but lifeless. They tend not to think by analogy, thus fail to detect the figurative language in literature; they distrust emotion as a basis for thinking, and therefore, distrust the language of literature. Perhaps the most serious problems of the constricted thinker are those stemming from his inability to see relationships. His lecture notes make no sense: they consist of a series of details with no larger meaning. He knows the operations in trigonometry but doesn't know when to use them in solving a problem.

Once more the value of Survey Q4R will be apparent. When one surveys the whole before memorizing the parts, the whole-part relationship remains dominant. Each part is appreciated, not as a discrete unit, but as a contributor to a large idea.

Tension. The positive and negative effects of tension were discussed earlier.[1] On the positive side, tension appears to speed up the thinking of introverted people so that they may do better on examinations than they expect. For some it seems to help in spawning ideas and in discerning relationships. For the rest, the results of tension seem to be negative. A continuing high level of tension contributes to the disorganized thinking of the extravert, interferes with memory, and sometimes incapacitates him on an examination. It interferes with concentration, at best simply by taking one's mind off one's work, at worst, by keeping one's mind filled with morbid thoughts.

Two parts of the study procedure are especially helpful in controlling the negative contribution of tension. Questions force concentration, often in the face of a high tension level. And frequent brief reviews, by rearousing associations, reduce the negative effect of tension on remembering.

The following lesson includes specific directions for modifying your study procedure to fit chemistry, physics, math, and language. In addition, a number of practice materials in Lesson 15 provide an opportunity for mastering your method in the social and biological sciences.

Application: See Lesson 15.

[1] See Lessons 2 and 6.

LESSON 14

Suggested Study Procedures

1. CHEMISTRY*

"Love," it has been said, "is mainly a chemical reaction." While it would prove interesting to analyze love as a chemical reaction, it is more important right now to examine your reaction to chemistry.

Let's suppose you are registering for a course in chemistry. If asked why you are taking it, your answer might place you in one of two groups. One group *likes* science (Group L), and usually math, and plans to major or minor in it. Another group takes chemistry because the subject is *required* (Group R) and is likely to approach it with less than complete enthusiasm.

As has been suggested earlier, Group L would probably be composed of individuals tending toward introversion. They will be able to pick up details without much difficulty, but may gloss over some of the larger ideas or fail to see relationships between facts. Group R individuals, on the other hand, tend to be uninterested in small bits of information like formulas, chemical reactions, and tables of numbers. Just the prospect of opening the textbook and starting to study may be painful. And while they may grasp the larger ideas, chemistry demands knowledge of specific information and procedures and the ability to demonstrate that knowledge by solving problems.

A general approach to studying chemistry will be set forth below. Certain suggestions will be identified with an L or an R as a signal for those in each group to pay particular attention to what is being discussed.

Fundamentals. Your understanding of chemistry— and hence your interest—will increase if you have certain fundamental information at your finger tips. Knowledge of the symbols of chemistry, the structure of formulas, and the procedures for deciphering the names of compounds are the foundation of much of the advanced work.

While background information is important to any student taking a chemistry course, the R or "required" group may need some brushing up.

Atomic Theory. Since the concepts of atomic theory underlie modern chemistry, knowledge of this theory is essential. Do you know the following:

1. What an atom is? What it is composed of?
2. What a molecule is? How it differs from an atom?

* A primary source of ideas presented in this lesson is Lanford, Oscar E. *Using Chemistry,* New York: McGraw-Hill, 1955, pp. 16-43.

3. How atomic weights are developed?
4. What an isotope is?
5. How elements form compounds? (the laws of multiple proportions and definite composition)
6. What the periodic table looks like generally?
7. How the valence of an element is calculated?

If you are shaky on *any* of these concepts, you must learn them!

Symbols. Each element is represented by a symbol (C = Carbon, Ca = Calcium, Cl = Chlorine, etc.) and learning at least the common symbols can make working with chemical formulas much easier. Like the alphabet, these symbols can be learned by rote memorization. Most symbols bear a reasonable fascimile to the elements they represent, but a few, like K (potassium) and Fe (iron), come from foreign words. (Note that the second letter is always lower case.)

It is also helpful to know the atomic weights of some of the more common elements.

Formulas. A formula is nothing more than a chemical shorthand, or the distilled essence of a larger idea. Understanding the larger idea depends on the ability to decipher the various symbols, subscripts, and numbers. For instance, H_2 (hydrogen gas) indicates two hydrogen atoms joined together to form a molecule. On the other hand, 2H means two unjoined hydrogen atoms.

Much information is compressed in a formula. For instance, from the formula C_2H_6, the following data can be derived:[1]

1. Elements which are present	Carbon and hydrogen
2. Relative number of atoms in the molecule	One C to three H
3. Actual number of atoms in the molecule	Two C and six H
4. Weight ratio of the elements	C 24 to H 6 (4:1)
5. Relative weight of one molecule	Two carbon atoms weigh $2 \times 12 = 24$ Six hydrogen atoms weigh $6 \times 1 = 6$ Weight of one molecule $= 30$
6. Percentage composition	$24/30 \times 100 = 80\%$ carbon $6/30 \times 100 = 20\%$ hydrogen

Since formulas contain a great deal of information, it is obvious that the reader must go through them slowly and thoroughly rather than skim over them.

Chemical Equations: While formulas are static, equations are dynamic and deal with chemical changes. Before a chemical change can be described, the following factors must be known:

1. Whether or not the reaction does occur.

[1] Ibid., p. 30.

2. The substances which react to produce the products, and their formulas. A substance that reacts is called a reactant.
3. The products formed by the reaction and their formulas.
4. External conditions necessary for the change to occur (e.g., heat).

Names of compounds. The names given to chemical compounds follow definite rules, and generally the elements are named in the same order as that in which their symbols appear in the formula.

Method of Attack

With the fundamentals in hand, you can tackle the chemistry text. Again the SQ4R method can be used with advantage, for, while the reading material is somewhat different, the learning machine, you, remains the same. Each step of the method is listed below with special suggestions as to how it can be adapted for chemistry:

Survey. Very important for L (constricted) group. The survey gives the overview, the major ideas of the chapter. Be sure to look at the title of the chapter, the major sections (there may be more than in nonscientific texts), and the summary. Pay particular attention to charts, diagrams, and tables, for very often they will help make a difficult concept understandable.

Questions. Besides converting subheadings into questions, there will sometimes be questions at the end of the chapter or in the workbook. In addition, problems can be used as a form of question and can serve as a concrete example of the more general concept.

Read. As before, read to answer your questions. Be sure you understand equations and can see the relationship between major ideas and examples of them. Remember that formulas and equations contain compressed information and must be read slowly and thoroughly.

Recite. Relate what you have read to what you already know. See if you can remember the formula or equation and how it was derived. Sometimes it helps to draw diagrams of molecular arrangements as an aid to remembering them. *Now* is the time to work out the appropriate problems so often included at the end of the chapter. Can you apply the formulas in solving the problem? If so, you've learned them!

"Rite." Try to reduce notes to key ideas. In chemistry, formulas can serve as cues for larger ideas. Cards (3 × 5) can make a convenient pocket file for formulas and equations to be learned. If formulas are difficult to remember, trace and say just as though the formula were the spelling of a difficult word.

Review. Go over the material after finishing the section you have been working on and then do the same thing later in the week. See how much you can remember without looking at your notes. Remember, if tension is high, reviews must be frequent and spaced somewhat like this:

Study◄(10 minute interval)►review◄(60 minute interval)►review◄(6 hour interval)►review◄(two day interval)►review.

Application: See Lesson 15.

2. MATHEMATICS AND PHYSICS

Difficulties which arise in the study of mathematics and physics can be classified into two broad categories: (1) difficulties which may be attributed to the nature of the student, and (2) difficulties which may be attributed to the nature of the subject matter itself. In this article, we cannot make adequate provision for overcoming some of the major difficulties of the first type, i.e., those specifically associated with inadequate background, lack of motivation, personality structure, and the like. Rather, we will pay particular attention to those difficulties which arise because of the nature of the subject matter and the way in which the student approaches it.

Part I of this article will be concerned with the origins of difficulties in studying math and suggestions for improving the study of math. Part II will consider the problems in the study of physics and suggestions for overcoming or reducing them.

Part I: Mathematics

We will consider two main areas of difficulty in the study of mathematics: (1) difficulties which arise from the definitive, explanatory, or illustrative material; and (2) difficulties which arise with the attempt to test or apply knowledge through the solution of problems.

What causes difficulty in the reading, understanding, and remembering of the explanatory portions of a mathematics textbook? To assist us in answering this question, consider the following fictitious example which might be representative of any of the specific kinds of mathematics to which you are exposed.

AN EXAMPLE FROM MARTIAN MATHEMATICS
TAKEN FROM A TEXT IN SPYLOCTGY

In this chapter, we will be concerned with a study of the Pexlomb. A Pexlomb is defined as any Zox with pictanamerals which flotate the Zox into five berta Zubs where each Zub is supramatilate to the Rosrey of the Ord. For example, consider the Zox defined by 3 berta Ooz. It is obvious that any pictanameral which is Blat must necessarily be Cort to the Ord. This follows from our knowledge of the relationship of a dentrex to its voom. However, if the Ord is partivasimous then the Zox must be Zubious. Thus, if we kizate the dox pictanameral, our Zox will be flotated into 5 berta zubs. But remember, each zub must be supramatilated to the Rosrey of the Ord. If any one of the zubs is not supramatilated, we then have a pixilated Pexlomb which requires a completely different procedure.

We can represent the necessary conditions by the following:
1. Q??---- ϕ (note: Q is nubbed according to the principle of Plasimony)
2. By Axdrellation we arrive at: X Q/??---!!-°
Thus, it is evident that the solution must be:
3. M---/?? (Really quite simple *if* you remember to obscone in step 4 of the Axdrellation process.)

By this example we are immediately made aware of the importance of language. Mathematics employs at least 3 kinds of language: (1) general—words which are a part of our general vocabulary; (2) special—words which have a precise mathematical meaning; and (3) symbolic—words and ideas converted to letter or number symbols and relations.

Lack of comprehension of any of these expressions of language leads to extreme difficulty. Referring again to the example, we see that adequate understanding of new material is dependent upon how well we understand and remember previous material. A Pexlomb is defined as a special kind of Zox. Therefore, we should know what a Zox is. The statement beginning "it is obvious that . . . " would certainly not be obvious if you didn't know the meaning of a pictanameral, Blat, Cort, or Ord, or how a dentrex was related to its voom. The same thing may be said for translating the verbal material to letter or numerical signs and symbols. The symbolic language is the most highly condensed and concise form of expression in mathematics. It is absolutely mandatory that you know *what symbols are used, what they mean, and how they are interrelated.*

It is entirely possible to understand and remember the explanatory or illustrative material and yet be unable to work the problems. It is also possible to calculate and compute the answers to many problems mechanically, without any real understanding of the processes involved.

It is highly probable that students who are poor in mathematics are expending too much time and energy on the problems and not enough on the explanations and illustrations. If you consider for a moment, you will realize that each problem is a miniature test and these tests are used to measure the extent and quality of your mathematical knowledge. Therefore, we might say that the most important part of a text is not the problems (since they are only a means for checking on our ability to apply our understanding or serve to consolidate our past learnings by providing practice materials), but rather the material which precedes the problems.

Following is a list of steps or procedures to be utilized to reduce difficulties in the understanding of the body of the text, assuming that intelligence, motivation, interest, or emotional problems are not the real difficulties.

Procedures for Attacking Explanatory Material with Understanding (To Be Carried Out in the Order Presented)

1. Survey the assigned portion of the text paying particular attention to boldface type, graphs, or diagrams, and the problems listed at the end of the assignment.

2. Survey the first paragraph, page, or section to determine both the kind of information being given and the location of important parts.

3. Raise questions based on the survey and the material itself. What does this term mean? Why did they do that? What formulas, equations, or processes are discussed? Do the problems give any clue as to the kind of information that is important?

4. Read the text slowly and thoughtfully to answer questions you have raised, pausing to recite pertinent material in order to understand or discover the relationships among the data involved.

5. *Work through the steps of an example yourself* to see what is being done, how it's being done, and why. Ignoring or simply reading through an example is usually fatal.

6. Do you understand the symbols, formulas, graphs, diagrams, equations, and procedures used to explain the example? If not, go back to earlier portions of the text, the appendix, class notes, or the instructor for assistance.

7. Having completed one paragraph, page, or section in the above manner, you should now be able to formulate one or two concise questions and recite the answers to these. What is this section about? It is about. . . . What procedures or steps are involved in dealing with this example? I must first do this, then that. I need to use 2 formulas and treat them in this manner. (See Lesson 5 of Part I for recite and write.)

8. If the topic, example, or explanation appears important and may be hard to remember, summarize the pertinent information from Step 7 into notes. Then repeat the whole procedure for the next section.

Procedures for Attacking and Solving Problems

The recommended procedure for attacking verbal problems is to employ SQ4R in miniature. With minor modifications, this will lead to success. Perform the following steps in the order in which they appear.

1. Read the problem rapidly to obtain a general idea of its nature. Try to answer the questions: What is it about? What does it involve?

2. Read it again carefully noting the details. Underline the parts that you think will be needed to solve the problem. You should now be trying to determine the conditions and the requirements of the problem.

3. Try to restate the problem using only the necessary information. Be sure you have identified the unknown.

4. What symbols, formulas, or equations will be needed? You may be uncertain about the necessary equations at this point. If so, wait until Step 7 for that information.

5. Convert the data to appropriate symbols so that each given and required part of the problem is represented.

6. If possible, try to represent the problem by drawing a figure. Label its parts.

7. Select the equations necessary to solve the problem.

8. Estimate your answer before computing.

9. Manipulate the equations, checking each step for carelessness in basic arithmetical processes, i.e., mistakes in adding, subtracting, multiplying, dividing, dropping of signs, and the use of wrong signs.

10. Check the final answer obtained and see if it meets the conditions of the problem.

The following information is taken from Polya's book entitled *How to Solve It*. Polya raises questions which he classifies into 4 categories: understanding the problem, devising a plan, carrying out the plan, examining your solution. While there is some duplication between Polya's questions and the procedures cited above, we believe it will be helpful to list the major questions he asks in solving problems.[1]

I. *You have to understand the problem.*
    a. What is the unknown?
    b. What are the data?
    c. What is the condition?
    d. Can you represent the problem by a figure?
    e. Can you convert the words to symbols?

II. *Devise a plan—find the connection between the data and the unknown.*
    a. Have you seen this same problem before?
    b. Do you know a related problem?
    c. What theorem would be useful?
    d. *Look at the unknown.* Can you think of a familiar problem having a similar unknown?
    e. Can you restate the problem in simpler form?

[1] Adapted from Polya, G., *How to Solve It.* Garden City, N. Y.: Doubleday & Co., Inc. (Doubleday Anchor Books), 1957, 2nd. ed., pp. xvi–xvii.

f. Can you solve part of the problem?

g. Did you use all the data?

h. Did you use the whole condition?

III. *Carrying out your plan.*

a. Check each step.

b. Can you see that the step is correct?

c. Can you prove that it is correct?

IV. *Examining the solution.*

a. Can you check the result?

b. Can you check the argument?

c. Can you use the result, or the method, for some other problem?

Summary

We have indicated some major sources of error in the study of mathematics. Some of these are personal and some are related to the subject matter itself. The two major areas of difficulties regarding the subject matter were divided into reading and understanding explanatory material and solving problems.

Suggested procedures were given for attacking explanatory material with understanding. Basically a modified SQ4R procedure is necessary. The key to understanding is active involvement utilizing an organized approach.

Finally, we recommended and listed the steps to be taken for solving problems. None of the above is necessarily easy nor will it make up for deficiencies in background, intelligence, or personality; however, where these deficiencies are nonexistent, mastery of these procedures will lead to reduction in frustration and anxiety, and eventual mastery of mathematics.

Part II: Physics

Our treatment of difficulties which arise in the study of physics will be short. The reasons for this will soon be apparent.

When students of physics are discussed by their instructors, the most frequent complaints are inadequate preparation, inability to work problems, lack of motivation, inability to read with understanding, no knowledge of how to study, and little or no interest in exercising the mental functions.

From the student's viewpoint—again assuming that adequate background, motivation, and intelligence are not the real problems—we find two major difficulties: (1) inefficient or complete lack of adequate study procedures, and (2) inability to solve the mathematical problems. The latter difficulty was discussed in Part I of this article. The same procedures suggested there can be utilized for attacking the mathematics which arise in physics.

To overcome inadequate study procedures, the student should utilize the SQ4R approach. However, one caution must be exercised in applying SQ4R to physics. As with the other natural sciences, physics has a language of its own. Special terminology with specific meanings for physical laws and functions occurs throughout the physics texts. Particular attention must therefore be given to building up and understanding the vocabulary of physics. The student who is having difficulty will be well advised to devise a glossary of his own choosing consisting of those technical terms and definitions which either have a high frequency of occurrence or which are likely to cause some misunderstanding if the student cannot remember them.

Other than the specific recommendation to seek out, identify, and record the technical terminology and to make provisions for frequent review of this personal glossary, nothing more need be done beyond the usual SQ4R approach. Thus, if you will follow the suggestions in Part I of this article for handling the mathematics of physics, use SQ4R for the rest of the material, and provide for the learning of the technical language, you will no longer be troubled by lack of understanding and the receipt of poor grades in your study of physics.

3. FOREIGN LANGUAGES

Reading this section may be a rather unpleasant experience for you, simply because it won't be easy. The content is neither obscure nor complex. On the contrary, it is quite concrete, specific, detailed. But it is just these qualities which many students, stumped by the task of learning a foreign language, find troublesome in *any* written material, whether it be in English, German, French, or Sanskrit! Effective foreign language study requires attention to fine detail, a methodical, well-organized approach, and ability to memorize. The same skills are necessary for effective reading of this article, for it presents, point for point, a series of specific study guides which must be *attended to in detail, memorized,* and then *applied in a methodical, deliberate way* if they are to result in more efficient handling of the problems posed by foreign language study.

If you are like many students who have difficulty learning foreign languages, the problem results at least in part from the fact that you tend to grasp large ideas easily, to excel in speculative thought, to jump quickly from one idea to another, to learn "less and less about more and more" (remember the test of "learning style" at the beginning of the book?). You also tend to skip details, to have trouble memorizing, and to be more or less disorganized (probably more!).

The suggestions presented below are designed to help you to counteract your unconscious natural tendencies through the *conscious* use of specific techniques. They will be organized under three general headings: (1) How to apply SQ4R in learning to read a foreign language; (2) How to use certain methods in attacking special problems in foreign language study; and (3) How to organize your time most efficiently for studying foreign languages. And remember, you will perhaps need to expend more *conscious effort* in attending to the details of these techniques than would that disgusting roommate who gets A's in ancient Aramaic without even trying!

Using SQ4R in Foreign Language Study

1. Survey. Even with foreign languages, learning the parts is easier if they are seen in relation to the whole. It is easier to master a new lesson if first you make a superficial acquaintance with *all* the new things covered in the lesson (for example, twenty new words, the passive voice, and ten idiomatic uses of the new words in the passive voice). Skim through the whole lesson, noting as usual the title and subheadings. Then skim *quickly* through the story or conversation at the beginning of the lesson to see how much you can understand on the basis of what you've already learned, and to begin anticipating a more careful examination of the words and forms which are new to you.

2. Question. The chapter title and your first skimming of the story or conversation will provide you with your *first* questions (more will come later, in connection with the third step, Read). For example, if the title is "The Passive Voice," you might well ask, "What *is* the passive voice in English?" and so on. If the skimming reveals some new words or forms, you can begin asking, "I wonder what that word means?" or "Why is the word order in this sentence different from anything we've had before?" Here, as in the study of any subject, the important result of asking questions is that of arousing a degree of interest, and of becoming *actively and thoughtfully involved* in the task at hand.

3. Read. Now is the time to read through the story or conversation more carefully. Move along as quickly as you can, but *don't* look up the words or forms you don't know. Skip them until you have read through the rest of the sentence, and then guess the meanings of these unknowns, using the context in which they appear to guide your guessing. Sometimes a sentence is all you need to help figure out the probable meaning of a word or phrase, and sometimes it may be necessary to read a whole paragraph before a logical possibility occurs to you. The important point is this: when you make such guesses you are automatically raising the question, "Am I right?" and when the time to *look up* the word finally arrives (at the end of the paragraph, or even at the end of the whole selection if

it is a short one), you will see the word not as an isolated item in a vocabulary list, but as a meaningful symbol which you have already seen in context. And even more important, you will react with a feeling of satisfaction (if your guess was correct) or of dissatisfaction (if you were wrong). You may even reprimand yourself if you made what you consider to be a rather stupid mistake. You will, however, react—and we have already seen in an earlier chapter how important it is for retention to become emotionally involved in the task at hand.

4. Recite and "Rite." As you look up the words (*after* having seen them in context and made a guess at their meaning), try writing the word without looking at the text. Got it? If not, try the tracing procedure mentioned in an earlier section on spelling. When the word can be visualized as you say it, and then as you say its English equivalent, it has been learned. When all the new words have been learned in this way, you are then ready for the step that will clinch the whole procedure—review.

5. Review. In this case review consists of reading again through the story. Since you have already made one quick and one slow trip through the material, and since you have learned all the new words by guessing, checking, and tracing, this third contact with the story as a whole should go almost as smoothly and quickly as if you were reading English. As an added test of your mastery, try reading the material *without* translating. By this time you should be able to get the *ideas* directly from the foreign words and phrases, without having to go through the process of translating into English first. If this review reveals any details which are still a bit vague, now is the time, of course, to repeat the process outlined above until everything is mastered. One additional point: every week or so review the preceding week's work by reading through the stories you studied during that week. This procedure will help to keep things fresh in mind, and to reveal those aspects of the language which still give you enough trouble to be included in the "nuisance" category discussed below.

Special Problems in Learning Foreign Languages

1. Nuisance Words. All students occasionally run across words that for one reason or another cause an unusual amount of trouble. We all have certain words in our own language which we consistently spell incorrectly, and for which we often forget the meaning. It is not surprising, therefore, that the same is true in any foreign language. Two techniques are particularly helpful here. The first is the tracing technique discussed earlier in this and another section. It is especially useful for mastering the spelling of a word, and if the tracing and visualizing process is accompanied by frequent associations with the English equivalent of the word being learned, the strength of the association between the word and the idea for which it is a symbol is increased. The second technique is that of making and using vocabulary cards (small slips of paper will do), the foreign word on one side, its definition on the other. Review sessions employing these cards should be brief (no more than five or ten minutes at a time) and frequent, and should consist of looking at one side of the card, guessing what is on the other, and then immediately checking to see if you were right. Three or four brief sessions of this kind in the course of a day should enable you to master even the worst dozen or two "demons" on your list. A caution: this procedure should not be adopted for *all* your new vocabulary, for it will be too time consuming, and completely unnecessary. Use it only as a last resort for those few words that yield to no other method of attack.

2. Taking Dictation. This is a real problem for some students. Learning new vocabulary by the tracing procedure should help considerably in this area, but two other methods may provide additional assistance. One is to trace the *whole sentence* in which any new word appears, simultaneously thinking of the English equivalent, and then to "recite" by writing the sentence without referring to the text. The other is to have another student in the same course read the story to you slowly while you take dictation. In this way you can quickly identify those words which you spell incorrectly, and which can then be learned by using the tracing technique. And remember, you should *say* the word as you trace it, thus "building in" the association between the sound of the word and its printed form. This procedure is far more effective (and much quicker!) than reading through the material repeatedly in an attempt to learn the correct spellings by a process of osmosis.

3. Conversation. In courses which emphasize the importance of learning to *speak* the language, silently reading a written conversation ten times will be far less effective than reading it orally twice. The main point to be made here is a simple one: since *oral* reproduction of the language is the objective, *oral* practice is the only sensible way to achieve that objective. In other words, *practice out loud!* Read through a whole conversation in order to get the meaning—but do it out loud. Now go back to the first sentence; read it orally, and then look away and try to repeat what you have just read. Check. Any errors? If so, repeat the process until you've mastered the sentence, then go on. This process, incidentally, is similar to that involved in learning to recite a poem, or in learning lines in a play. Divide the material into small sections; learn the first

in the manner just described, then go on to the second. When that is learned, repeat the first and second sections together, go on to the third, and so on until the whole conversation is under control. Then review *immediately* by talking (not reading) through the entire section again. Sound time consuming? It is, for a while, but as you become more and more familiar with the language you will find that learning to speak it gets easier and easier, and the time required becomes less and less.

Efficient Use of Time

In other sections we have frequently discussed the importance of *timing* in the learning process. It is particularly important in learning a foreign language to study *frequently*, and to keep your study sessions *brief.* You need to expend a lot of energy in the close attention required for foreign language study, and after a half or three-quarters of an hour the energy supply begins to dwindle. Also, the amount of memory work involved can become pretty dull. Moral? Study six days a week (even if you have your language class only three or four days a week), but study only about an hour or so each day. If this hour per day can be broken up into two half-hour periods, so much the better. And when working on nuisance words with the tracing process or with flash cards, you will get even better results by splitting the process up into four or five fifteen-minute sessions per day.

If you've gotten this far in this lengthy and detailed dissertation, we may assume that you *really* want to improve your status in that language course! One more suggestion, then: go back to those parts of this section which deal with your problem areas. Read the suggestions again—*carefully.* Memorize them *thoroughly.* Then apply them—*regularly.*

LESSON 15

Applications of Survey Q4R*

1. *Economics: Easy, Intermediate, Difficult*
2. *History: Easy, Intermediate, Difficult*
3. *Psychology: Easy, Intermediate, Difficult*
4. *Sociology: Easy, Intermediate, Difficult*
5. *Zoology: Easy, Intermediate, Difficult*

* The content of Lesson 15 has been prepared by Mrs. Nancy Beresford in consultation with college instructors in the various subjects. The aim was to present material representative of existing textbooks.

FUNCTIONS AND PROCESSES OF ECONOMIC SYSTEMS

I. The General Nature of an Economic System

To the student:

1. To *survey*, read the title, main heads, and sub-heads (usually, the first and last paragraphs also)
2. *Question* by asking: "Why is an economic system necessary?"
3. *Read* to answer
4. *Recite* in your own words
5. *"Rite"* (jot down) *brief* notes

Need for an Economic System. In a society where each person supplies for himself all of his wants, there is no need for an economic system. A Robinson Crusoe could gather his own food, build his own shelter, and provide his own recreation, in short, fulfill his economic needs, without dependence on any other individuals. But in a complex society, where occupations are divided into many categories, such as food suppliers, builders, etc., each individual performs by and large in only one, or in just a few capacities. He, therefore, becomes dependent upon many others for the basic necessities of his life. When such a situation occurs, there is need for a system to regulate the activities and provide order, ensuring that the many parts will function harmoniously and adequately.

Kinds of Economic Systems. The occupational structure and the relationship of these activities to one another is often the same from one society to another. However, responsibility for handling three important tasks of economic systems tends to vary greatly from one system to another. These tasks are the responsibility for production, the control of natural resources, and the division of the total product. Because of this variance, many different types of economic systems have been developed. Generally speaking, they consist of two types, the managed economy and the free economy. These terms refer to the extent to which the functions of the economic system, the responsibility for production, control of resources, and division of produce, are assumed by private individuals upon their own initiative (free economy) or by a central agency such as government (managed economy).

II. Tasks of the Economic System

2. *Question* by asking: "What are the tasks of an economic system?"
3. *Read* to answer
4. *Recite* in *your* words
5. *"Rite"* brief notes

You're on your own!

The efficient production of goods is the first responsibility of the economic system. In order to produce goods there must be *enterprise*, the willingness to take the initiative and provide the leadership required for production. In a completely managed economy, the central agency both initiates productive activity and maintains the leadership of the enterprise. In a free economy it is left to private citizens to decide to undertake production, to raise the necessary capital, and to guide the actual production. In the case of capitalism, for example, wealth takes the initiative and hires labor to carry out the program which those with wealth supervise.

In addition to enterprise, the system entails one or more solutions for the problem of *incentive*. Many different motivations may prompt individuals to engage in production. Some of the more obvious of these are fear (as in the case of slave labor), patriotism, social approval, advancement of the arts and crafts, and, of course, personal profit. A capitalistic system relies largely on income as a motivating force, the profit motive for the enterpriser and the wage motive for the worker.

Guiding the use of natural resources is the second basic function of an economic system. This involves the allocation of the resources among the various projects which require it, the utilization of these resources in most suitable locations and with suitable tools (including the workers and their skills and aptitudes), and the movement and distribution of these resources.

6. *Review* by: *reading* the question, *covering* the notes, and *reciting*

Then, take the test (check text for answers)

In the last-mentioned category, the system is concerned both with speed and proper destination.

Distribution of the end and total products is a third function of the economic system. There are, of course, many different ways in which the goods of production can be allocated and distributed, but it is only in a managed economy that his function is separate from the first two functions we have discussed. When production and use of resources rest upon private initiative and incentive, the nature of distribution will be an outgrowth of these factors. When an economy is based on a price system, as, for instance, capitalism in America, costs and profits regulate distribution of goods.

QUESTIONS

1. Why is an economic system necessary in a complex society?

3. What are the three main functions of an economic system?

2. Name the two main types of economic systems and give an example of each.

4. Explain the terms "enterprise" and "incentive."

Subject: Economics

Level: Intermediate

INTRODUCTION TO FINANCE AND ACCOUNTING

I. *Expression of Financial Status*

In order to demonstrate the nature of securities and their value, dividend practices, and corporate capitalization, let us first take an imaginary corporation and devise a balance sheet to show its financial status.

The Michigan Company, let us say, is organized to undertake a manufacturing project requiring $1,000,000 of plant equipment, inventories, and cash. Ten thousand shares of common stock are issued (par value $100) to raise the necessary money. Supplies and a building are purchased and laborers and staff hired. At this point the Michigan Corporation's situation (highly simplified) could be represented as follows:

TABLE I

Assets		Liabilities & Proprietorship	
Cash	$ 20,000	Capital stock	$1,000,000
Inventories	370,000		
Plant & Equip.	610,000		
	$1,000,000		$1,000,000

After a period of time in which the corporation has been successfully operating, the situation has altered. Products have been sold, some on credit. Wages are

paid, additional funds borrowed from a bank to aid expansion, supplies and materials purchased, some not fully paid for. The balance sheet now reflects some of these changes in financial status:

TABLE II

Assets		Liabilities & Proprietorship	
Cash	$ 30,000	Acc'ts. Payable	$ 40,000
Acc'ts. Rec.	40,000	Notes Payable	40,000
Inventories	460,000	Capital Stock	1,000,000
Plant & Equip. (at cost) (710,000)		Surplus	70,000
less depreciation (90,000)	620,000		
	$1,150,000		$1,150,000

II. *The Balance Sheet*

The balance sheet, such as the simplified one we have drawn up for the Michigan Corporation, is a measure of wealth. It tells nothing specifically about the revenue or expenses of a business (these matters are dealt with in the "income statement"). Its purpose is to view the same set of factors from two standpoints, assets and liabilities, to show the *present position of wealth* of the firm.

Assets. Assets include all valuable possessions of the

firm: *fixed facilities*, such as buildings, land, and equipment; *circulating capital,* that is, stocks of materials, partly finished products and goods awaiting sale; *cash,* either on hand or in the bank; *claims* against other firms or individuals—that is, sales for which payment has not been received, usually shown on a balance sheet as "Accounts Receivable." Assets may also include *intangibles,* such as patents, although these were not included in our sample above.

Liability-Proprietorship. This side of the balance sheet, also called "equities," is not by accident the same in total as the asset side. Everything owned by the corporation is owed *to* someone or else represents the equity or interest of the stockholders. At first, only the banks (Notes Payable) and suppliers (Acc'ts. Payable) have acquired claim against those assets. The remainder, surplus and capital stock, belongs to the stockholders.

Surplus. Surplus is a particularly important concept in finance. Surplus exists because a firm has been successful, and has made money. It is *not* cash, however, which is an asset, something valuable in the company's possession. It is, rather, an extension of the equity of the stockholders. The company's prosperous state is reflected in its increased net assets, in new machines, larger inventories, expanded cash, and accounts receivable. *The surplus reflects this enlarged interest of the stockholder.* Consequently, it appears on the liability-proprietorship side of the ledger.

QUESTIONS

1. What single most essential information does a balance sheet give?

2. Give three examples of assets, three of liabilities:

3. Explain why surplus is not an asset:

4. Can you think of two reasons why a company might decide to sell additional shares of stock?

SECURITIES AND THEIR CHANGING VALUES

I. Book Value and Dividends

The book value of a stock is measured by the *net assets per share,* which can be computed from the balance sheet. For example, a company with total assets of $1,150,000 and debts of $85,000 has net assets (the total of capital stock and surplus) of $1,065,000. If the company has issued ten thousand shares of stock, the net assets per share, and hence the book value of the stock is $106.50. This situation is precisely that of the Michigan Corporation after its period of operation which was described in Table II of the previous section.

Dividend. When a company decides to return a portion of its earnings to its stockholders rather than to use the earnings for further expansion, it declares a *cash dividend.* The dividend for the Michigan Company, let us say, is declared at $3.00 a share. This means that the cash and surplus of the company will be reduced by $30,000 when all the stockholders have been paid, and consequently the book value of the stock will be reduced. In the case of our example, the net assets are now $1,035,000 and the book value of the stock will be $103.50.

Stock Dividends. The company may decide to declare a stock dividend. This means that the net worth of the company will be represented by more shares of stock. This is frequently done to enable a company to appear profitable, or to reduce the market value of the shares in order to encourage trading. If a stock dividend of 50% is declared, this means that for every two shares he now holds, a stockholder receives one additional share. The net assets of the company remain the same, since the company has neither added something nor lost something in declaring the dividend. On the liability side of the balance sheet, the surplus has been decreased and the capital stock increased by a proportionate amount, and the total is the same as before. Hence, the equity of the stockholder is unchanged (and consequently the stock dividend is not considered income, not even by the tax collector). However, you can see that the book value of the stock will be lower.

II. Par Value and Capitalization

Par Value. The par value of a bond states the amount of the debt to the holder of the bond, that is, the amount the corporation will pay when the bond matures. For preferred stock, the par value is that amount that the holder is entitled to claim if the company is liquidated. The preferred stockholders are paid their claim after the bondholders are paid, and before common stockholders are paid, in the event of liquidation.

For common stock, there is no prescribed amount for par value, since the common stockholder is entitled to whatever remains when other claims have been satisfied. The absence or presence of a stated par value on a stock does not alter the stockholders' interest in the company; for example, if a stockholder owns 100 shares of stock in a company which has issued 10,000 shares, his equity is 1% regardless of the nature of the company or its wealth. Any particular figure on the stock will not alter the company's facilities or ability to produce, hence, the par value of the stock gives no indication of the actual value of the security to its owner.

Capitalization. The word "capitalization" is used in this context to refer to the securities of a corporation as they appear on a balance sheet. A statement of capitalization tells which securities in what amounts have been issued to raise capital and to represent the interest of the owners, the stockholders and bondholders. Since securities are entered in the books at their par value, capitalization is figured by par value, but some specific amount, usually representing the amount paid for them, is entered on the statement of capitalization.

Overcapitalization. If a company were to issue $100,000 worth of stock (that is, stock with a total par value stated as $100,000), in exchange for property or materials worth only $50,000, the company would be "watering" its stock, and the resulting condition would be called overcapitalization. Since the company would list on its balance sheet the property so obtained as worth $100,000, the assets of the company would, in fact, be overvalued, and a false impression created as to the net worth of the company.

Overcapitalization as such is not necessarily a dangerous practice; however, this type of dealing gives rise to other forms of speculation and extreme practice, and may lead to an unstable market; consequently, it is generally frowned upon.

III. Market Value of Securities

The *price* at which securities are bought and sold is a more accurate estimate of their *real worth* than either book value or par value. Market value is based on an estimation of what earnings the owner of the securities can expect from them. This is admittedly a much less accurate figure than either book value, based on the actual past performance of the company,

or par value, which is a definitely specified figure. However, market value reflects future tendencies, book value and par value only the past.

The price at which a security is bought is determined, then, by and large by what rate of return the prospective earnings of the company will give, and therefore it might be expected to fluctuate with conditions other than the capitalization and production of the company itself. This is exactly the case; with boom conditions in the economy as a whole, the price of shares is likely to be overly high, and in depressions may fall unreasonably low.

QUESTIONS

1. List the three types of value ascribed to stocks and explain briefly how each value is computed:

2. Explain briefly why a stock dividend is not considered "income."

3. What is meant by "watering" stock?

4. List two reasons why the market value of a stock might drop in a time of economic depression:

5. Which "value" gives the best estimate of the immediate future of a concern? of the present financial status?

THE DECLINE AND FALL OF THE ANCIENT WORLD

I. Pax Romana

To the student:
1. To *survey*, read the title, main heads, and first and last paragraphs
2. *Question* by asking:
   "What did Rome conquer?"
   "Which dictators rose?"
3. *Read* to answer
4. *Recite* in *your* words
5. *"Rite"* (jot down) *brief* notes

You're on your own!

Rome Conquers. The Italic Alliance (390-264 B.C.) united the provinces of Italy under Roman rule. During the next 100 years, Rome added to her empire the Carthaginian domains of Sicily (241 B.C.) and Spain (201 B.C.), the city of Carthage herself and her African territories (146 B.C.), then the Greek City-States, a large portion of Asia Minor, Syria, and finally Egypt. Following these annexations there began a period of peace in the Mediterranean world, peace but not prosperity.

The Rise of the Dictators. Despite the ending of warfare in the empire, conditions were not prosperous. The rich grew richer, largely through corruption, and the poor grew poorer. The governors of the provinces were exploited by the Senators in Rome, who demanded payment brought home after their terms as governors. The governors had to pay not only these ransoms but, of course, their living expenses; they, in turn, exploited their subjects. Plunder, extortion, and usury were the means of the powerful to increase their power. The establishment of capitalist farms deposed many peasants. They were unable to find suitable work in the cities, for the urban dwellers were themselves suffering from a glutted labor market, caused by the influx of slaves from the conquered provinces. Such conditions quite naturally made the rise of a dictator, Julius Caesar, an easy matter.

Julius was murdered two years after his rise to power, in the name of liberty, and his reign was followed by twelve years of civil war. Then his grand-nephew, Augustus, succeeded him. While in name he was "princeps" (first citizen), he was, in fact, also a dictator. Both Julius and Augustus did much to curb Senatorial corruption and to give Rome honest and efficient administration. The 250 years of the Pax Romana, marred only by an uprising of generals (68 A.D.) and some minor wars which resulted in the annexation of Britain, Rumania, and parts of Mesopotamia, saw progress in the development of the empire.

The Growth of the Empire. During the Pax Romana, many improvements were made. New cities grew up in Italy and in the outlying provinces. Older cities expanded and covered far greater areas of land. Public water supplies were developed, and many public buildings, baths, theaters, fountains, etc., were boasted by the urban centers. Municipal self-government was common, and archeological evidence, especially some ancient posters discovered in the ruins of Pompeii, indicate there was considerable interest in local elections. In particular, trade expanded.

The Expansion of Trade. Free circulation of trade throughout the empire, which now extended as far north as Britain, south to Africa, eastward to Spain, and west to the Russian border, helped the empire to thrive. Roads connected Rome with all portions of the provinces, and money was spent in improvement of these roads and the building of new ones. Harbors were improved. Shipping was a thriving industry. The northern barbarians provided slaves and furs for Rome; the southern Arabs sent spices and jewels; from China came the luxuries, dancing girls, parrots, ivory, pearls, and drugs. Trade with Russia was effected across the Black Sea. With the western provinces, Rome exported items of manufacture, particularly textiles, glass, and metal work. Because of the limitations of transportation and the nature of the societies in the Far East, these items were not appropriate, and Roman export in these areas was almost solely in good gold coin.

6. *Review* by: *reading* the questions, *covering* the notes, and *reciting*

Then, take the test (check text for answers)

Communication. A remarkable amount of communication went on between the areas of the empire. Trade itself, of course, was responsible for much of this exchange of ideas. In addition, civil servants and military personnel were recruited from all parts of the empire and customarily served in places other than their native lands. Craftsmen frequently traveled to the provinces, either for temporary visits or to establish their crafts in new areas. Yet it should be noted that despite an unprecedented amount of interchange between various groups over a wide geographical area, Rome's profit from this communication was solely in terms of trade and strengthening of political ties. Intellectual development in Rome was not changing. No new theories were developed, no great inventions made, no innovations in architecture or medicine appeared.

Summary. During the 250 years following the Roman conquest of Egypt, the Roman Empire developed its agriculture, trade, and building. Cities grew in size and number. Despite this, the conditions of the majority of the population, both in Rome and in the provinces, remained unprosperous.

QUESTIONS

1. What is the meaning of the expression "All roads lead to Rome"?

2. List five aspects of Roman life which prospered under the Pax Romana:

3. Why were the Roman provinces, on the whole, so poorly governed?

4. What benefit derived from the rise of dictators?

Subject: History

Level: Intermediate

THE DECLINE AND FALL OF THE ANCIENT WORLD

II. Internal Foundations Weaken

Industrial Lag. While it is true that the manufacture of glass and textiles was a thriving industry in Rome and that the arts and crafts provided employment for large numbers of people in the provinces, several factors associated with industrial progress were absent. First, industry was not "modernized" by the Romans. Manufacture continued much as it had for the previous several hundred years. Nothing resembling "mass production" was invented; there was no increase in specialization. More important, industry was not considered respectable. There was no incentive for those with money to invest in industry. They, rather, purchased and developed land, and prestige was accorded on the basis of land ownership. With no encouragement to expand and develop industry, money was naturally lacking and improvements were consequently not made. Still another factor was the migration of craftsmen. Instead of increasing production and exports of crafts to the provinces, the artisans themselves migrated and established their trades in new areas. Cities began to decrease in size.

The Decline in Agriculture and Trade. The agriculture in the provinces was still carried on by primitive means. The capitalist farms were gradually being turned into self-sufficient households as the land holders enlarged their estates, acquired more slaves, and attempted to circumvent the problems of importing goods from Rome. These enlarged villas turned into manors, and became the precursors of the feudal estates which were to become so common in the Middle Ages. The increase in size brought no increase in technology, and the peasant class remained as poor as they had been in the time before the Roman conquest.

Internal markets (within the empire) were not increasing. Since the lower classes remained unprosperous, they were not increasing their buying power. Standards, even in the cities, were low. The ordinary man subsisted on wheaten bread, figs and olives, lived in miserably furnished rooms heated by braziers and lit by oil lamps. There was no advertising to make him dissatisfied with his lot and eager to become a consumer of new goods. External markets already covered all of the "civilized" world. Since the market could no longer expand, it began to contract. By the year 250, prosperity had gone entirely. This was reflected by a decline in fertility within the empire. It is to be noted that classical civilization was already moribund, if not actually dead, 150 years *before* the invasion of the barbarians from the north.

Downfall Approaches: During these 150 years, the situation continued to grow worse. Financial difficulties beset the Romans. As has been noted, trade with the Far East had resulted in the shipping of vast quantities of gold coin in return for luxury items such as spices and drugs. This vast export of gold bringing in return relatively little for the prosperity of the empire weakened the financial base. Many minor civil wars sprung up, and a large and well-equipped army was once again necessary. Large deficits were incurred in raising these armies. Nero found it necessary to debase the currency in order to keep his administration from becoming bankrupt. Roman coin was no longer the symbol of stability and the standard of exchange.

An important result of this diminishing prosperity was the loss of desirability suffered by civil office. It had been the custom for civil servants to pay their own expenses, much as ambassadors do at the present time. Men of wealth, and often wisdom, were attracted to seek civil office. As it became more and more difficult to meet the financial responsibilities of the office, good men no longer sought to hold such office, and civil government, once the pride of the Roman State, became first the tool of the rascals, and finally virtually nonexistent.

Life was less free for the craftsmen. Whereas once their guilds had served to protect them, they now became the tools of the state. In order to attempt to increase, and even simply maintain, production, the state compelled artisans by law to follow certain trades. In effect, the trades became castes. The farmers fared no better; they became literally tied to the land. Emperor Constantine in 322 forced the tenant farmer to be virtually a serf by denying him the right to leave the farm on which he worked. Freeholders who had been ruined joined with the wealthier land owners on the manors for their own safety, and the rise of the feudal lords was only a short step beyond.

Finally, under Constantine, the church is officially joined to the state, and the last vestige of freedom has been removed from the once glorious state of Rome. The capital had by this time been moved to Constantinople, and the barbarian sack of Rome left the Byzantine Empire under Constantine to carry forth the tradition of the empire.

1. Give three reasons for the failure of Roman industry:

2. Why did the capitalist farms turn into feudal estates?

3. What two factors caused the weakening of Rome's financial base?

4. This period of history has been characterized as a "failure of nerve." Who failed to show nerve?

5. If it is true that Roman civilization was dead 150 years before the invasions, why do you suppose the traditional view of the Sack of Rome as the ending of the empire has been perpetuated?

Subject: History

Level: Difficult

CHRISTIANITY AND THE DARK AGES

The Rise of the Christian Church. Undoubtedly there are many complex factors which led to the establishment of Christianity. Certainly the time was ripe. Rome in her heyday, with the wealthy few living high, and the masses impoverished, had already proved a fertile field for other religious cults, particularly those imported from the Far East. These oriental cults and mystical groups fused with early Christian groups, and lent them ideas and ritual. The Christian dogma must have had considerable appeal to the serfs and slaves, and to the proletariat of Rome, who saw little to be gained in this world except by plunder and extortion, and who were glad enough to renounce earthly leaders, such as the long line of Caesars, who demanded hard tribute. The state, of course, resented this usurpation of its powers. However, the persecution of the Christians which it fostered only tended to attract people's attention to it, to increase sympathy for it, and to draw converts to it.

As the number of converts grew, a need for organization within the religion became apparent, and the foundations of the official church were laid, dogma was written, hierarchies of workers within the church were established, and the more formal aspects of the religion and its worship naturally grew up. To defend their arguments against their critics, the Christians used Aristotelian logic, which had, like so much else from the Hellenistic world, been preserved almost without alteration through the days of the Roman Empire. And as controversies arose over interpretations and innovations, groups split off, and the major sects took their beginnings.

The establishment of the church contributed its share to the crumbling of the empire. It turned the loyalties of the people away from the secular monarchs, and their thoughts away from the improvement of their earthly lot toward other kingdoms and afterlife. At the same time, it was the church, by and large, which preserved many elements of the Greek and Roman culture through the dark ages.

The Dark Ages and Glimmers of Light. Civilization was not, in actuality, destroyed by the invasion of the barbarians. True, the western part of the Roman Empire was no longer the hegemony it had been. The eastern empire, under Constantine, with its capital at Constantinople, however, continued to thrive. Culture advanced, conquests increased the power of the state, and in fact, up to 1100 the Moorish provinces continued to extend the stream of Hellenistic civilization.

In Europe the churches kept alive much that was Roman. Springing from the Roman culture, the religion itself embodied much of that civilization. The monks kept alive the art of writing, and copies of manuscripts were made which are still extant today. Cities grew up around the cathedrals. The great art of glass manufacturers continued and expanded. While it is true that communication no longer existed on the grand scale it once had, and that the overwhelming proportion of people were poor, illiterate and unenlightened, the dark ages were by no means totally without light.

The Roman Empire Revived. In the minds of the people, Rome never died, for Daniel's prophecy about the Fourth Kingdom made the Christians "know" that the empire would last to the end of the world. Since the world had not ended, the population of the dark ages assumed Rome had not fallen. When Charlemagne established a great new empire in the west, it was thought to be a restoration of the great Roman Empire. He had a Frankish kingdom, without Roman roads, legions, or laws, no cities and no Senate, but he had the Church. The Church crowned him emperor in 800, and later canonized him.

Charlemagne's successors were a shoddy lot, and his empire soon was dissipated. Vikings, Magyars, and Saracens attacked, and the chaos of Europe exceeded that preceding Charlemagne's creative effort. In 962 Otto, the German king, again restored the empire. The Byzantine emperors were considered pretenders, unable to trace their lineage back to Augustus. In the twelfth century, Frederick I exalted the empire further by calling it "Holy."

Unity and the Church. The great pervading spirit of the Middle Ages was that of unity. There was practically universal agreement on the basic ideas by which men lived, or professed to live. The Church was not only the spiritual and moral guide, but the inspiration of art, the main source of education, and the accepted base for all philosophy, science, economic and political theory. Chivalry had the same practices everywhere, and everywhere the serf had the same hard work to perform. Literary forms were shared by all countries and common myths were found in all classes and countries.

While this unity, created and fostered by the Church, helped to make the Dark Ages a time of little earthly endeavor, narrow thought, isolation and unenlightened masses, it can also be viewed as a quiescent period, laying the groundwork, if only in the discontent it bred, for the "middle ages," the rise of Charlemagne, the awakening of intellectual forces, and eventually the Renaissance.

QUESTIONS

1. List three factors which may have influenced the sudden rise of Christianity in the ancient world:

2. In what way did the Church aid the downfall of the ancient Roman Empire?

3. What aspects of Roman life continued to dominate life in the Dark Ages?

4. What reason can be offered to explain the Church's active involvement in "matters of empire" during the Dark Ages? Middle Ages? to the extent of canonizing emperors?

5. Can you give two reasons why the Church did not encourage literacy?

Subject: Psychology

Level: Easy

THE MEASUREMENT OF INTELLIGENCE

I. What Is Intelligence?

To the student:

1. To *survey*, read the title, main heads, and first and last paragraphs
2. *Question* by asking: "What is intelligence?"
3. *Read* to answer
4. *Recite* in your own words
5. *"Rite"* (jot down) *brief* notes

2. *Question* by asking: "How do you compute the I. Q. score?"
3. *Read* to answer
4. *Recite* in *your* words
5. *"Rite" brief* notes

You're on your own!

Binet, who developed the first intelligence test, thought that intelligence was the ability to adjust to a problem situation. All specific abilities, such as judgment, abstract thinking, word usage, and so on, he felt to be reflections of a general strength of mind. In the fifty years since Binet's work, it has been found that some of the traits that are included in his definition of intelligence are almost completely independent of each other, and that a person may be "intelligent" in one field or area but not in another.

II. Determining the I.Q. Score

One way of expressing the mental capacity of an individual is by computing his mental age from the Stanford Binet test, which consists of many problems which have been given to a very large group and for which standards have been computed. For any item on the test, it is possible to say at what age the average respondant can successfully answer. In this manner, the over-all mental age is divided by his actual chronological age. The quotient is then multiplied by 100, and this result is called the Intelligence Quotient (I.Q.). For example, if a 9 year old tests at the mental age of 9, his I.Q. is $9/9 \times 100$, or 100, which is average. If the 9 year old had a mental age of 12 (that is, could do tasks on the test performed by the average 12 year old), his I.Q. would be $12/9 \times 100$, or 133, which is considerably above average.

I.Q.'s are normally distributed in the population. This means that the largest number of people have 90 to 110, and fewer and fewer have scores approaching the lower and higher extremes. Below 70 are found the feeble-minded, the imbeciles, and the idiots. It is generally found that to be a successful college student requires an I.Q. of about 120.

III. Other Measures of Intelligence

Because the Binet was developed for children, it does not give an adequate picture of adult intelligence. The Wechsler-Bellevue (W-B) scale was designed for adults, although there subsequently was a children's form of the test developed. The scores from this test can easily be converted by means of a table into I.Q. scores comparable to those from the Binet. In addition, the W-B gives a measure of deterioration. That is, it consists of several sections testing different abilities, so that it can show the degree of impairment of particular factors as is often found in senility or in various forms of mental disorder.

Both the Binet and the W-B are, however, subject to a severe limitation; they are verbal in nature, even though some of the subtests are performance tests. Naturally someone from a home where English is not spoken, or someone whose command of language is limited for either physical or psychological reasons, will not do well on the verbal sections of the test. And if the handicap affects ability to understand instructions, even the performance tests may not reflect the subject's true abilities.

Tests have been developed which are totally performance in nature; others have been used which require no verbal instructions as well as being pictorial for the actual items, but these tests are few in number, and the variety of abilities which can be measured in this way is, of course, curtailed.

IV. *Limitations of Intelligence Testing*

As has already been pointed out, any language handicap prevents the subject from making a good showing on most intelligence tests. In addition, it should be stressed that cultural factors invariably influence the construction of a test of intelligence. To illustrate this factor, suppose you were to ask a group of children from French Equatorial Africa to perform two tasks, tieing a shoe and telling the time of day from a clock. Since the children have never worn, or perhaps even seen, shoes, and the clock is not an item of use in their native society, undoubtedly these tasks could not be performed successfully even by 12 year olds, whereas American children can do the former by the time they are about 6, and the latter not long thereafter. On the other hand, all 12 year old boys in the native culture would be able to tell the time of day by the sun, and to sharpen a spear. How many American 12 year olds would appear intelligent if those items were on their test?

V. *The Values of Intelligence Testing*

6. *Review* by: *reading* the questions, *covering* the notes, and *reciting*

Then, take the test (check text for answers)

Despite the biases of the tests, their verbal weighting, and the many errors of validity and reliability to which tests are subject, we continue to use them. This is because we have found that measures of intelligence are good predictors of a number of things, including success at school, aptitude for certain types of work, etc. They also enable us to discover whether an individual's problems are due to deficiencies in basic ability or whether we need to look further at other aspects of the person in order to assist him. If we know, for example, that a problem child at school actually shows a high I.Q. when he is tested, we can then assume that problems of another sort—perhaps emotional problems—are interfering with his abilities.

QUESTIONS

1. What is meant by the statement "intelligence is what an intelligence test measures"?

2. What is the I.Q. of a boy of 15 whose mental age is 12?

3. What are the chief limitations of intelligence tests?

4. Name two standardized tests of intelligence:

5. Of what value would it be to a high school teacher to have I.Q. scores for his students?

Subject: Psychology

Level: Intermediate

THE NATURE OF LEARNING

I. *What Is Meant by Learning?*

Learning as Improvement. Many times it is evident that when something has been learned, an improvement is shown. By learning you are able to perform some act more proficiently than you previously could. However, a moment's thought will yield many examples of learning that cannot be classed as improvement. For instance, a man learning to play golf often learns many things, such as slicing or hooking, which is in no way improving his game.

Learning as the Product of Rewards. It is frequently observed that receiving a reward, either material or in terms of praise or security or satisfaction, tends to increase learning. But learning frequently occurs in the absence of any reward, indeed, often in the presence of its opposite. If you walk to class some morning and are bitten by a ferocious dog, you may quickly learn to take a different route, or to carry a large stick for warding off strange dogs, or to issue a complaint to the owner of the dog. Your fear is what has prompted you to make new responses to this situation.

Learning as the Result of Motivation. In the case of the encounter with the dog, we have seen that fear motivated you to learn. Can we say all learning is the result of motivation? While it is true that motivation seems to be present in all learning situations, it is sometimes so small a factor that it cannot be used to explain anything about the learning. Recall, for example, the "optical illusion" pictures in which your first glance shows you a staircase, and a second glance shows, quite spontaneously, the staircase in reverse perspective. In adjusting your perception you have "learned" to see the picture in a new way, but the motivation for this change, if present at all, is scarcely evident.

Learning as Changes in the Nervous System. Since we see the effects of learning by *changes in ways of responding* to stimuli, it can be hypothesized that any changes in the nervous system which lead to changes in response constitute learning. This definition is not specific, and little is as yet known about the actual changes occurring in the nervous system, but we can at least avoid the objections raised in the first three commonly used definitions. Considerable work has been done in describing the conditions under which the changes occur and what factors facilitate or hinder them.

II. The Fundamentals of the Learning Process

Drive. Drive is the impetus to make a response, a strong stimulation to act. When we speak of motivation, we are referring to the existence of drives. A drive may be *primary,* that is, relating to innate needs such as pain, hunger, fatigue, and sex; or it may be *secondary,* dealing with desires for praise, acceptance, security, financial gain, etc. It is possible for societal inhibitions to suppress a drive, in which case it no longer acts as a motivating force.

Response. The ability to make a response must be present in the individual in order for him to react to a drive or stimulus. It is not possible to elicit a response that has never before been made. In teaching a child to talk, for example, the parent can only repeat and reward sounds which the child makes, so that he will learn to repeat them. The parent cannot get the child to make a totally new sound. For this reason, the frequent occurrence of a sound leads to frequent re-

ward and thus to still more frequent occurrence. Learning, by and large, consists of learning appropriate times and places for making particular responses, not in learning totally new responses. In a new situation, responses are likely to be made in trial-and-error fashion, with those responses which have been effective in other situations being tried first.

Cues. Cues are stimuli in the environment that direct the response which shall be made, and when and where it shall be made. A traffic light may cue a motorist to come to a stop; a neon sign may direct a hungry man to come inside for a meal. A stimulus may have both an eliciting (drive) function and a selective (cue) function. The traffic light, for example, may motivate the man to be a law-abiding citizen, and to be concerned for his personal safety. At the same time, the red light cues the specific response of applying the brake.

We also react to combinations of cues; this "patterning" is shown by the situation in which you see dark clouds and have made plans to be away from the house for the afternoon. You might, therefore, decide to shut the windows. The perception of either one of these factors alone might not call forth this act. Perceptions of changes or differences may also become cues.

Reinforcement. An act that is repeated without reward will eventually be dropped in favor of some other act. If patting yourself on the stomach fails to satisfy your hunger, eventually you will cease making that response and try something else in hopes of eliminating your hunger. When satisfaction is found, the hunger will abate. This "drive satiation" permits you to engage in other activities, that is, to stop making the rewarded response. When the drive occurs again, the response which satisfied it in the past (eating food, in this example) will be tried again.

It should be noted that many rewards are learned, and their satisfaction may be indirect. An adult, for instance, may be satisfied to receive money in return for some act, whereas a child who has not yet learned the value of money would receive no satisfaction from this type of reward.

Summary. The general nature of the learning process, then, revolves around drive, cue, response, and reinforcement. A strong drive or motivating force causes the individual to make a response. This response is guided by cues in the environment relating to which response shall be made and when to make it. A successful response is rewarded by a reduction of the original drive, allowing the individual to engage in other activities, and enabling him to meet successfully future needs by repetition of successful responses.

QUESTIONS

1. How do we ordinarily tell when learning has occurred?

2. List the 4 fundamentals of the learning process:

3. List 4 primary and 4 secondary drives:

4. What is meant by saying that a stimulus may have both an eliciting and a selective function?

5. What is "drive satiation"?

Subject: Psychology

Level: Difficult

VISUAL PERCEPTION

I. The General Nature of Visual Perception

How the Eye Works. The human eye has often been compared to a camera. Like the camera, the eye has a sensitive surface upon which an inverted picture of the world is projected, a lens for focusing rays of light, and an adjustable aperture to regulate the amount of light admitted. In addition, the eye has two things not found in a camera, fluids and three pairs of muscles to control the direction in which it points.

The image which is projected onto the sensitive surface (the retina) is transmitted to the brain via the optic nerve. Since there is no right or wrong-side up to the brain, the image is perceived as a faithful copy of the external world.

Every person, however, has had many experiences which show him that frequently he thinks he sees something which actually is not in the external world, or which exists there in some form other than that in which he sees it. These "optical illusions" have many causes.

Perceiving Parts as a Whole. We tend to see a series of impressions as part of a whole or configuration. Indeed, if we did not, we would be unable to recognize in the lines making up constant patterns the familiar objects of our everyday world. There is controversy over whether or not this tendency to see unities is present from birth or merely learned from a very early age; it is certain, however, that by the time you can talk, all of your perception is of this type. When a series of totally unfamiliar impressions is presented, you will tend to gather them into some kind of recognizable form. Your conception of this total form may in turn affect your perception of the separate parts, and this adjustment to the configuration may give rise to "errors" of perception.

Physiologically Based Errors of Perception. The construction of the eye itself and its mode of operation may give rise to common errors in seeing. For one thing, the point at which the optic nerve enters the eye causes a "blind spot" in your field of vision. You are so accustomed to seeing despite this blind spot that you are rarely conscious of its presence. Another example is seen in the figure below of a cross. Because of the fact that it is more difficult for the eye to move up and down than from side to side, the vertical line below appears to be longer than the horizontal line, whereas in actuality a test with a ruler will show you that it is the same length.

The Effect of Attitude or Set in Perceptual Distortion. Your general frame of reference, including the vast impressions left by your society in mores, traditions, and folkways, can influence how you will perceive your external world. For example, men and women often have differing ways of viewing the same events. In one study done with college students, an ambiguous stimulus (that is, one which could not be positively identified as any particular object) was presented to a group of men and women. A series of choices was given, and the subjects were asked to select the object which they thought the stimulus represented. It was found that the women in the study frequently chose the answer "spool of thread" while almost no men chose this alternative. On the other hand, nearly 50% of the men chose "an electro-magnet" while less than 4% of the women made this choice. This is one example of how set, in this case, masculinity-femininity, can affect perception.

There are some psychologists who feel that the stimulus itself, even when ambiguous, contains all of the necessary factors for eliciting the visual response.

Others, in growing numbers, feel that many factors other than the stimulus itself, or even the nature of the eye and its processes, may be responsible for what we see. In particular, the needs of the individual, whether conscious or unconscious, seem to affect how he will perceive in a given situation.

II. How Needs Affect Perception

Seeing What We Want to See. It has been found that, for example, if a group composed of very hungry subjects and others who have just completed a full meal are shown certain ambiguous stimuli, the very hungry individuals give a significantly greater number of responses dealing with foods and with eating than do those whose hunger drive was recently satiated. It seems, therefore, that the operation of basic drives within the individual may affect how he perceives his environment. Other studies dealing with different drives, thirst and sex, substantiate this finding.

This finding may seem less strange to you if you will recall how these "drive states" can affect other aspects of a person's behavior. You have heard often of someone who was feeling annoyed at some event, say, the failure of his wife to be ready on time, who kicked his cat. The cat itself had done nothing to annoy the man, nor was there anything about the cat to suggest his wife or tardiness. His kicking was prompted by his internal state; the hostility he felt at being kept waiting motivated this act. If a drive can influence a man's response to his cat, it is not so strange to find that it can also influence the response made by his eye and the visual center of his brain in response to a stimulus which, like the cat, may not be directly related to his actions.

Nonconscious Factors. It has been shown that subconscious attitudes or needs may also affect perception. In an interesting study done at the University of Michigan, four words of about equal length, spaced around a center point on a card, were shown to a subject on the tachistoscope at a speed sufficiently rapid that the subject reported he was totally unable to make out any of the words, seeing nothing but four grey blurs. Two of these words were "neutral" and two of them had important meaning for the subject (for example, were words which he had used in describing his own personality). These words, in varying positions, were shown over and over again, and each time the subject, despite his protests that he could not

see them, was asked which of the four words seemed to stand out the most. The experimenter found that an overwhelming number of times the subject chose the two words which had important meaning to him.

III. Summary

While the eye is very much like a camera in its construction, it is liable to many sources of distortion. Some of the errors of perception to which we are all accustomed arise from the nature of the eye itself. Others arise from the fact that we tend to see patterns or configurations even with unfamiliar stimuli, and from the important fact that our attitudes and sets and our conscious and unconscious drives or needs exercise an influence on what we see.

QUESTIONS

1. What is the most important way in which the eye differs from a camera?

2. Why does the figure below appear to be a square and not simply a series of dots?

    •   •

    •   •

3. Give an example other that the one cited in the text of how attitude or set influences perception:

4. List 4 causes of perceptual error:

5. Can you venture a guess as to the meaning of the term "perceptual defense"?

Subject: Sociology

Level: Easy

THE CONCEPT OF RACE

To the student:

1. To *survey,* read the first 2 paragraphs, last paragraph, and the main heads
2. *Question* by asking: "What is the meaning of racial differences?"
3. *Read* to answer
4. *Recite* in your own words
5. *"Rite"* (jot down) *brief* notes

2. *Question* by asking: "What are the problems in classifying by race?"
3. *Read* to answer
4. *Recite* in your own words
5. *"Rite" brief* notes

You're on your own!

I. *The Meaning of "Racial Differences"*

It is obvious even to the casual observer that differences exist between certain groups of people, differences which the anthropologist calls "racial." By racial he means differences which are hereditary and beyond the control of the individual. The Negro's dark skin and wooly hair have nothing to do with the country in which he lives, the food he eats, or the school he attends.

At first glance it seems easy to identify a member of the Negro race, or to tell a Chinese from an Italian. You might therefore assume that the scientist can give you a simple guide for determining racial affiliations. While it is true that a number of inherited physical characteristics are used to classify individuals into the major groupings of *Caucasoid, Mongoloid,* and *Negroid,* there are several reasons why this division is far from complete and accurate.

II. *Problems in Classification by Race*

Gaps in Historical Evidence about Causes of Racial Differences. The early history of mankind is known to some extent by the findings of archeologists, from the discovery of bones and artifacts from which inferences about prehistoric man are drawn. The evidence, however, is scanty, and even the question of whether all men spring from a single *homo sapiens* ancestor is not yet answered. Scientists do not know whether the characteristics we call racial were originally caused by the adaptation of men to a particular environment (over, of course, a very long period of time), or are due to a mutation of genes in the original stock. Questions such as how these characteristics came about and whether they have always existed in their present form may be crucial for reaching proper conclusions about the meaning of race.

Overlapping of Traits among Racial Groups. A second difficulty is found in the fact that racial traits overlap, that is, are found to greater or lesser degree among all groups. For example, while Mongoloids are generally thought of us shorter in stature than Caucasians, many individuals of Mongoloid classification are, in fact, taller than many individuals classified as Caucasian. The use of traits in classifying is a technique relying on *averages,* and while this often enables the investigator to draw a general picture of a race, it may lead to trouble in categorizing any particular person.

Inbreeding. A third major problem is that of the inbreeding of races. It is possible, even likely, that at one time in man's history the major races were much more isolated than at present, and had little opportunity for contact with one another. Under such circumstances, the racial stock would remain pure. But with intermarriage, characteristics of each race are blended in the offspring, and isolating racial factors becomes an impossible task. Today there are almost no groups in existence in the world that are known to be pure, in the sense that the stock has been unaltered by intermarriage.

Unclassified Peoples. Still another factor to be considered is the fact that there are at least three groups of people who do not conveniently fit into any one of the three major classifications. The *Ainu* of Japan, the *Australian natives,* the *Polynesians*—each has, as a group, certain racial characteristics, but in each case these appear to be combinations of some of the predominant traits of two or more racial groups. This may be due to some very early contact between the original group and some other racially pure group—for example, in the case of the Ainu, probably an original Mongoloid group with a Cauca-

6. *Review* by: *reading* the questions, *covering* the notes, and *reciting*

Then, take the test (check text for answers)

sian group—but again, the lack of historical evidence makes such theories purely speculative.

Thus while we see that there are racial differences, that is, hereditary differences between certain groups of peoples, the effectiveness of the concept of "race" is influenced by our lack of complete historical knowledge, the overlapping of traits, the inbreeding of racial stocks, and by the incompleteness of the categories.

QUESTIONS

1. What is meant by "racial differences"?

3. What are two possible causes of racial differences?

2. *List* the four major difficulties encountered in the use of the term *race:*

4. List the three major classifications of race, and name the three major groups of peoples who do not precisely fit this classification:

Subject: Sociology

Level: Intermediate

THE CONCEPT OF RACE

III. Indices of Racial Differences: An Evaluation

The traits most commonly used in classifying racial types are stature, cephalic index (the relation of length of head to breadth of head), hair texture, skin color, hair and eye color, prognathism (the jutting of the jaw), length and breadth of nose, and hairiness of the body. A further examination of some of these traits will reveal the factors which affect the usefulness of these traits.

Stature. No racial group has an average height of less than five feet, nor greater than 5 feet 10 inches. This, it is evident, is a small range of differences, and, as was pointed out earlier, the overlap is considerable. Another problem in relation to stature is the effect of nourishment, which we know today to be more than negligible, though its exact effects are not yet known.

Cephalic Index. This measurement appears to be free from environmental effects, and it has the added advantage that measurements can be accurate and relatively unvarying from one observer to another. Further, the dead as well as the living can be measured. However, while it is useful in identifying subgroups, it cannot be universally applied. Thus, Nordics are characteristically narrowheaded, Alpines, broadheaded, but there is no typical Caucasian head shape.

Hair Texture. Hair texture is determined by the diameter of each hair and the curvature or straightness of the root sac; it has the advantage of being unaffected by age, sex, climate, or diet, and is consequently regarded as the most valuable of the traits in racial classification.

Skin Color. While this trait is certainly conspicuous,

its many shades and variations make it difficult to describe by a standard measure; further, the effect of environment, the sun in particular, on this factor is not known.

Despite the difficulties cited, it is obvious that differences do exist, and the question immediately arises as to whether there are other differences between races as a result of these physical variations. The primary obstacles to answering this question has been ethnocentrism, the tendency for an investigator to look at the world from his own point of view, with the values inculcated in him by his own culture. A great portion of the research in this area has been done by citizens of the Western world, who tend to regard the "White Man's Culture" as the most advanced, a point of view which, correct or incorrect, affects their ability to make their investigation genuinely scientific.

IV. The Question of Racial Superiority

The question of whether one race is superior to another is, even after many years of consideration, beset by problems of basic understanding. Consider, for example, how our very language gives rise to some of these problems: the frequent misuse of the word "race" (which, you will recall, refers to groups with certain hereditary traits in common) to apply to nationalities ("the French race"), to cultural groups ("a race of gypsies"), to language groups ("the Anglo-Saxon race"), and to religious groups ("the Jewish race").

The word "heredity" is frequently used in connection with cultural traits, which, of course, are not inherited in the biological sense at all. Other phrases, literary but inaccurate, add to our confusion: "good breeding" refers to manners that are taught, not to any genetic process; we speak frequently of "generating" when we do not imply biological reproduction; and the phrase "to inherit a fortune" certainly has nothing whatsoever to do with the alteration of chromosomes.

Let us now examine some of the arguments that are frequently put forth by exponents of theories of racial superiority.

Physical Distance from the Apes. If we could establish that one race had evolved further from the original ancestor, a case might be made for superiority on that ground. The evidence indicates that, for example, the Caucasian has less prognathism than the Negro—prognathism being the characteristic of the ape. But it is also true that, like the ape, the Caucasian has more hair on his body than the Negro. And the Negro's thick lips and wooly hair are less anthropoid than the Caucasian features. The Mongoloid has the least hair on his body. Careful examination of all the traits used to differentiate races indicates that each race shows some traits far removed from the simian ancestor and others less evolved, and no evidence for superiority on this account can be established.

Mental Achievement. Does any one race show more intelligence than another? Any measure of intelligence must be in a language understood by the subject, dealing with matters that are familiar to the culture from which he comes. Just the designing of adequate measures for any race and cultural group, therefore, is a monumental undertaking. Further, care must be exercised that native capacity is not confused with education, cultural heritage, or other environmental factors. Few such tests have been used, and what evidence there is seems to point to the fact that within each culture standards are developed for judging intelligence, and no racial group lacks qualifying members. It seems reasonable to suppose that, given environmental changes, a Hottentot could also be classed a genius by Western standards.

Historical Accumulation. Occasionally the argument is advanced that certain races have, over time, accumulated "more culture," or seem to be more highly civilized, than their contemporaries, and this is used as proof of their superiority. The validity of this argument can be assessed by means of an analogy: imagine a citizen of the ancient Roman Empire claiming that countries such as England or France, at his time mere outposts of civilization, are populated by inferior groups who are unable to achieve a culture comparable to that of the Romans. How wrong such a view would be is clearly evident to us today. It is less easy to see that the same situation may apply to, say, the Congo. So far as is known, there is no evidence that

hereditary factors of racial difference are the direct cause of civilization or its absence.

In summary, there are a number of traits which are used to classify people into racial types, despite the complications caused by the problems of measurement, the effects of environment, and the small ranges of differences. These differences are used to support theories of racial superiority, although at the present time there is no evidence that any race is further evolved, more intelligent, or capable of more civilization than any other.

QUESTIONS

1. Which index of racial difference is regarded as the most useful?

2. List three factors which affect the usefulness of a trait for purposes of racial classification:

3. Name and evaluate briefly three kinds of evidence for determining racial superiority:

4. Define briefly ethnocentrism:

Subject: Sociology

Level: Difficult

RANK STRATIFICATION

I. Status and Stratification

When a value judgment is made, by the society as a whole or by any subgroup of that society, about some social role, that judgment is called status. A role may have low or high status or may be viewed as both of these by differing groups, consequently, "relativity" is a common attribute of status. For example, some people consider college teachers as professionals without sufficient skill or ambition to practice in their fields —low status; while others think them to be devoted to the advancement of learning without regard for financial recompense—high status.

Some factors which are not actually roles but which are accorded the same types of judgments are called "role-related" positions, for instance, income, or race and nationality. These factors often affect what roles a person can assume in a society, but are not in themselves roles or positions which are role-related.

If one examines a society in terms of various of its parts which vary in status, one abstracts its vertical structure, or stratification. Some very common examples of stratification are the army, consisting of a hierarchy of ranks with varying status from private to general; a lodge such as the Masons, with 33 degrees of status; a college, divided in its faculty into Professors, Assistant Professors, Instructors, etc. In our culture, the occupation of physician is rated more highly than that of factory worker.

II. Rank Systems

Comparisons between various roles are generally made among positions of the same type, for instance, physician with factory worker, or an income of $20,000 with an income of $5,000. One cannot directly compare positions from different systems and arrive at a meaningful rank. How, for instance, does being of Polish descent compare with earning $5,000 a year? If a number of positions are of one type, we shall consider them part of a system, and if they vary in the status accorded them, we shall call this stratification a *rank system.*

A rank system is composed not of people but of positions. True, particular people hold the positions in actuality, but the position and the person are not identical. A position is more than a person since many people may hold the same position; and a person is more than the position, since he holds many roles in the society. A person with high status as, say, a lawyer, and as a college graduate, may also have low status with respect to other positions he holds, for instance, his nationality.

III. Differences in Rank Systems in Various Societies

All societies have rank systems, though different positions are stratified in different societies. The systems commonly referred to in the United States are income, occupation, education, racial descent and, in some places, family descent. Many small societies do not stratify income or occupation, because there is no sufficient differentiation between these positions to warrant it.

In some cultures the status of men is higher than that of women, and different age groups have varying status, although this does not appear to be a rank system found to any great degree in this country. In simple societies, as for example the Andamanese, rating scales may be based on such factors as physical prowess, hunting skills, the number of enemies slain, and the possession of supernatural powers.

Societies differ not only in which positions they stratify but also as to the particular status accorded to a position within the rank system. It has been found, for example, that considerable difference exists in the way certain cultures view the same occupations. In a small study done several years ago in Russia

it was found that the Russians tend to view the occupations of banker and priest as much lower in status than these occupations are regarded in this country. It is evident that the basic value scheme of the culture will affect the ranking given to positions; the anticapitalist and antireligious orientation of the Russian culture makes the above findings hardly surprising.

Another example of variation in the status of a particular role is that of educational accomplishment. In the past, Chinese culture accorded a place of high honor to the scholar; the East-European Jews also have traditionally regarded advanced learning as praiseworthy, perhaps because it involved a study of religious materials. In our culture, where there is still respect for "the self-made man" much less premium is attached to formal education, to the "egg head."

Thus we have shown that rank stratification varies culturally with respect to both the types of positions which are stratified and the relative status which is accorded to any particular rank within the system.

IV. Investigation of Rank Systems in Our Culture

Those systems which are easily expressed in some units of measurement are easy to assess: income, in terms of dollars, education in terms of number of grades of schooling. For systems where the differences are not quantitative, as in occupation, for example, special rating systems have to be devised. Further, some of these systems contain such a large number of positions that to be exhaustive an investigator would have to spend an inordinate amount of time and energy.

Another factor which affects our ability to investigate rank systems is the variation found between different groups within the culture, for example, from one region of the country to another. Studies have been made of occupational status and educational status with an attempt to show the differences caused by the age, regional location, and, to some extent, economic level of the respondents.

Studies have also been made of ascribed status. While such positions as occupation and income are achieved, others such as family descent and racial descent are "hereditary" and not necessarily the choice of the individual who holds them. Studies of rank systems of ascribed traits have also to consider the problems of units of measurement, the large number of positions in some of the systems, and differences found between varying age groups, regional groups, etc., in according status.

The stratification of role and role-related status of various positions into rank systems has been shown to differ among societies. Problems of investigation of rank systems include the unfeasibility of quantification, regional variations in status accorded a role, and the great number of positions within some rank systems.

QUESTIONS

1. Define (in one sentence) status:

2. List any three examples of rank systems other than those mentioned in the text:

3. List the two main aspects in which rank systems differ from one culture to another:

4. Give an example of each of the above (list only type of position and cultural group):

5. List three factors affecting the investigation of rank systems in a culture:

Subject: Zoology

Level: Easy

AN INTRODUCTION TO ZOOLOGY

To the student:

1. To *survey,* read the first two paragraphs, last paragraph, and the main heads
2. *Question* by asking: "What is the subject matter of zoology?"
3. *Read* to answer
4. *Recite* in your own words
5. *"Rite"* (jot down) *brief* notes

2. *Question* by asking: "How are animals divided by mode of life?"
3. *Read*
4. *Recite*
5. *"Rite" brief* notes

You're on your own!

The Subject Matter of Zoology. The animals most familiar to the ordinary person are those which are comparatively large and common, such as the four-footed beasts, the birds, and the fish, snakes, and insects. Many other animals inhabit our earth as well, some of them so minute that a powerful microscope is needed to see them. All of these animals are studied and classified by the zoologist.

For the sake of convenience, all animals are divided into two main categories, the *vertebrates* and the *invertebrates.* The vertebrates have a vertical column, or backbone, and the invertebrates do not. Because the vertebrates are generally larger, and include most domestic animals, they are better known. However, there are far more invertebrates in our world, both in kind and in actual numbers. Hence, in the eleven main phyla (or classes) of animals generally used in classifying animals, only part of one class deals with vertebrates, and the rest of that phylum and the remaining ten phyla are composed of invertebrates.

Division of Animals by Mode of Existence. One general way of classifying animals is by the habitat in which they are found. Four principal types of habitat can be defined: (1) marine animals living in the salt water of the sea; (2) fresh-water animals, found in streams, ponds, and lakes; (3) terrestrial animals; (4) parasites, living on or within the bodies of other animals.

Millions of animals of all sizes inhabit the sea, ranging in size from the enormous whale to the microscopic floating organisms called plankton. Salt-water animals live in restricted areas of the sea; some of them are on the surface, others live at varying levels of the ocean, down to a depth where light does not penetrate. Generally a salt-water animal is unable to survive in fresh water.

Each pond, lake, brook, and stream contains a host of fresh-water animals. For example, in a pond can be found the eggs of the mosquito, in a raft-like mass on top of the water; frogs and salamanders live in the vegetation of the pond; crayfish crawl at the bottom of the pond; many small animals swim about the pond in search of food; and thousands of tiny microscopic forms can be found in a single drop of pond water.

The vast number of animals which move about on the surface of the earth are at least partially known by nearly everyone. Animals, like the mole, which live underground, are said to be *subterrestrial;* and those like birds and butterflies, which fly above the earth, are called *aerial.*

Parasites are far more widespread than many people suspect. Almost every animal is infested with others that prey upon it. One of the smallest and most important parasites is the malarial fever germ. Fleas and lice are examples of external parasites. Man's internal parasites include the round worm, the tape worm, and the *Trichinella* (the cause of trichinosis). Hyperparasitism, the condition of parasites preying on other parasites, is a common condition, and even hyperparasites may be parasitized. Hence the famous lines:

> Great fleas have little fleas
> Upon their backs to bite 'em,
> And little fleas have lesser fleas,
> And so on *ad infinitum.*

Evolutionary Order. Practically all zoologists believe that the complex animals evolved from simpler forms at some period of history. How this evolution occurred is not yet answered. It is presumed that the first animals on the earth were single-celled creatures, similar to these now classified as *protozoa.* In some way these animals gave rise to multiple-celled animals. In the millions of years following, the complexity of some animals increased, so that all those existing at present can be arranged in a kind of family tree. Some of the links connecting present forms with earlier ones have been lost, but many have been found as fossils in rock. The simpler animals living today probably do not resemble exactly the ancestral forms, since undoubtedly many changes have taken place. Thus we say that man, for example, is descended not from the apes, but from ape-like ancestors, the birds from reptile-like ancestors, and the insects from worm-like ancestors.

6. Review by: *reading* the questions, *covering* the notes, and *reciting*

Then, take the test (check text for answers)

QUESTIONS

1. How are vertebrates distinguished from invertebrates?

2. What are the four general classifications of animals by mode of existence?

3. Give an example of an animal for each of the four classifications:

4. Explain why the statement "Man is descended from apes" is not strictly accurate:

Subject: Zoology

Level: Intermediate

THE PHYSICAL BASIS OF LIFE

I. Living Matter Compared with Nonliving Matter

All plants and animals, which is to say, all living matter, have certain peculiarities which distinguish them from nonliving things. Not all of these characteristics pertain exclusively to life, but taken as a whole, they are sufficient to determine whether or not an object is lifeless or alive. The seven most important of these factors are described below.

1. Definite Size. Every animate object has a speci-

fied limit to size. Although animals actually range in size from the microscopic blood parasite, the smallest animal known, to the whale, which is the largest, each animal has a characteristic size. Nonliving objects, on the other hand, may be of any size. A drop of water and an ocean are the same matter, but the possible variation in size is almost unlimited.

2. Definite Form. Just as animals have a constant size, they have also a constant form. If they did not, we would be unable to distinguish one from another. Nonliving objects may have indefinite numbers of forms, or may, like water, take the form forced upon them by environmental factors.

3. *Definite Chemical Composition.* The elements found in living matter are also found in nonliving matter, but the particular combination of elements which produces *protoplasm* is found only in living bodies. These elements are found in a typical animal in the following proportions:

99% of the weight	Carbon Oxygen Nitrogen Hydrogen Sulfur	1% of the weight	Phosphorus Chlorine Potassium Sodium Magnesium Calcium Iron

4. *Definite Organization.* The protoplasm found in living matter is generally divided into small units called cells. A cell is a small mass of protoplasm containing a nucleus. Very simple animals, such as the protozoa, are made up of a single cell. Most animals are more complex, and composed of literally countless numbers of cells. Inanimate matter has no units of structure comparable to the cell.

5. *Metabolism.* Metabolism is the process of converting food into protoplasm, an activity carried on by all living matter. Growth takes place by the process of intussusception, that is, by the addition of these particles of protoplasm to the already existing particles. If inanimate objects grow at all, they do so by addition of particles on the outside, by accretion. They are, therefore, not metabolic.

6. *Reproduction.* Animals are able to reproduce other animals like themselves. Nonliving bodies cannot reproduce their kind.

7. *Irritability.* By irritability is meant the ability to react or respond to stimuli, which are changes in environment. This responsiveness is termed "behavior." Animals are irritable, inanimate objects do not behave.

II. Protoplasm

Protoplasm has been called "the physical basis of life" since all vital phenomena are due to its presence. All living matter is composed of protoplasm, and it is never found in inorganic matter. There are several theories regarding the structure of protoplasm, the *alveolar,* the *reticular,* and the *granular.*

The alveolar theory states that protoplasm consists of two substances, one of which is in the shape of spheres embedded within the other. The reticular theory holds that protoplasm is a network of living anastomosing fibers, among which are nonliving substances such as fat and water. The granular theory considers protoplasm to be innumerable living gran-

ules arranged in various ways. It is not known which, if any, of these theories is correct.

The composition of protoplasm is oxygen, carbon, hydrogen, and nitrogen for the most part (97%). Oxygen makes up 65%, carbon 18.5%, hydrogen 11%, and nitrogen 2.5%. The nonorganic compounds are (a) water, which comprises more than 50% of the weight of most animals; (b) salts, such as the chlorides, phosphates, and carbonates; (c) gases, such as oxygen and carbon dioxide. The organic compounds are the proteins, carbohydrates, and fats.

III. The Origin of Life

No one knows when or where life on this earth originated. Creation by divine providence (the theory of special creation) is not accepted today by the zoologist. The idea of spontaneous generation which was believed by the ancients held that animals originated directly from nonliving matter; for example, frogs were supposed to have sprung from the muddy bottoms of pools under the effects of the sun, and insects from the dew. The experiments of Redi (1668), Pasteur (1864), and Tyndall (1876) overthrew this theory completely, and scientists now believe that life springs only from pre-existing organisms. The most likely guess as to the place of life's origin is the meeting point of the sea and the land.

QUESTIONS

1. What are the chief features distinguishing life from nonliving matter?

2. Rocks often change in size over the years. Why is their growth not considered metabolic?

3. What are the four main elements composing protoplasm?

4. Why is protoplasm considered to be the physical basis of life?

5. Why do you think scientists feel the meeting point of land and sea is a likely place for the origin of life?

Subject: Zoology

Level: Difficult

THE CELL AND CELL THEORY

I. The Structure of the Cell

The cell is a microscopic unit which is a small mass of protoplasm with a nucleus. The size of a cell may vary considerably; the blood parasite is extremely tiny, whereas the egg of a bird, for example, is quite large. In shape, the cell may be columnar, spherical, flat, or long and thin. As far as number is concerned, complex animals are composed of uncountable millions of cells. It is estimated, for example, that the gray matter of the human brain is composed of 9,200,000,000 cells. On the other hand, the protozoa are single-celled creatures. The size of an animal depends not upon the size of the cells, but upon the number of cells which compose it.

The largest part of a cell is the cytoplasm, within which is embedded the nucleus. Vacuoles, plastids, mitochondria, chromidia, and nonliving bodies may also be found in the cell. A membrane may or may not surround it. The cell nucleus contains a network of thin linin fibers. Along these fibers are scattered granules of chromatin, a substance with a strong affinity for certain dyes. This phenomenon enables scientists to dye specimens of protoplasm and study this minute and intricate structure. Frequently several granules of chromatin unite, forming a network (karyosome). In addition to the regular bodies, one or more bodies known as nucleoli may be present. Occasionally cells may contain more than one nucleus, and a few cells have no definite nucleus at all.

II. Physiology of the Cell

There is a division of labor among the parts of the cell. The nucleus, in addition to being the key factor in cell division, seems to control the activities by which the protoplasm is elaborated. The cytoplasm, which has a direct relation to the outside world, is the seat of such functions as irritability, absorption, digestion, excretion, and respiration. The cell covering may serve for support or protection, or, if extremely delicate, may have significance chiefly as a control over the absorption of fluids. Plastids may represent waste products or stored food; some of them have more complex functions, such as the chloroplasts, which carry on photosynthesis in plants.

III. Cell Division

Cells multiply by direct division (amitosis) or by indirect division (mitosis). Amitosis may be effected in one of several ways: the nucleus may be pinched in two in the middle; a plate may be formed in the plane of division which later doubles and separates in two; or two nuclear membranes may be built up inside the old membrane. The cell body then divides. The amitotic process is most common in old cells.

Mitosis is the far more common method of cell division. A complex process, it can be roughly arranged into four phases.

a. Prophase. The chromatin granules scattered through the nucleas become arranged in the form of a long thread (spireme). At the same time, the centrosomes move apart. Radiating lines appear around them, which later become a spindle. At this time the nuclear membrane disintegrates and the spireme segments into a number of bodies called chromosomes.

b. Metaphase. The chromosomes now split in such a way that each of their parts contains an equal amount of chromatin.

c. Anaphase. The chromosomes now move along the spindle fibers to the centrosomes. Thus half the chromatin of each chromosome is sent to either end of the spindle. Just what mechanism causes this occurrence is still in doubt. The fibers which are usually left between the separating chromosomes are called the interzonal fibers.

d. Telephase. This is the stage of reconstruction, in which the chromatin becomes scattered throughout the nucleus, again enveloped by a membrane; the centrosome divides and takes a position near the nucleus. Finally, the constriction of the cell into two daughter cells is completed.

IV. Cell Theory

Cells were first described by an Englishman, Hooke, in 1665. By 1838 the idea had been advanced that all plants and animals were made up of cells. At first it was thought that the cell wall was the most important part of the cell, but by 1861 the protoplasm was recognized as the principal constituent. Credit for the cellular theory is usually given primarily to Schleiden and Schwann, who in 1838-39 put forth the idea that cellular structure was the key to understanding life.

Cell theory enabled scientists at last to bring together in one point of view both plants and animals. It opened the way to understanding embryological development and the basis of inheritance. It revolutionized pathology and physiology by showing that disease and health were outward reflections of cell activities. And, finally, it solved the riddle of fertilization and the mechanism of hereditary transmission. According to E. B. Wilson, an eminent investigator of cells, "No other biological generalization, save only the theory of organic evolution, has brought so many apparently diverse phenomena under a common point of view, or has accomplished more for the unification of knowledge. . . ."

QUESTIONS

1. What functions are performed by the cell nucleus? by the cytoplasm?

2. List three major contributions made to the understanding of the biological world by cellular theory:

3. What is meant by the term "mitosis"?

4. Explain why a knowledge of the behavior of cells is vital to understanding human life:

V

Timed Readings

OUR NEW BREED OF KNUCKLEHEADS

Harry Golden

The Quiz Champion is the keeper of the fool's paradise, the Almanac. In order to be a Quiz Champion, you must be concerned only with that which is past. If Columbus had been a Quiz Champion he would have never discovered America. He would have been heavily laden with the words of countless others who said the world was flat, and he could also tell you in which cities those fellows flourished, and how many children each of them had produced.

The Quiz Champion is not a self-thinker. He is too busy trying to recollect the words and thoughts of others. Mere feats of memory are of little or no use at all. Voltaire could not recall the name of the mayor of his town. Thomas Jefferson and Benjamin Franklin, our two greatest philosophers, made a particular point of not cluttering up their minds with stuff that could be looked up at a moment's notice when, as, and if needed.

Albert Einstein, who never remembered where he put his eyeglasses, liked to play the violin. If you asked him where Vivaldi was born, and how many children he had, the professor would have retreated to the other end of the room, and pleaded with you: "Please, let me just play it for you on my violin."

The Quiz Champion is part of the current decline of the intellectual and the distrust of the scholar. He is our new knucklehead. He has succeeded in reducing scholarship to the level of knowing the population of Tokyo, and the batting average of Babe Ruth—and thus, unwittingly perhaps, he has helped to shut the door a bit tighter on Original Thought and the exploration of a New Idea.

286 words. See Rate Chart, page 136.

QUESTIONS

1. To be a quiz champion, one must be concerned only with events of (a) the past (b) the present (c) the future (d) all of these.
2. If he had been a quiz champion, Columbus would have (a) found India (b) sought fame at home (c) thought the world was flat (d) sailed south and east.
3. Feats of memory (a) are necessary for creative thinking (b) were typical of Jefferson and Franklin (c) did not help Voltaire remember the mayor's name (d) are of little or no use.
4. To Einstein, the most important thing about a composer was apparently (a) his thought processes (b)

OUR NEW BREED OF KNUCKLEHEADS From *Only in America* by Harry Golden. Copyright 1958 by The World Publishing Company. Reprinted by permission of The World Publishing Company.

his music (c) his family (d) the musical period to which he belonged.

5. The author seems to feel that the current emphasis on quiz champions reflects (a) a new era of scholarship (b) the failure of the schools (c) the end of original thinking (d) the decline of the intellectual.

Key on page 136.

GATEWAY TO THE ANIMAL MIND

Arthur C. Clarke

Some years ago the great physiologist Lord Adrian went the witches in *Macbeth* one better. He took the eye of a toad, and instead of dropping it into a caldron he connected it to an amplifier and loud-speaker. As he moved about the laboratory, the dead eye imaged him on its retina, and the changing pattern of light and shadow was converted into a series of clicks from the loud-speaker. The scientist was, in a crude and indirect manner, using his sense of hearing to see through the eye of an animal.

This somewhat eerie experiment hints at much more exciting possibilities which may have effects far beyond the realm of science. All our knowledge of the world around us comes through a limited number of senses, of which sight and hearing are the most important. We often assume that these senses give us a complete picture of our environment, yet we must be tone-deaf and color-blind—or worse—in a universe of impressions beyond our direct experience.

What must the world look like to those animals which have developed quite different senses from our own? The bee, for example, has an eye which can detect the polarization of light—something we can do only with instruments. Bats and porpoises have built-in echo locators, so that they are aware of obstacles even in the dark by the pattern of reflected sound waves. And there are still-odder gateways to the animal brain—the infrared detectors which enable the rattlesnake to "home" at night on the warm body of its prey, the pressure-and-electricity-responsive organs which guide fish through their watery world. And, perhaps most mysterious of all, there are the unknown instruments by which migrating birds navigate across the seas.

One day, if we wish, we may know what it is like to possess such sense organs. Since the messages from them, in the final analysis, are electrical, it follows that any sense organ of any animal could be wired into an appropriate area of a human brain. It would take some

time to interpret the incoming messages (it might be rather like learning to read) but with practice it could be done.

One can thus imagine the development of sense-telemetering devices which could be attached to any sufficiently large animal without harming it, and which would allow a man at the receiving end to become—as far as his impressions and experiences were concerned—that animal. At last we would know the way of an eagle in the sky, or of a space dog in a satellite. This would be of great philosophical interest, for it would give us insight into minds quite different from our own.

It would also open up ranges of experience which would be accessible in no other way, and which hitherto have been only dimly imagined. What man would not thrill to the thought of inhabiting the mighty body of Moby Dick, as he plows through the waves or hunts his dreadful prey deep below the surface of the sea? Not all, perhaps, would care to follow that search to its climax, when in the eternal night the sperm whale and the giant squid meet in what must be the most awesome combat since the dinosaurs vanished from the earth. Yet the time may come when men will know every move of that battle, and will be able to monitor the actions and experiences of all the creatures of land and sea.

The conquest of this vast new realm of experience may take centuries, and will change us in many ways. It will give us an outlet for emotions and impulses which, for better or worse, we have forgotten or deliberately repressed. When we can look at ourselves through other eyes, respond to the thoughts and desires of other minds—however primitive they may be—we will regain our lost kinship with the animal world. We will remember once more that man does not exist alone, but is merely the topmost peak of the great pyramid of terrestrial life.

Though art and literature will be immeasurably enriched when we possess such almost magical powers, this new revelation may not be wholly for the good. Face to face with the passionless cruelty of nature, we may ourselves become hard and indifferent to suffering; yet it is equally possible that the opposite reaction may occur.

For a million years man, alone of all the primates, has been a hunter and an eater of flesh. How strange it will be if the power of his own instruments turns him from his ancient ways, when the supreme hunter feels in his own heart the terror of his victim, when the lover of the T-bone steaks and filet mignon knows what it is to rear and buck at the first scent of the slaughterhouse.

1000 words

QUESTIONS

1. Lord Adrian's experiment allowed him to "see through the eye of an animal" by (a) recording light waves on a screen (b) changing light to sound (c) attaching the eye to his own nervous system (d) attaching the eye nerves to a lens.
2. The author's contention that we are color-blind means (a) there are senses which we don't have (b) some animals perceive colors which we don't notice (c) our picture of the world is complete except for color (d) we are aware only of light and shadow.
3. Porpoises are able to avoid obstacles by means of (a) unusual vision (b) response to electrical waves (c) warmth receptors (d) echo locators.
4. The sense which birds use during migration is (a) instinctive (b) chemical (c) visual (d) unknown.
5. The author suggests that unusual senses can be directly experienced by man (a) through existing senses (b) by transplanting areas of brain (c) by learning to interpret incoming messages (d) by observing animals' responses to signals.
6. An experience worth having would be a fight between (a) a school of sharks and a whale (b) a shark and a squid (c) a shark and a dinosaur (d) a whale and a squid.
7. One result of the new experience will be (a) the indirect experiencing of new feelings (b) an outlet for forgotten emotions (c) new ways or repressing old feelings (d) a higher level of happiness.
8. Furthermore, we will regain our (a) sense of man's superiority (b) sense of man's inferiority (c) kinship with animals (d) ability to communicate with other animals.
9. Experiencing the cruelty of nature may make us (a) cruel (b) indifferent to suffering (c) poorer artists and writers (d) poorer artists but better humans.
10. The new experience may influence man's (a) hunting methods (b) appreciation of conservation (c) valuation of each other (d) diet.

Key on page 136.

ADJUSTMENT IN COLLEGE: SEPARATION FROM PRIMARY GROUPS

Roger W. Heyns

There is a whole set of problems, such as homesickness, indecisiveness, and fear, that owe their origin in large part to the fact that college represents separation from family and other primary groups. This separation is often accompanied by a movement from a

small, intimate situation to a large, complex community. Different skills are required in these two situations and the process of acquiring the new ones is often difficult.

Separation from the family has different meanings for different people. For some it means loss of emotional support; these people have remained emotionally tied to their parents and relatives and have not formed effective relationships to others outside this circle. Lacking practice in thus forming relationships, they find it difficult to do so in the new situation. Homesickness does not, as often believed, result from an unusual amount of love in the home but rather from emotional dependency, a lack of psychological weaning. It is a relative matter. The home is not necessarily, nor even probably, such a highly attractive, loving place. Rather, given the inadequate skills for relating to others, it is more attractive than the emotional isolation of college life.

Usually homesickness and kindred emotions are thought of as exclusively freshman maladies and indeed they are probably found most frequently among this population. However, if one views the capacity to relate emotionally to others as an ongoing process, it is apparent that the rate of development is not the same for all people. For some, acquiring the ability to establish effective relationships is a slow, painful business and after a year or less of unsuccessful effort, the person gives up and returns to the nest. For others, the misery of emotional isolation is stretched over the four years of college, though it never reaches the intensity that results in flight from the situation. For still others, whose early lives gave them preliminary successful practice in emotional relationships, the process of establishing them in college is a rapid one.

Separation may have another meaning, that of separation from the decision makers. The person is now free to make his own decisions and direct his own conduct. No one supervises and controls him in so exhaustive and definitive a fashion as did his parents, although one can usually find administrators who will gladly try to fill this gap. New areas of freedom are now open to the student. This state of affairs is anxiety producing, as we noted earlier. Decision making is hard work. Being responsible for decisions and having to live with their consequences is frightening, particularly if one lacks the kind of practice that gives confidence in one's own judgment.

There are many aspects to this problem of freedom and we can go into several of them only very briefly. One aspect concerns definitions of the limits: just which kinds of behaviors are permissible and which are not? No situation is completely free and we feel most safe when we know what the limits are, when sanctions will be applied, and what kind they will be. Experienced teachers have noted that some children become very anxious until they know what the ground rules are. The same observation has been made in connection with delinquent boys: some of the flagrant behavior represents the youngster's effort to determine what the rules are, to determine how free the situation really is. The same response is found at the college level. Many instances of extravagant and irresponsible behavior result not from the fact that the person is now freed from restraints that kept him from satisfying some of his needs, but from efforts to determine what the standards are. It is important, though often difficult, to determine which reason is at the root of the behavior. It makes a great deal of difference in determining what action steps are going to be effective in preventing a recurrence.

There are many other responses to the anxiety created by freedom. One is searching out and rigidly conforming to the standards of a parent substitute; still another is rigid conformity to the norms of some group. Although many students maintain these patterns with a modicum of success, there are often pressures that make them unsatisfactory in the long run. These students begin to feel that they lack true independence and become dissatisfied with themselves. Typically these patterns are then abandoned for more mature relationships to others, in which the person can be a successful member of a group and yet retain his individuality.

Returning to the point that separation from primary groups has a variety of meanings for students, we should also mention that for some students it means a loss in status. They have gone from positions of recognition and eminence, albeit in a small group, to anonymity in a large one. For some students this is a temporary loss: the skills that were useful in the past assert themselves and the old position is regained. For others the loss may be permanent: perhaps their previous eminence was based on skills that were not transferable, for example. Whether permanent or temporary, the situation is unpleasant while it lasts, especially if important needs are involved.

In this discussion of the problems attendant upon separation from primary groups, several points stand out. The first is the importance of the previous history, of what has gone before. When a person has had practice relating to others, making his own decisions, and so on, the transition may be stressful but it is not overwhelming. When he has had no such practice, the individual must telescope some important learning into a relatively brief period. Sometimes he needs help from experts. Since all students face some of these problems, the total community should be organized to provide help for all. It is not possible to prescribe a panacea, but an important first step is understanding the nature of the problem. Many instances of student happiness and inefficiency originate in the separation from primary groups that going to college involves.

1000 words

QUESTIONS

1. The "primary group" referred to is the (a) neighborhood "gang" (b) dormitory group (c) age group as a whole (d) family.
2. To some people, according to the writer, separation has the meaning (a) a loss of emotional support (b) a change in one's ways of thinking (c) a temporary removal from home (d) a long-term removal from home.
3. Homesickness results from (a) too much love in the home (b) not enough love in the home (c) dependency (d) interdependency.
4. Dropping out of school is interpreted by the author as (a) fear (b) attack (c) flight (d) defeat.
5. Another interpretation of separation results from viewing the parents as (a) love givers (b) decision makers (c) administrators (d) counselors.
6. Being responsible for the results when one is free to govern himself may induce (a) anxiety (b) bravado (c) recklessness (d) emotional crippling.
7. The concept of limits concerns (a) the amount of freedom allowed (b) the person who is the ultimate authority (c) the amount of responsibility one can carry without cracking (d) the kinds of hours college students are allowed to keep.
8. Irresponsible behavior by college students probably results from (a) lack of knowledge about what behavior will not be tolerated (b) freedom from authority (c) rigid restrictions (d) all of these.
9. One response to new-found freedom is (a) lax behavior (b) disorganized thinking (c) rigid conformity to the norms of a group (d) rebellion against all authority.
10. Which meaning of separation is not discussed? (a) loss of status (b) opportunity for self-development (c) new-found freedom (d) loss of someone to lean on.

Key on page 136.

SOCIAL RELATIONSHIPS: DYNAMICS OF FRIENDSHIP

Roger W. Heyns

When are two persons friends and when are they not? Some of the conflicts between people arise over

SOCIAL RELATIONSHIPS: DYNAMICS OF FRIENDSHIP From *The Psychology of Personal Adjustment* by Roger W. Heyns. Copyright, 1958. Reprinted by permission of Holt, Rinehart, and Winston, Inc.

different definitions. The person who says, "If you do that you are no friend of mine," is stating that there are certain kinds of behaviors that do not fall within the category "friend" as far as he is concerned. In the research on friendship this problem has been handled very simply. The researcher just asked people who their friends were and then proceeded to study these choices. In a sense this method places a real limitation on the data. It is quite probable that people chose on different bases and used different definitions of the term "friend." Nevertheless, our knowledge of friendship is increased by the results of this kind of study.

These investigations show that some friendship pairs are characterized by marked similarities in interests, attitudes, and values. The total personality pattern is very much the same. In other pairs, rather than similarity there is complementarity. One person is quite different from the other but the differences are reciprocal: each supplies what the other lacks. In other friendships the two-way relationship is less clearly present. The person may regard as his friends those who serve him. There are many more kinds of friendships and even the ones already mentioned can be described in different terms. It seems reasonable to say, however, that the common characteristic running through all of them is this: friendship is a relationship of mutual need satisfaction. Friendships are stable or unstable depending on how much mutual satisfaction of needs is provided and how permanent the needs are. The old adage to the effect that old friends are the best friends is true only if the needs and the mutual capacities to satisfy them remain the same. Many a college student has returned home during a vacation period and found that his relationships to former close friends had changed; they were no longer so satisfactory. This experience is often disturbing and the individual feels guilty about neglecting old friends. It is probable that during the period of separation changes took place in the interests, values, and needs on the part of all concerned, thus reducing the mutual satisfactions in the relationship.

Our description of friendship as a strong, affiliative tie in which there is mutual need satisfaction may seem to have a strong hedonistic and egocentric tone. We seem to be saying that friendships are essentially exploitive: we form them with persons who satisfy us. This reading of the definition arises partly from too little emphasis on the word "mutual." The need-satisfaction process works both ways. More important, however, is the fact that the definition does not specify the kinds of needs that may be satisfied. Actually they are well-nigh limitless and not all of them are selfish and exploitive.

The whole problem of whether or not our behavior is ever anything but selfish has served as a topic for dormitory bull sessions since colleges began. The answer one gives depends on the point of view with which one begins. All motives are ultimately personal. A person does something because of an internal state; in that sense all behavior is selfish. Some of the things we do, however, may result in happiness for others. Looked at from the standpoint of the recipient, the behavior is altruistic. Some needs then, involve concern for others—the need to nurture and care for others, for example. These needs often operate in the interests of others, even though they remain strongly personal. In short, merely because a need is personal and is satisfied in friendship, it does not follow that all friendships are exploitive, in the sense that one person is being manipulated or exploited.

It is clear from this analysis that many different kinds of friendship relationships, serving widely varying needs, are possible. Some satisfy the need of one person to dominate and of the other to be submissive. Others satisfy the aggressive impulses of one and the masochistic tendencies of another. If we arbitrarily limit our definition of friendship to the kinds of relationships we ourselves have with people we call friends, the friendships of others often seem mystifying. We find it difficult to see why the relationship is referred to by the participants as a friendship and, more importantly, why it is close and stable. The answer lies in our inadequate understanding of what the needs are in the particular case.

CAUSES OF FRIENDLESSNESS

It will be apparent from the following brief discussion of some of the causes for friendlessness that not all of the difficulties necessarily lie within the single individual. Friendship is a reciprocal business and we must scrutinize the social situation as well as the person when we encounter friendlessness.

The Non-Conformer. Some people are friendless because they have habits, interests or physical attributes that differ from the prevailing group norm. The newcomer to neighborhoods who deviates from traditional practices often finds it difficult to form close friendships. The same phenomenon occurs in a college community. Persons may avoid friendships with a non-conformist for any of several reasons. One is the fear of losing social prestige by such an affiliation. Given the general social insecurity that characterizes the young person, conformity is one way of being sure that one is behaving acceptably. This applies as much to the choice of friends as to anything else. Later in life and in other settings, being different is not so much of a barrier to acceptability. In college, however, there are usually many who are not sufficiently secure in their social relationships to accept the non-conformist as a close friend. The different person, then, remains friendless not because his behavior itself directly interferes with friendship but because his difference makes him a social liability, judged by the values of the group. Marked lack of physical attractiveness is an illustration of the kind of difference that may interfere with acceptability as a friend.

Egocentrism. Another kind of friendless person is one who is so preoccupied with his own needs that he is unable to satisfy the needs of others. He cannot handle the mutual aspect of friendship. The egocentricity operates to interfere with stable friendships in a number of ways. This person's relationships are likely to be exploitive: people are means to his own satisfactions and friendship is not an end in itself. When the goal has been attained the relationship is no longer necessary. These people are usually uninterested in making the relationship mutually satisfying. The needs of the other person are unimportant. Indeed, sometimes the individual concentrates so exclusively on his own happiness that he does not even note the signs that indicate the presence of needs in another person.

1000 words

QUESTIONS

1. Some researchers define friendship by (a) observing how individuals act toward one another (b) asking each person who his friends are (c) using a social choice scale (d) requiring each person interviewed to specify his meaning of friendship.
2. Which friendship pair is not mentioned? (a) similar personalities (b) opposites (c) servant-served (d) authority-dependency.
3. Friendships have one thing in common (a) similar goals (b) mutual need satisfaction (c) exploitation (d) divergent viewpoints.
4. Old friends might not be best friends because (a) people's needs change (b) boredom often occurs (c) people generally are not steadfast (d) friends lose their ability to satisfy us.
5. All motives are (a) personal (b) exploitive (c) altruistic (d) selfish.
6. We are sometimes unable to understand why certain people are close friends because of (a) personal animosity (b) lack of knowledge of their needs (c) mental blocks toward some people (d) failure of those individuals to satisfy our needs.
7. The person who is "different" may be friendless because he is (a) frightening (b) unable to fulfill others' needs (c) a social liability (d) potentially dangerous.
8. The exploitive person is called (a) egocentric (b) dominant (c) aggressive (d) hedonistic.
9. The author apparently feels that friendship is a subject to be (a) studied scientifically (b) played down by college authorities (c) discussed more thoroughly in "bull sessions" (d) all of these.
10. A dominant person is likely to be friendly toward a person who is (a) conforming (b) egocentric (c) submissive (d) aggressive.

Key on page 136.

FRATERNITIES

Stephen Birmingham

"Neither a borrower nor a lender be" was one of the canons of my fraternity. Still, from that great grab bag of communal living that was my fraternity house, I emerged, upon graduation, with several articles of dubious ownership—a single white athletic sock, a pitch pipe, a size seventeen-and-a-half shirt, an ash tray monogrammed H, two towels, one marked Gymnasium and the other marked Hotel Meurice, Paris, and a copy of the official fraternity pledge training book marked *Do Not Remove From Library*.

I rediscovered this little volume the other day and read, "Your fraternity chapter will be your home; for four years it will take the place of parents, and, as its mysteries and ideals are unfolded to you, it will come to occupy a place of unequaled importance in your heart." I was swept back into the world of seal and ritual, songs, badges, official flowers, colors, calls and whistles, flags and mottoes, secret vows and handshakes. And I decided to visit this world again to see what had happened to it since I left it.

The house that was my home for four years at Williams College, and that took the place of my parents during that time, was a square, solid, unpretentious red-brick building. It had two and a half floors in varying states of dis-repair caused by the fifty-odd pairs of feet that tramped in and out each day. On the first floor there were a living room, a library, a sun porch, dining room, kitchen and telephone room. The walls of the last were inscribed with the names and telephone numbers of young ladies from Smith, Vassar, Wellesley and Mount Holyoke, along with pertinent statistics, comments, warnings and endorsements. The upper two floors contained perhaps a dozen sleeping rooms, accommodating about two dozen members of the upper two classes. The décor of the house would best be described as Early Alumni.

Most of the furniture was massive, unmovable and donated. Some of the larger, more permanent pieces bore bronze plaques engraved with their donors'

FRATERNITIES From "Are Fraternities Necessary?" by Stephen Birmingham. Reprinted by special permission from *Holiday*, copyright 1958, by The Curtis Publishing Co.

names, their class numerals, and scraps of poetry in praise. On the living-room mantel was a collection of silver cups and trophies, usually unpolished, representing athletic or scholarship awards our house had won. In a special library cabinet was a file of old exams, maintained in the wistful hope that through some fluke, Physics 12 would be given the same exam in 1949 that it had been given in 1948.

Downstairs, in the dark and secret bowels of the house, was our Chapter Room or "Goat Room." In some fraternity houses the location of this *sanctum sanctorum* can be spotted from the outside—wherever you see a long and windowless expanse of wall. But in our house the Goat Room's location was less apparent, since it was carved out of the subsoil and was approached through a long, twisting cellar passageway. The door to the Goat Room was always locked, and no one but an initiated member was permitted inside. As pledges we used to speculate wildly on what it contained; only hard wooden benches, jammed against concrete walls, we later discovered. The walls were painted, for dramatic effect, with lamp-black, and in cold weather when they sweated, we often emerged from meetings weirdly streaked with black. The room was unventilated, and sometimes held a faintly noxious odor caused, we thought, by a plumbing defect. Filing out of this room, swearing, soiled and gasping for air, our appearance suggested far more fiendish goings-on than voting to hire a jazz combo for House-party weekend.

Although keeping house in this building had many of the problems and much of the excitement of an all-male camping trip—the peccadilloes of the coal-burning furnace, the mysteries of the fuse box, the arbitrary appearance of ceiling leaks—it is not always thus in a college fraternity. In my recent study of the fraternity world I discovered that perhaps the greatest single truth about college fraternity houses is that if you have seen one, you have *not* seen them all. Most chapter houses are owned by alumni corporations, and the size and splendor of each house is governed by the state of its alumni pocketbooks. At Penn State several fraternity houses look like low, sprawling country clubs. At the University of Pennsylvania they are mostly trim, elegant town houses. At Purdue you will see a tall Gothic castle with crenelated walls and gargoyles; at Tulane, a bungalow. At the University of Oklahoma one fraternity house looks far grander than the United States Supreme Court building. At U.C.L.A. there is one that resembles, appropriately, a huge motel. There are fraternity houses with billiard rooms, music rooms, conservatories, gymnasiums, bowling alleys, and Turkish baths. A Dartmouth fraternity excavated for an indoor swimming pool, but when the college objected on grounds of safety the hole was turned into an underground night club.

Precisely how these pleasure domes of youth came to college campuses from Brunswick, Maine to San Jose, California—and even sent colonies northward to Canada—is an American phenomenon. Certain English public schools in the early 18th Century may have contained secret societies with Greek letters, grips, vows, and passwords, but the first college fraternity was formed at the second oldest American college—William and Mary—in 1776. This was Phi Beta Kappa and, though it is now a nonsecret scholastic honorary society that takes in both men and women, it was, in the beginning, a men's social fraternity. It even had a well-heeled alumnus, Elisha Parmele, who, through a bequest, established other chapters at Harvard and Yale.

The idea caught on, and Phi Beta Kappa spread to Dartmouth, Union, and Bowdoin. At Union, three more fraternities were started—Kappa Alpha, Sigma Phi, and Delta Phi—the so-called Union triad. From then on, there was no stopping fraternities. Through the 19th Century they blossomed like wild-flowers. They spread across the Allegheny Mountains, across the Mississippi River, across the plains, over the Rockies, the Sierras, and into California. They are still spreading.

1000 words

QUESTIONS

1. "Neither a borrower nor a lender be." The author implies that this maxim is (a) hard to live up to (b) symbolic of the fraternity way of life (c) a warning to pledges of what's to come (d) found on page one of the training book.
2. The author's description of his fraternity house results from (a) having visited many others (b) a recent visit (c) memories (d) speculation concerning the future.
3. The décor of the house was (a) stipulated by the college (b) determined by alumni gifts (c) designed by an interior decorator (d) planned to be appropriate for college life.
4. The author's house accommodated (a) members and guests (b) members only, during secret meetings (c) junior and senior members (d) usually some fifty members.
5. The only item in the library worth mentioning is (a) the trophy collection (b) the wall inscribed with phone numbers, etc. (c) certain bronze plaques containing poetry (d) a file of old exams.
6. The "Goat Room" contained (a) wooden benches (b) paraphernalia for secret rituals (c) the furnace (d) plumbing fixtures.

7. Black streaks on the members resulted from (a) old furniture (b) sweating walls (c) the initiation ceremony (d) the kind of lamps which were used.
8. The condition of a fraternity depends upon (a) the size of the membership (b) its popularity (c) the amount charged for dues (d) the wealth of the alumni.
9. One fraternity's proposed swimming pool was turned into a (a) *sanctum sanctorum* (b) night club (c) guest suite (d) smoke house.
10. The first social fraternity to be formed was (a) Phi Beta Kappa (b) Kappa Alpha (c) Sigma Phi (d) Delta Phi.

Key on page 136.

DON'T BE A PAL TO YOUR SON

Art Buchwald

There are many different attitudes on how to treat American youth. One we heard recently comes from Al Capp, the cartoonist, who was once a boy himself. Mr. Capp, father of three, told us in what might be his last interview:

"When I was six years old my parents put me in a clean shirt, pointed out the direction of school and told me not to come back for eight years. They never expected to see my teachers and the teachers never expected to see my parents. Each one had a function. My parents were supposed to feed and clothe me; my teacher was supposed to teach me how to read and write. Neither group had any effect on the other. The only thing my parents knew about my teacher was 'she was always picking on me.'

"My teachers graded me on arithmetic, English, history, and geography. Since I failed all of them, it was obvious I was going to be a cartoonist. But we never were graded for adjustment, emotional stability or 'Does he get along with the other children?' My parents knew I got along with other children just by virtue of the fact I came home every afternoon with a bloody nose or a black eye. We didn't worry about emotional stability in those days. All children were emotionally unstable. They were full of hatreds and frustrations. Who wouldn't be if you were half the size of the rest of the world and didn't have a nickel to your name?

"In my day, it wasn't a question of which was the best school to send a kid to; it was which was the nearest one. All schools were good just as all churches were good and all teachers were good.

DON'T BE A PAL TO YOUR SON Reprinted by special permission of The New York Herald Tribune and the author. Copyright 1958.

"We never heard of words like adjustment, environment, rejection, and 'community of children.' Sure we were unloved. We took it for granted it was natural for everyone to hate us. No one paid any attention to us. And we, in turn, didn't pick up our father's shotgun and wipe out the whole family.

"The child today is wise to the adult jargon and as soon as he thinks his parents are paying any attention to him the monster swells up in him. The child who is held in proper contempt by his family is grateful for anything he gets. All he needs is food and shelter. If he's loved, he becomes drunk with power, flexes his muscles, and takes over. Those parents who concern themselves with their children's problems are crazy. The problems of a nine-year old cannot be solved in any way except by becoming ten. The problems of a sixteen-year old will only be solved by turning seventeen."

Mr. Capp believes that the emphasis on teen-agers has been damaging. "Teen-agers are repulsive to everybody except each other. We all know that children pass through various stages of insanity, so why try to understand them?"

But aren't teen-agers unhappy?

"Sure they are. Let them stay that way. We've put too much emphasis on security. The teen-agers today have been told they have rights. Why should they have rights?

"In Europe kids have no rights. If they ever asked for any they'd get belted by their fathers. But in America things have been all switched around. Children used to try to please their parents—now the parents try to please the children."

What is your solution?

"It is my humble belief that we should give American children something they desperately need and crave for—brutality. We must make them feel neglected, insecure, unwanted, and unloved. In return we'll get courtesy, obedience, good scholastic records. They'll be so eager to be wanted that they'll do everything in the world to please us."

Is there anything else?

"Yes. Don't be a pal to your son. Be his father. What child needs a forty-year old man for a friend? And forget about teaching him the facts of life. There is nothing that a boy could discuss with his father that he couldn't discuss much more openly with his gutter-snipe friends.

"Keep in mind we owe children nothing. We'll supply them food, shelter, and clothing only because we're gambling that some day these sub-humans will turn into civilized beings and possibly make reasonable and honest citizens."

725 words

QUESTIONS

1. Capp contends that his parents and teachers were (a) strangers (b) born enemies (c) experts in their specialties (d) of no use to him educationally.
2. When Capp was a boy, people didn't worry about emotional stability because (a) they didn't know enough to worry about it (b) children had no problems to speak of (c) parents had too many other problems to worry about (d) all children were emotionally unstable.
3. Children were less likely to revolt because (a) they were better treated (b) they had no rights to be violated (c) they were afraid of the world (d) parents were too powerful.
4. In general, Capp implies that love (a) is bad for children (b) won't solve today's problems (c) is a poor substitute for hate (d) conquers all.
5. What children need most is (a) money (b) neglect (c) wisdom (d) brutality.

Key on page 136.

TEACHING MACHINES: THE COMING AUTOMATION

Edward Fry

"Why should the classroom be less automated than the family kitchen?" This is the taunt thrown at us by B. F. Skinner of Harvard, a leader in the development of teaching machines.[1]

His question is especially relevant in this headlong technological age. By the year 2000 A.D., we are told, our world will be automated beyond the wildest dreams of H. G. Wells. But by the year 2000 students now in first grade will be no older than the average Phi Delta Kappan is today. Obviously, education must not continue to lag behind by the traditional fifty years.

Fortunately, developments in educational psychology—or, more accurately, theoretical and experimental psychology—are providing educators with some new tools and facts bearing on their use. Most dramatic of these new tools are the several varieties of teaching machines now being developed.

Teaching machines are not just any audio-visual device, such as the motion picture projector, the phonograph, or even the sleep-teacher we see advertised in newspapers these days. Teaching machines have as a common characteristic the automatic feed-

[1] Skinner, B. F. "The Science of Learning and the Art of Teaching," *The Harvard Educational Review*, Vol. 24, No. 2, 1954.

TEACHING MACHINES: THE COMING AUTOMATION Excerpted from *Phi Delta Kappan*, October 1959, XLI, No. 1, pp. 28, 29, 30, 31. Reprinted by permission of Phi Delta Kappa and the author.

back of information to the student. "Feedback" is a term borrowed from the electronics field. A simple illustration is the automatic feedback found in the thermostat for a heater: when the room becomes too hot or too cold, the thermostat relays information to the heater so that it can "sensibly" regulate or control its own behavior.

One of the important elements for the teacher in accelerating human learning is feedback. Normally, teachers get feedback from giving examinations, asking oral questions, and listening to student discussions in class. By interpreting this feedback, the teacher can intelligently vary the flow of information or further instruction. One of the prime difficulties with the motion picture machine (or the lessons of a poor teacher) is that rates of presentation and repetition are not varied to suit the student's needs. Even under the best circumstances in group instruction the rate of presentation may be too slow for the fast student and too fast for the slow student. Teaching machines can almost completely correct this difficulty. (This does not mean that teachers or motion picture machines are about to be outmoded, of course. It means that we have at hand another useful device to individualize instruction.)

Research long ago emphasized the importance of rewards as motivation for learning. Knowledge of correct response is perhaps the most important reward the teacher can give. It is satisfying to the student to know that he has answered a question correctly, to know that he is understanding. We have also learned that the more frequent the rewards the better the student assimilates material. Ideally, he should be rewarded for answering each question correctly, even each part of each question. Also, it has been proved that more learning takes place when errors are corrected *immediately*. Fortunately, a basic characteristic of teaching machines is "immediate-knowledge-of-results."

It might be noted here that rewards obtained from a motion picture or lecture, while not absent under good conditions, are somewhat random, intangible, and sometimes even spurious (that is, they may reward the wrong bit of learning as much as the right one). To paraphrase Skinner, "the teacher has been outmoded as a rewarding device." Here again let us state that there is no danger of the teacher being replaced by machines; rather, some parts of some subjects may quite possibly be taught better by machines than by a teacher. Before you become irritated or fearful, let me point out that few people get emotional about washing machines replacing hand-washing. Technological advance in education will no more replace the teacher than washing machines have replaced the housewife. They will help emancipate her for work that no machine can perform.

The progressive educators were and are right when they emphasize encouragement over punishment. Research backs up the hypothesis that more learning occurs when praise is given for right responses than when punishment is given for wrong responses. There may be exceptions to this principle, but as a general rule of teaching it is correct. Machines always and only give rewards.

Progressive educators also emphasize student activity. Teaching machines require activity, and most of it is mental activity.

Conservative educators who prefer to stress "mental discipline" and academic subject matter can also find much of value in the proper use of teaching machines. Curriculum material programmed into the machine can be as factual, as thought-provoking, or as "academic" as they care to make it.

Machines allow for a more complete individualization of teaching. Why shouldn't a good student be learning the multiplication tables up to the "twenty-five's" while the average student is struggling to get up to the "twelve's"? Or a brighter student can be learning German vocabulary while waiting for the duller class members to finish their regular work.

Most teachers prefer not to be classed as either progressive or conservative, but they certainly have a right to ask, "Will curriculum material presented by teaching machines be as effectively taught as by present methods?" For some material, at least, research done at Ohio State, Harvard, by the U.S. Army, and by the U.S. Air Force all answers in the affirmative.

Whatever type of teaching machine is used, it has its limitations. Only certain types of material should be put into it. The art of the teacher is tested in making the statements and questions that go into a machine-teaching program. Much material now in use, such as teachers' quizzes, workbooks, and teachers' manuals, can easily be adapted to machine use. Generally speaking, it is desirable in the programming process to take small and consecutive steps, missing none. Motivation is higher when the student is often successful.

1000 words

QUESTIONS

1. One of the leaders in the development of teaching machines is (a) H. G. Wells (b) Edward Fry (c) B. F. Skinner.
2. With the use of machines, the teacher contributes to the learning by (a) determining the materials to be learned (b) caring for the machines (c) evaluating the learning (d) praising the learner.
3. One of the advantages of the machine is its "feedback," that is (a) provision for varying the rate of presentation (b) a self-correcting feature (c) a system of rewards and punishments (d) the ability to work the student harder.
4. Teaching machines (a) are similar to "sleep-teaching" in ineffectiveness (b) promote learning with less effort by the student (c) will eliminate teachers (d) help to individualize instruction.
5. Possibly the most important reward to the learner, according to the author, is (a) receiving a good grade (b) knowing he has answered correctly (c) acceptance by his teacher (d) a feeling of having "beaten the machine."
6. Most learning occurs when (a) learning aids are used (b) errors are corrected immediately (c) reviews follow the initial learning (d) the teacher does not arouse anxiety.
7. One limit of the teaching machine is (a) the inability of its "programmed" material to ask thought-provoking questions (b) its cost (c) its size (d) its dependence on a person to provide it with teaching material.
8. Apparently, the learner can use the machine to (a) test himself (b) find short-cuts to knowledge (c) learn at his own rate (d) get by with rote learning.
9. The best learning occurs when (a) praise is given for right and wrong answers (b) punishment is given for wrong answers (c) wrong answers are eliminated (d) right answers are rewarded.
10. The main problem with movies and lectures is that they (a) often miss the important points (b) sometimes reward both right and wrong learnings (c) always seem to be unavailable when most needed (d) fit all learners equally well.

Key on page 137.

THE MECHANICAL MAN

Arthur C. Clarke

During the last few centuries, the human body has become progressively mechanized. The process had been so insidious that most of us are quite unaware that it has even started, but in the past two or three decades it has begun to speed up. Maybe it is time that we considered, with some trepidation, where it is going to end.

It all started with the invention of spectacles about seven hundred years ago. Then, some time later, came dentures and hearing aids, followed quite recently by

THE MECHANICAL MAN © 1958 by Curtis Publishing Company for *Holiday* magazine. Reprinted by permission of the author and the author's agents, Scott Meredith Literary Agency, Inc.

the various gadgets which surgeons have started to insert into our bodies when some part needs a replacement. New valves for the heart are just a beginning; one day there will be new hearts, new lungs, new limbs. . . .

So far, all these additions or replacements, internal and external, have been made in response to bodily defects; but this may not always be the case. The time will come when artificial organs and prosthetic devices may be so much better than the flesh-and-blood originals that the latter may be abandoned, or at least bypassed.

It is a general principle that the products of biological engineering must always be far less efficient than those of mechanical engineering. The choice of materials is fantastically restricted, and the entire organism has to meet the extraordinarily difficult requirement of self-reproduction. With such handicaps it is almost a miracle (and some would delete that "almost") that living creatures can exist at all. Imagine trying to design an automobile or an electronic computer which contained no metal, and which had to grow from a tiny seed!

The human eye provides an excellent proof of this proposition. Regarded purely as an optical instrument, it is a pretty poor piece of work; the great physiologist Hermann von Helmholtz once remarked that if his instrument maker handed him a telescope with as many defects as the human eye he would refuse to pay the bill. It is the feat of making a telescope out of flesh, blood, and water instead of glass and metal that is so incredible. Without these admittedly unavoidable limitations of working materials, our eyes could give us much better service.

The same argument applies to almost every part of the human body. All feats of strength and precision which we are able to perform can be far exceeded by some mechanisms specifically designed for the job. It is true at the moment that any electrically powered arms, hands, or legs which we can build are extremely clumsy and unreliable, but this will not be the case in a few hundred years. Eventually it will be possible to give a man the strength of a bulldozer, the delicacy of touch of a micrometer gauge, the speed of an automobile. And the new limbs which provide these powers will seem as much a part of our bodies as do our present limbs of flesh and blood.

Even this is only a beginning. It is a truism that our senses are able to observe only a small part of the universe around us. Our eyes and ears are unable to detect vibrations of light or sound outside a comparatively narrow band. Perhaps most serious of all, we have no senses whatsoever which can detect radio waves, nuclear radiations, and electric or magnetic fields. In the world that we are building, such senses would have a high survival value—and they could be provided by wiring suitable instruments, such as Geiger counters or radio receivers, directly into the nervous system.

Is there any point at which this process will stop? Frankly, no. The science-fiction dream (or nightmare) of a brain encased in a machine which has completely replaced the body may be nothing less than a matter-of-fact prediction. The time may come when we will trade in last year's mechanical body for a new and improved model as casually as we now dispose of a worn-out automobile. This indeed may be the next stage in human evolution when flesh and blood meet the limits of their potentialities, and man encounters the challenge of strange environments on other worlds—environments in which his natural body could not survive.

Even without this last incentive, there is another reason why this ultimate form of mechanization will continue. We are killed by our bodies; the brain, even if not immortal, can far outlive the rest of the human organism. Why, therefore, should it be doomed to die when the body fails?

This thought gives us a hint of the far future, when medical science has reached its apotheosis. One day men will be born and live as creatures of flesh and blood for—oh, say a hundred years—reproducing the next generation, and experiencing fuller and richer lives in mind and body than we can ever know. But this will be only the larval or chrysalis stage of their existence; when their bodies begin to fail, they will discard them to take up strange and varied forms of metal and plastic, with senses and powers beyond our imaginings. Perhaps their brains will move to their new homes; it is equally possible that only the memories and psychological patterns which, after all, are the real essence of personality, will make the transfer to purely electronic storage units.

And so they will put aside, firmly but with tenderness, the phase of childhood which we have not yet learned to leave.

1000 words

QUESTIONS

1. The author begins with the contention that the body is becoming more (a) frail (b) healthy (c) mechanized (d) archaic.
2. The first replacements for the body were needed to compensate for (a) defects (b) the stress of life (c) more complex work (d) war injuries.
3. Biological engineering is inferior to mechanical engineering because (a) it occurs by chance (b)

choice of materials is limited (c) man's mind is superior to his body (d) biology depends on mutations for change.

4. The eye is criticized for its function as (a) a decoder of messages (b) a transmitter of messages (c) an optical instrument.

5. One will feel no different after mechanization than before because (a) some of the organs will remain (b) mechanical devices can be made well enough to fool us (c) the same brain will remain (d) learning will occur.

6. The changes will influence our senses by (a) increasing the number of them (b) decreasing the number (c) increasing their quality (d) decreasing their quality.

7. The predicted changes must occur because of man's (a) discovery of new worlds in which the body cannot survive (b) insatiable imagination (c) need for everlasting life (d) dissatisfaction with his present body.

8. The ultimate change would be (a) the installation of Geiger counters (b) replacement of the brain (c) a reversal of the aging process (d) the movement of mind through space electronically.

9. The author looks at the move from flesh to metal as (a) a natural stage in man's evolution (b) a horrifying possibility (c) a ridiculous idea (d) a predictable occurrence in our lifetime.

10. The new body is compared with (a) a radar device (b) a radio receiver (c) an electronic storage unit (d) an automobile.

Key on page 137.

Appendices

APPENDIX 1

Construction and Validation of Diagnostic Tests

I-S Scale. The two scores derived from this scale provide an index of "learning style." The first score, taken from items 1-20, measures impulsivity-constriction as illustrated both in overt behavior and in style of thinking. The scale was constructed by starting with several items reported elsewhere to measure impulsivity.[1] It was assumed that impulsivity in behavior ("Are you inclined to be quick and a little careless in your actions?") is accompanied, to some extent, by impulsivity in thinking. Therefore, items thought to reflect impulsive and constricted thinking were constructed and tried out along with the original items. Those with high item-test correlations (i.e., those items which measure the same quantity which the whole test measures) were retained. Only those items which were effective in two quite different samples of students (arts and engineering) were kept. The reliability or consistency of the scale is indicated by a coefficient[*] of. Using this figure and a measure of the spread of scores, it can be shown that an individual's "true" score on the scale is probably within two points of his obtained score. Therefore, the scale may most safely be used as a screening device. Scores should not be considered different from average unless they are below the 30th percentile or above the 70th percentile.

The S or stability scale is a shorter form of a scale previously validated.[2] It is derived from items 21-40. The scale consists of neurotic symptoms. It is scored in such a way that a high score means *few* such symptoms. The present scale differs from the original one mainly in length, in minor changes of wording to increase clarity, and in the addition of new items tried out by the procedure described above. The coefficient of reliability is .73. Once more, a given individual's true score is likely to be within two points of his obtained score. Therefore, scores should not be

[1] Goldman-Eisler, F. "The Problem of Orality and Its Origin in Early Childhood." *J. Ment. Sci.* 97, 1951, 765-782.

[*] Split-half, N = 100 students in college reading classes. There is reason to believe that a large part of the inconsistency here is due to the dimension being measured, i.e., impulsive people are unreliable while constricted ones tend to be reliable. Attempts to increase the reliability of an earlier form were unsuccessful. It was found that standard measures of reading ability are much less reliable for extraverts than for introverts.

[2] Smith, D. E. P., Wood, R. L., and Carrigan, P. *Manual for the SA-S Senior and Junior Scales.* Bureau of Psychological Services, University of Michigan, 1958.

considered different from average unless they are below the 30th percentile or above the 70th percentile.

Several years of experience with measures of extraversion-introversion and stability by Smith and others[3,4,5,6,7,8] have demonstrated the usefulness of such scales in academic counseling. For example, Ironside found anxious extraverts to be especially prone to exam panic;[9] Carrier found extraverts, especially anxious ones, to be penalized by artificially induced stress during exams and for stable introverts to "over-achieve."[10] Smith and others found that anxious extraverts gain more in reading skill when taught directively than when taught nondirectively.[11] Watson reported that introverts prefer a structured learning environment and extraverts an unstructured one, even though such environments may penalize their learning.[12] For other relevant studies, see Smith *et al.*[13]

As shown by Guilford[14] and by Sanford *et al.*,[15] a primary component of extraversion-introversion is impulsivity-constriction. Following their lead, the present scale was developed. Its relationship with the previously mentioned extraversion measure (N-160 members of college reading classes) is substantial,[*] thus indicating that extraversion and impulsivity are closely related. College students tending toward impulsivity have a higher rate of reading than do constricted students both before and after special training in a reading course. On the other hand, constricted students are superior to impulsives in academic

achievement at the end of their first college semester.

Rate Flexibility. It was assumed that rate flexibility is limited by perceptual speed and familiarity with selective reading procedures. Thus measures of each were prepared. Part 1 is similar, on the face of it, to perceptual speed measures. It requires attention to detail and ocular-motor control during visual tracking. Part 2, the skimming test, on the other hand, gives a speed advantage to the selective reader, as follows:

1. Sensitivity to key words presented in the question.
2. Translation of "score" in the question into a number and a per cent.
3. Realization of the cue value of italics in highlighting important information.
4. Ability to suppress competing purposes, i.e., to ignore interesting content.
5. Realization of the cue value of a superscript to indicate a footnoted reference.

Normative data is presented on the diagnostic chart. Other evidence of validity has yet to be determined.

Context Test. This scale was prepared by Ironside[16] and was used in a study of directed concept formation. Try-outs and revisions resulted in a split-half reliability of .76 (N=300 reading class students). Correlates of the scale are as follows:

TEST	PART	N	r
Diagnostic Reading Test	Vocabulary	300	.36
	Paragraph Comprehension	300	.42
ACE Psychological Examination	Linguistic	131	.56
	Total	131	.60

It appears that the ability to use the context to induce meanings as sampled by this scale is most closely related to verbal reasoning. There is some evidence that improvement in the use of context clues is greatest among anxious extraverts (5:91ff.).

Reading Test. Parts of Mill's essay, "On Liberty," were selected for this test. Some sentences with unusually complex structure were simplified. Twenty multiple-choice questions on the context were prepared to sample main ideas, significant details, inference, organization, and conclusions. The fifteen selected have item-test *r*'s ranging from .47 to .74. There is reason to believe that the test difficulty is great enough to make it a good measure only for superior readers. It should be considered a rough estimate of reading skill.

[3] Carrier, N. A. "The Relationship of Certain Personality Measures to Examination Performance under Stress." *J. Educ. Psychol.* 48, 1957, 510-520.

[4] Ironside, R. A. "Relationship of Exam-Panic to Scores on the SA-S Scales." Unpub. study, University of Michigan, 1954.

[5] Ironside, R. A. *A Study of Directed Concept Formation: The Teaching of Context Clues for Vocabulary Development.* Unpub. doctoral dissertation, University of Michigan, 1958.

[6] Smith, D. E. P., Wood, R. L., Downer, J. W., and Raygor, A. L. "Reading Improvement as a Function of Student Personality and Teaching Method." *J. Educ. Psychol.* 47, 1956, 47-59.

[7] See footnote 2.

[8] Watson, R. P. *The Relationship between Selected Personality Variables, Satisfaction, and Academic Achievement in Defined Classroom Atmospheres.* Unpub. doctoral dissertation, University of Michigan, 1956.

[9] See footnote 4.

[10] See footnote 3.

[11] See footnote 6.

[12] See footnote 8.

[13] See footnote 2.

[14] Guilford, J. P. and Guilford, R. B. "An Analysis of the Factors in a Typical Test of Introversion-Extraversion." *J. Abnorm. Soc. Psychol.* 28, 1934, 377-399.

[15] Sanford, N., Webster, H., and Freedman, M. "Impulse Expression as a Variable of Personality." *Psychol. Mono.* 71, (No. 440), 1957.

[*] r = .68 (corrected for attenuation, .85).

[16] See footnote 5.

APPENDIX 2

How to Write a Term Paper *

A term (or research) paper is primarily a record of intelligent reading in several sources on a particular subject. The task of writing the paper is not formidable if it is thought out in advance as a definite procedure with systematic preparation.

The procedure for writing such a report consists of the following six steps:

Choosing a subject
Finding sources of materials
Gathering the notes
Outlining the paper
Writing the first draft
Editing the paper

Now let's look at each of them.

I. Choosing a subject

Most good papers are built around questions. You can find subjects in any textbook. Simply take some part of the text that interests you and examine it carefully. Ask yourself the following things about it to see if you can locate a question to answer in your paper. Does it tell you *all* you might wish to learn about the subject? Are you sure it is accurate? Does the author make any assumptions that need examining? Can two of the more interesting sections in the text be shown to be interrelated in some useful way? Your paper is an attempt to write a well-organized answer to whatever question you decide upon, using *facts* for the purpose of proving (or at least supporting) your contention.

The most common error made by students in choosing a subject for a term paper is to choose one that is *too general*. A subject must be quite specific to be adequately treated in a short paper. (The most specific subject will always have enough aspects to furnish a long paper, if you think about it for a while.)

II. Finding sources of materials

A. Limitations. Tradition suggests that you limit your sources to those available on the campus and to those materials which are not more than 20 years old, unless the nature of the paper is such that you are examining older writings from a historical point of view.

* The content of Appendix 2 has been prepared by Professor Alton L. Raygor, University of Minnesota.

B. Guides to sources.

1. Begin by making a list of subject headings under which you might expect the subject to be listed.
2. Start a card file using the following form:

SAMPLE BIBLIOGRAPHY CARD
FOR A BOOK

Subject	Propaganda—History
Author	Jones, James Allen
Title	American History and Propaganda
Facts of publication	N. Y., Rutledge Press, 1955
Library call number	HJ 267.3R

SAMPLE BIBLIOGRAPHY CARD
FOR A MAGAZINE ARTICLE

Subject	Propaganda—Memory
Author	Erskine, Peter Samuel
Title	"Memory of Emotionally Loaded Words vs. Neutral Words"
Facts of publication	J. of Elem. Psych., Oct. 1954, vol, 23, pp. 83-89
Library call number	230.8 AT62

SAMPLE BIBLIOGRAPHY CARD
FOR A NEWS STORY

Subject	Propaganda—Cost
Facts of publication	New York *Times*, Apr. 21, 1955, p. 1
Headline	"Proposed Budget for Voice of America Doubled"

For periodicals, record author, title, name of periodical, volume and page number, month and year.

Sort these cards into (a) books and (b) each volume of periodicals. Then look up call numbers of the periodicals and sort out those for each branch library. This sorting saves library time.

If the list looks very large at this point, reduce further the generality of your paper. Take one main division of it as your subject. However, remember that several of the references you have will be discarded when you see the actual material, and you may not have too much useful material even if you have a large working bibliography.

3. Consult the card catalogue in the library to locate books—record author, title publisher, date of publication, and call number.
4. Consult guides to periodicals, such as:
   Education Index
   Reader's Guide
   International Index to Periodicals

Psychological Abstracts

There are aids to finding articles on any subject. They list subject headings, with various titles of articles under them, together with the location of each article.

III. Gathering the notes

A. Examine the books and articles—several volumes at a time will save steps.

Skim through your sources, locating the useful material, then make good notes on it, including *quotes* and *information for footnotes*. You do not want to have to go back to these sources again. Make these notes on separate cards for each author—identifying them by author.

B. Take care in note-taking—be accurate and honest. Be sure that you do not distort the author's meanings. Remember that you *do not* want to collect *only* those things that will support your thesis, ignoring other facts or opinions. The reader wants to know other sides of the question.

C. Get the right kind of material.

1. Get facts, not just opinions. Compare the facts with the author's conclusions.

2. In research studies, notice the methods and procedures, and do not be afraid to criticize them. If the information is not quantitative in a study, point out the need for objective, quantified, well-controlled research.

IV. Outlining the paper

A. Do not hurry into writing. Think over again what your subject and purpose are, and what kind of material you have found.

B. Review notes to find the main subdivisions of your subject. *Sort the cards into natural groups, then try to name each group.* Use these names for main divisions in your outline. For example, you may be writing a paper about the Voice of America and you have the following subject headings on your cards:

1. Propaganda—American (History)
2. Voice of America—funds appropriated
3. Voice of America—expenditures
4. Voice of America—cost compared with Soviet propaganda
5. Voice of America—statement of purpose
6. Voice of America—structure and organization
7. Voice of America—offices and duties
8. Voice of America—effect on Soviet people
9. Voice of America—voluntary contributions

10. Voice of America—plans for the future

The above cards could be sorted into 6 piles, furnishing the following headings:

1. History   (card 1)
2. Purpose   (card 5)
3. Organization   (cards 6, 7)
4. Cost   (cards 2, 3, 4, 9)
5. Effects   (card 8)
6. Future   (card 10)

You will have more cards than in the example above, and at this point you can possibly narrow down your subject further by taking out one of the piles of cards.

C. Sort the cards again under each main division to find subsections for your outline.

D. By this time it should begin to look more coherent and to take on a definite structure. If it does not, try going back and sorting again for main divisions, to see if another general pattern is possible.

E. You may want to indicate the parts of your outline in traditional form as follows:

    I.
        A.
            1.
                a.
                    (1)
        B.
    II.
        A.

Use these designations only in the outline and not in the paper itself, or it will look more like an extended outline than a paper.

V. Writing the first draft

You are now ready to write.

A. Write the paper around the outline, being sure that you indicate in the first part of the paper what its purpose is. Follow the old formula:

1. Tell the reader what you are going to say (statement of purpose).
2. Say it (main body of the paper).
3. Tell the reader what you've said (statement of summary and conclusions).

B. A word about composition:

1. Traditionally, any headings or subheadings included are nouns, not verbs or phrases.
2. Keep things together that belong together. Your outline will help you do this if it is well organized. Be sure you do not change the subject in the middle of a paragraph, and be sure that everything under one heading in your outline is about the same general topic.
3. Avoid short, bumpy sentences and long

straggling sentences with more than one main idea.

C. This is the time to decide upon the title of the paper.

VI. Editing the paper

You are now ready to polish up the first draft.

A. Try to read it as if it were cold and unfamiliar to you. It is a good idea to do this a day or two after having written the first draft.

B. Reading the paper aloud is a good way to be sure that the language is not awkward, and that it "flows" properly.

C. Check for proper spelling, phrasing, and sentence construction. *Be sure that pronouns clearly refer to nouns.*

Ex. Labor believes in a guaranteed annual wage while management is opposed. The facts clearly indicate that *this position* [which?] is unwise.

D. Check for proper form of footnotes, quotes, and punctuation.

E. Check to see that quotations serve one of the following purposes:

1. Show evidence of what an author has said.
2. Avoid misrepresentation through restatement.
3. Save unnecessary writing when ideas have been well expressed by the original author.

F. Check for proper form of tables and graphs. Be *certain* that any table or graph is self-explanatory.

APPENDIX 3

Vocabulary Development: Context Clues

The sentences and paragraphs on the following pages are designed to give you practice in the use of five *context clues*. A context clue shows the way in which words are ordered in a sentence or paragraph so that we see relationships among them. We need to practice using these clues so that we become *consciously aware* of them and their usefulness. It should be noted that these clues do not appear in all contexts; but if we learn the clues, we can use them when they do occur. The greatest improvement in ability to attack new words seems to depend upon conscious effort to distinguish and learn the methods involved.

Clue 1. Definition. Often a word is defined or its meaning is described by the words around it; however, this definition does not look like a dictionary entry.

Clue 2. Experience. Our background of direct experience (or experience through reading) helps us to know the meaning of a new word, since we are often already familiar with the type of situation which the new word helps to describe.

Clue 3. Comparison and Contrast. The context may tell us the meaning of a word by telling us what it does not mean, or by comparing it with a familiar word.

Clue 4. Synonym. For variety, the same ideas are often expressed by two or three different words or phrases. If we know the easier, familiar term, we can learn the new word.

Clue 5. Summary. After a situation or an idea has been presented in different ways or on different levels, it is sometimes summed up with the use of one word. We can learn the new word's meaning by being aware of what it is summarizing.

Directions: Read each sample, and before looking at the choices of meaning, try to give a tentative definition for the italicized word. Then circle one of the four choices given which comes closest to the correct meaning. After you have checked the answers in the Key, page 137, pay special attention to any you may have missed. Go back to the item and see how the clue helps to make the keyed choice the correct one.

Clue 1: Definition

1. Well, no, it was more than just saving his money. He just didn't spend any. And money that a *parsimonious* man stores away makes him unhappy and anxious, you know.

Parsimonious: (a) ranting (b) extravagant (c) spicy (d) miserly

2. It was hard for the agent to *relinquish* his insurance business. After it was gone, what would he have to rely on? Only three sons-in-law and two War Bonds. . . .

Relinquish: (a) maintain (b) give up (c) inherit (d) announce

3. Never had I heard such a *carillon* as in the Bok Tower. Its bells must have been cast in the finest foundry, for their sounds were crystal clear with a rich, full resonance.

Carillon: (a) melody (b) set of chimes (c) high pitch (d) clapper

4. Even though he was *admonished* not to go, the captain felt a sense of semi-duty about those maidens in distress. Disregarding the advice of his sailors, and oblivious of the inconvenience involved, he raced off.

Admonition: (a) charge (b) trial (c) recommendation (d) warning

5. No one could have done a better job of taking the money quickly and quietly and hiding it so well. And no one would have been less suspected of *absconding* with the company's profits.

Abscond: (a) to speculate (b) to disappear (c) to deceive (d) to disobey

6. The *queue* was orderly and unusually straight. Normally when many people gather to buy movie tickets, they push and shove. . . .

Queue: (a) waiting line (b) dock (c) geometric figure (d) entrance

7. There are many *criteria* that must be considered in successful job getting. One must meet certain requirements in intelligence, interests, experience, and physical qualifications.

Criteria: (a) habits (b) standards (c) materials (d) alternatives

8. To *refute* the accusation against him, the dentist called upon all his powers of oratory, all the testimonials of his good name that he could pay for, and all his relatives.

Refute: (a) to acclaim (b) to confide (c) to disprove (d) to outline

9. The rushing torrents of rain over the dry, baked earth cut out a strange pattern of *arroyos*, such as the desertlands see every spring with the "big rains." Some of them are as many as 40 feet deep!

Arroyo: (a) path (b) sediment (c) river bed (d) gully

10. The experimenter discovered the primary cause for the strange sickness. The bottling company had *adulterated* its product by adding a harmful coloring matter. In order to take the case to court, however, he needed further evidence.

Adulterate: (a) to purify (b) to correct (c) to contaminate (d) to alter

11. The old newspaper was now *defunct*. It had seen its best days back in the goldrush era, and now had been literally run out of business.

Defunct: (a) eroded (b) traditional (c) fighting (d) dead

12. The sociologists tell us that every community has its reprobate, its genius, its dissembler, and its politician. But there's the *sycophant*, too—the man who weedles and flatters his way into favored positions.

Sycophant: (a) parasite (b) tyrant (c) salesman (d) slanderer

13. You can make use of the *vicarious* experience you obtain through reading. When you travel by book to Persia or ancient China; when you learn from a brochure the changing aspects of the Belgian stock market; when you feel the excitement of climbing K-6; you can be living and enjoying these experiences even though you are only reading.

Vicarious: (a) artificial (b) substitute (c) vivid (d) spurious

14. Although the girl had been recalcitrant (and she knew it), she posed a *blasé* attitude when her faults were dragged out on the carpet. She left with a look of "why-should-I-care?"

Blasé: (a) unconcerned (b) unafraid (c) blustery (d) humorous

15. In *repudiating* the demands of the distant relatives of his client, the lawyer adamantly insisted that, legally as well as morally, they had no chance of making their claims good.

Repudiate: (a) to spurn (b) to agree (c) to accept (d) to imitate

16. In science we need a *pragmatic* as much as a theoretical approach. We must be concerned with the results of an experiment and with the usefulness of those results.

Pragmatic: (a) necessary (b) ideological (c) practical (d) paradoxical

17. One of the first requisites for good speech making is the ability to gain good *rapport* with an audience. Both the speaker and the listeners will learn and enjoy more if there is an atmosphere of co-operation and working together toward certain goals.

Rapport: (a) enthusiastic approach (b) set of catchy jokes (c) intelligent insight (d) harmonious relationship

18. In the middle of the argument, the husband stormed petulantly out of the house, even though he admitted to himself that the whole affair was his fault. It was a somewhat *puerile* demonstration on his part.

Puerile: (a) welcome (b) childish (c) justified (d) amateur

19. The conclusion reached by the judge was far off base from what was expected. He had apparently thought about the case carefully, considering more aspects than the newspaperman had. Net result: no one agreed with his *abstruse* decision.

Abstruse: (a) easy to understand (b) looking suspicious (c) difficult to fathom (d) invalid

20. Of course, you must remember that the author's main purposes in writing are to convey his general thoughts and perhaps to perfect his style of writing. Making his vocabulary understandable without the use of a dictionary is most often *ancillary* to the main purposes, if indeed it enters into the author's consideration at all.

Ancillary: (a) important (b) useful (c) contradictory (d) subordinate

Clue 2: Experience

1. Now Maggie could be said to be a *querulous* wife. Jiggs is the one who could really tell us about that—nearly every day!

Querulous: (a) bragging (b) satisfied (c) efficient (d) nagging

2. Madame Pompadour was never quite married to

Louis the King. As his *paramour,* however, she hung around the palace quite a lot.

Paramour: (a) mistress (b) housekeeper (c) doctor (d) daughter-in-law

3. After a week on the range, the cowpoke smacked his lips and took his fork in hand as the hot *viands* were set before him.

Viands: (a) articles (b) foods (c) glasses (d) pokers

4. A review of history indicates that many nations have been in a *chronic* state of war or preparation for war.

Chronic: (a) uncertain (b) brief (c) justified (d) constant

5. In one night Scrooge was mystically changed from a *penurious* crank into a patient and kindly man.

Penurious: (a) miserly (b) liberal (c) irreligious (d) horrible

6. Mr. McGoo certainly never fails to make a *ludicrous* mess of any situation he gets into. Remember the time he climbed the Matternot?

Ludicrous: (a) repulsive (b) melancholy (c) quaint (d) ridiculous

7. "It's a simple fact," the women's club speaker said, "that very many women *vegetate* after marriage. They become too settled down."

Vegetate: (a) to grow fat (b) to become irritable (c) to plant gardens (d) to lead inactive lives

8. To feel *replete*—this is what happens to anyone who overeats at a Thanksgiving Day dinner.

Replete: (a) happy (b) gorged (c) defeated (d) squeamish

9. It was the *truculent* handling of the Jewish people by the Nazis which led certain groups to deny the right of the Berlin orchestra to present its concerts in this country last year.

Truculent: (a) separate (b) timely (c) quick (d) cruel

10. The politician who knows which strings to pull and how hard, can engage in rackets and gross crimes with *impunity.*

Impunity: (a) freedom from punishment (b) danger (c) machine guns (d) scorn and defiance (stubbornness)

11. It is to be hoped that you will no longer find vocabulary improvement as *jejune* as reading the dictionary from cover to cover. It can be an exciting and interesting process if you use your head!

Jejune: (a) scholarly (b) devoid of interest (c) tiring (d) fruitless

12. Don't be discouraged in the beginning by gaps in your knowledge and experience. Your growth and broadening is *ineluctable* (like death and taxes) if you are alert and aware of the world around you, and if you read widely.

Ineluctable: (a) unpleasant (b) possible (c) inevitable (d) unlikely

13. The principal purpose of the European missionaries—the fanatic Spaniards in particular—was to *proselyte* the natives of South America and the West Indies by force or cajolery if necessary.

Proselyte: (a) to kill (b) to control (c) to convert (d) to aid

14. Not even a letter from the President can do much to *mitigate* the grief of a Gold Star mother.

Mitigate: (a) to cause (b) to lessen (c) to make harsh (d) to intensify

15. As the two little boys walked along the *esplanade,* they imagined they were the whole Michigan Marching Band which they admired so much.

Esplanade: (a) large level space (b) pit (c) steel girders (d) stadium

16. Even 20 years after Amelia Earhart's brave flight over the Pacific, the story of her fate remains an *enigma.*

Enigma: (a) obstacle (b) defeat (c) tenseness (d) puzzle

17. "We will surrender everything but our faith and our language," the pertinacious Bohemian chancellor told the invaders. "On these two points, we will remain *obdurate.*"

Obdurate: (a) intolerant (b) hopeful (c) unyielding (d) discordant

18. Religion often asks that we *transcend* our earthly problems and concentrate on how spiritual values will benefit us in the afterlife.

Transcend: (a) to meddle with (b) to defeat (c) to rise above (d) to do

19. When Alexander Pope wrote that famous line, "Whatever is, is Right," he was making a *poignant* criticism of the upper classes of his day.

Poignant: (a) penetrating (b) weak (c) methodical (d) attentive

20. By a process of nefarious and *specious* reasoning, power diplomats like Hitler and Stalin are able to influence and then control the thoughts and passions of the people they rule.

Specious: (a) supported (b) deceptive (c) detailed (d) direct

Clue 3: Comparison and Contrast

1. Mandie's pie was clearly bitter and salty. It's no wonder that Belinda's *piquant* cherry pie won all the blue ribbons.

Piquant: (a) beautiful (b) tough (c) oven-browned (d) pleasantly tart

2. An individual must set up an *ultimate* vocational goal, even though along the way he needs temporary aims.

Ultimate: (a) responsible (b) final (c) appropriate (d) general

3. We always seem to remember the faults of our enemies, while we become *oblivious* of their contributions.

Oblivious: (a) proud (b) insolent (c) spiteful (d) forgetful

4. Compared with the robust and healthy faces of farmers in the midwest, many southern share croppers present a *sallow* appearance.

Sallow: (a) ruddy (b) sun-burned (c) sickly (d) obvious

5. In 1885 the steam engine was still a new and fascinating machine. By 1955 it was *obsolete,* just as in 1855 the ox cart was.

Obsolete: (a) extinct (b) out of date (c) overused (d) questionable

6. Although wars have always been cruel, there has seemed to be a steady increase in the *nefarious* nature of the plans and purposes of war.

Nefarious: (a) villainous (b) reckless (c) negative (d) deceptive

7. In one seat sat slow, careful and somewhat plodding Terry, working so hard to keep up with his classmates. And directly behind him sat *precocious* Marvin, with the work done in his head and time to spare, even though he was several months younger than Terry.

Precocity: (a) early mental development (b) maturity (c) hackling (d) high degree of intelligence

8. It was an *acrimonious* answer, like the kind a neighbor would get if he went calling at 1:00 A.M.

Acrimonious: (a) courteous (b) bitter (c) abundant (d) absurd

9. The Senator from Rhode Island seriously questioned the honesty of the proposal; and in thus *impugning* the President's integrity, he almost lost his seat in the next election.

Impugn: (a) to import (b) to deny (c) to consider (d) to praise

10. Roosevelt was noted for his *succinct* and effective speech. Truman, conversely, either spoke in unrelated or involved terms, or had someone write his messages for him.

Succinct: (a) deceptive (b) concise (c) hopeful (d) biting

11. Have you ever tried to drive a nail into a concrete floor? That should give you an idea of how *adamant* a typical conservative Vermonter is about new ideas.

Adamant: (a) frightened (b) favorable (c) resistant (d) verbal

12. Ach! In one family yet—two boys, and so very different. The one a compliant, obedient lad; the other

an envious, *recalcitrant* mongrel!

Recalcitrant: (a) careless (b) rebellious (c) docile (d) destructive

13. We seem to have the stereotyped notion that all big-city machine politicians gain their offices through sheer *dissembling* in their speeches, political conniving, or ballot-box stuffing.

Dissemble: (a) to sell a project (b) to lose face (c) to be opinionated (d) to pretend honesty

14. In reading classes, naturally and of course, everything that is said or done is essential to improvement or to understanding. Nothing is *extraneous* or extrinsic.

Extraneous: (a) important (b) unrelated (c) void (d) vague

15. A direct, honest, and rational approach to the engineer's personal problems never seemed to work. Instead, he had to be *cajoled* into facing the basic issues at stake, even though his counselor was averse to using anything that smacked of deceit.

Cajole: (a) to coax (b) to lead (c) to force (d) to experiment

16. Imagine McClarthy and Scrivvens in a debate! Scrivvens would be reserved, thoughtful, and gentlemanly; McClarthy would be expected to display an impetuous and *blatant* performance.

Blatant: (a) coarse (b) consistent (c) disapproving (d) colorless

17. That gal became my *nemesis,* believe me. I even spent my tuition money on her, and for what? Hah! It was like the time you said that painting was your undoing. But at least you could look at them without paying.

Nemesis: (a) meal ticket (b) pain (c) wife (d) downfall

18. There are doctors and doctors. Most of them are able and honest men who stick to the Hippocratic oath; but Lucas had to admit that there are also pretenders who deserve no better name than *charlatan.*

Charlatan: (a) buffoon (b) fall guy (c) imposter (d) friend

19. The situation demanded that he *acquiesce*—in favor of the bishop's plan. If he did not approve the proposal of his superior, he would be subject to restrictions under church law.

Acquiesce: (a) to restate correctly (b) to associate quickly (c) to attack violently (d) to comply unwillingly

20. It would hardly seem that communism even begins to look as though it's in a *moribund* condition, for its political parties flourish, its controls multiply, and its structure is of increasing strength.

Moribund: (a) near death (b) exaggerated (c) virile (d) seriously argued

Clue 4: Synonym

1. Every season has its *harbinger;* the crocus tells us spring is near; the first frost announces winter and the long days announce summer. Perhaps it is only a balmy wind that foretells the coming of fall.

Harbinger: (a) bad weather (b) certain date (c) advance notice (d) flower

2. Into the midst of the *melée* Jason flew, hoping to stop the bloody fray. Of course he himself had two knives and a bludgeon, but his was a mission of rescue.

Melée: (a) brawl (b) war (c) mystery (d) horse race

3. Compared with Satan's seat in hell, Jehovah's throne in heaven reflects an *effulgent,* resplendent, and overpowering light.

Effulgent: (a) gloriously radiant (b) seemingly bright (c) distantly effective (d) usually brilliant

4. For Rochester it wasn't hard at all to *circumvent* Jack Benny's amateur attempt to keep him locked out of the kitchen. All he had to do to foil Jack's plans was to climb through the milk coop.

Circumvent: (a) to outwit (b) to defend (c) to invent (d) to discover

5. Regardless of his many reforms and arguments, Mendès-France was forced into a *cul-de-sac* by his ministers. And what can a man—premier or petty official—do to retrieve himself from a blind alley?

Cul-de-sac: (a) battle (b) outlet (c) dead end (d) conversion

6. Unlike Malenkov, Stalin held *pertinaciously* to the old party line. He persisted in the belief of the supremacy of the state, the absolute necessity for competence in the farming program, and the thickness of the iron curtain.

Pertinaciously: (a) happily (b) suspiciously (c) unyieldingly (d) timidly

7. After a course like that, no one could tell Spike that there weren't any *inane* and pointless lectures on campus.

Inane: (a) senseless (b) terrific (c) critical (d) proper

8. "Yes, he has personality—but let's say that it's a rather *vapid* one." "Oh! You mean, sort of 'blah'?" "That would describe it well."

Vapid: (a) clever (b) empty (c) attractive (d) despicable

9. It seemed that every move the young actress made was aimed at receiving some flattering remark from the pianist. She needed his *approbation* and good wishes in order to maintain her self-confidence.

Approbation: (a) boisterousness (b) approval (c) courting (d) criticism

10. "I agree," the judge answered. "But we need evidence to *corroborate* this opinion. Can you supply any?" Lawyer Jensen then produced letters and re-cordings which supported the accusation.

Corroborate: (a) to define (b) to falsify (c) to settle (d) to confirm

11. "It was a clear case of *equivocation,*" the lawyer said, "bandying words about so that his double talk persuaded them to invest. He was a blatant deceiver."

Equivocate: (a) to excavate (b) to reveal (c) to bundle (d) to falsify

12. When I am in the swamp, I am like a duck; when I am in the Rockies, I am like a mountain goat. I can change to meet any situation. In fact, I am the ideal salesman, the *quintessence* of adaptability.

Quintessence: (a) ultimate (b) standard (c) residue (d) method

13. With direct verbal hits, the author violently attacked his critics. He *fulminated* against their ignorance of both his subject and his purposes and against their irresponsible conclusions.

Fulminate: (a) to react quickly (b) to argue cleverly (c) to censure mildly (d) to explode suddenly

14. Somehow the audience reacted only to the *extrinsic* parts of the speech, missing the meat of the senator's purpose. It often happens that a group of people will understand only extraneous material.

Extrinsic: (a) emotional (b) unessential (c) valuable (d) outmoded

15. As a freshman, he was only a *tyro* in the art of love. He was only beginning to learn that females have to be "managed."

Tyro: (a) an extravert (b) a novice (c) a connoisseur (d) a cheat

16. Stalin's power in the Yalta conference lay in his Sphinx-like silences. Because of this *taciturn* manner, there was little that anyone else could disagree with.

Taciturn: (a) cleverly quarrelsome (b) locquacious (c) wise (d) uncommunicative

17. Dulles made the year's most *puissant* efforts for the unity of the free world by his tireless travels in the Middle East and the Far East, delivering addresses and patching up relationships. This was a powerful attempt on the part of the west to consolidate its forces.

Puissant: (a) tentative (b) dignified (c) intruding (d) forceful

18. Often when you complete a chapter or section of a book, you pause for a few moments to rest and think over what you have read. In that *hiatus,* try thinking back over the new words you have encountered so that you will recognize them next time you see them.

Hiatus: (a) silence (b) gap (c) manner (d) recollection

19. You know that when you depress the surface of a cake with your finger it will spring back to its

original position, don't you? This *resiliency* is the quality that lets you know when the cake is baked.

Resilient: (a) cooked through (b) resistant (c) elastic (d) spicy

20. Those who *execrate* the job of vocabulary building must be those who have not learned to identify word meanings from context. If they would increase this skill, they would not curse so the process of uncovering meaning.

Execrate: (a) extoll (b) abhor (c) assist (d) neglect

Clue 5: Summary

1. Wilson had no words to thank the lad. Every accusation had been made, the grand jury was about to set up formal charges—and then this delivery boy proved that Wilson had been at a bar and not at the race track. The *exonerated* man went home with his reputation intact.

Exonerate: (a) to free from suspicion (b) to release from jail (c) to hastily condemn (d) to exaggerate

2. He foresaw all the difficulties and was able to circumvent them; in this way he accomplished the work of a genius although he was somewhat less than that, just a *sagacious* man.

Sagacious: (a) keen (b) inept (c) helpful (d) unimaginative

3. For Jerry it was not easy to stay home every night of the week. He needed a "variety of companions of the opposite sex," he told his wife, and assured her that he could find that in the local tavern. First she called him a *philanderer*, then a liar, and finally a downright home-breaker.

Philanderer: (a) ne'er-do-well (b) opponent (c) flirt (d) deceiver

4. Why, if you screamed "Fire!" he would saunter down the stairs. It's not that my father is unhappy or dull, but he simply does not hurry. It's part of his *phlegmatic* nature.

Phlegmatic: (a) animated (b) hardened (c) sluggish (d) funny

5. The young bride flitted from one activity to another. She was an excellent cook, a fine bridge player, and an accomplished violinist: indeed, a *versatile* wife.

Versatile: (a) having many aptitudes (b) lovely and charming (c) having time to spare (d) uncontrollable

6. Joe spoke with his counselor because he was confused by social restrictions. His parents and church did not allow him to smoke, drink, or dance. He reached the conclusion that the *mores* of his own provincial county have a real strength and effect.

Mores: (a) laws (b) illegal materials (c) customs (d) politics

7. She was 29. Her hair glowed. Her dress fit tight and her sequin-studded shoes sparkled in the moonlight. She beamed into the eyes of her first date. She was proud and awake and *resplendent* in the glory of this new experience.

Resplendent: (a) glimmering (b) brilliant (c) dizzy (d) lustful

8. Well, he was one of those flaccid boys who tell the same joke over and over, and I might add that everything he said could be classed as a dull, *banal* remark.

Banal: (a) flat (b) elegant (c) sweet (d) unkind

9. During the lecture Mel yawned and yawned. He crossed and uncrossed his legs, fidgeted and finally relaxed into near-sleep as his pencil fell to the floor. It would take no doctor to say that he was suffering from *ennui*.

Ennui: (a) neuroticism (b) circumstances (c) boredom (d) melancholy

10. The only time he clenched his fist was when he had a coin in it. He stood at attention in the relaxed way others stood "at ease." He was more flabby than solid, and altogether this would-be cadet presented a rather *flaccid* appearance.

Flaccid: (a) limp (b) straight (c) congenial (d) nervous

11. After Professor Primrose had left the church for a smoke between the acts, had set a trap for the baby, and fondled the mice—his wife petulantly complained, "These *contretemps* must cease!"

Contretemps: (a) absent-minded act (b) foolishness (c) careless choice (d) dangerous behavior

12. Tapers by the thousands flickered as the colorful procession made its way down the aisle. Every pillar was wreathed with flowers and through the splendid tracery of the windows the late sun blazed in red and orange. Never had little Ned seen such a *flamboyant* spectacle.

Flamboyant: (a) invisible (b) religious (c) graceful (d) ornate

13. No sooner had the boss opened his mouth than Marion snapped back at him. And she was that way outside the office, too. One time she imagined that her date had insulted her intelligence so she *impetuously* sent him home. She never got a call from him again.

Impetuously: (a) modestly (b) thoughtfully (c) impulsively (d) helpfully

14. It was an anxious situation. Here was his mother-in-law coming up on a surprise visit; he had not used the money she had sent for garden furniture; and on top of it all, his wife was out and he and the boys were in for a game of poker. But he successfully routed the "enemy" and easily explained everything with a surprising amount of *finesse*.

Finesse: (a) difficulty (b) smoothness (c) cultivation (d) quotations

15. Everything seemed to happen at once. The $14,000 was returned, Harry's arm healed rapidly, and the bandits were routed. It was indeed a *propitious* sign for the future of the business.

Propitious: (a) unfortunate (b) quick (c) favorable (d) stimulating

16. The nurse patiently explained to the doctor how the mistake occurred, and although she herself did not excuse the interne, she tried to point out that errors are easily made in the pharmacy department. In fact, she did everything she could to *mollify* the surgeon's rage.

Mollify: (a) entangle (b) incite (c) escape (d) reduce

17. In establishing his new "doctrine of life," Silvanus borrowed exactness from the physical sciences, theory from the social sciences, time perspective from religion, and creativeness from art. He was certain that this *eclectic* approach would fulfill his hopes.

Eclectic: (a) combining (b) educating (c) circling (d) defining

18. Or take that student over there. He is sprawled out in his chair as if it were his bed. He glances idly around him, doing nothing, thinking of nothing in particular. Wouldn't you say he is *otiose?*

Otiose: (a) excited (b) ill (c) lazy (d) comfortable

19. Sometimes fault finding can be helpful to you. Are you really using your brain and trying to think about the meanings of these words as you go along? Are you watching for new words in all the reading you do? Are you trying to remember some of them, or trying to use the most useful of them in your own conversation or writing? Are you learning new words? Now, I don't want to seem too *captious,* but maybe you need a shot in the arm!

Captious: (a) industrious (b) quarrelsome (c) hypercritical (d) verbose

20. Sometimes a new word describes in a single word the general atmosphere of the situation. When you have mastered vocabulary, you will feel content, your reading will be easier and more pleasant, and you will be more relaxed. Your state will be *euphoric.*

Euphoric: (a) state of well-being (b) state of confusion (c) state of exultation (d) state of complacency

KEY

LESSON 1: How to Be Brilliant with Limited Resources (920 words)

(Page 15)

Rate Chart

1:00—920	2:20—394	3:40—251
1:10—786	2:30—368	3:50—240
1:20—690	2:40—345	4:00—230
1:30—613	2:50—331	4:10—221
1:40—552	3:00—307	4:20—212
1:50—502	3:10—290	4:30—204
2:00—460	3:20—276	4:40—197
2:10—421	3:30—263	4:50—190

Comprehension

(Page 17)

1. A
2. E
3. intelligence, ability, capacity
4. lawful
5. survey
6. important
7. forgetting

Application

(Page 17)

1. Survey
2. Review
3. Question
4. Recite
5. Recite
6. Read
7. Review
8. Survey
9. Survey

LESSON 2: Survey (1400 words)

(Page 18)

Rate Chart

1:00—1400	3:10—442	5:20—263
1:10—1200	3:20—420	5:30—255
1:20—1050	3:30—400	5:40—247
1:30—933	3:40—382	5:50—240
1:40—840	3:50—365	6:00—233
1:50—763	4:00—350	6:10—227
2:00—700	4:10—336	6:20—221
2:10—646	4:20—323	6:30—215
2:20—600	4:30—309	6:40—210
2:30—560	4:40—300	6:50—205
2:40—525	4:50—288	7:00—200
2:50—493	5:00—280	7:10—195
3:00—466	5:10—271	7:20—191

Comprehension

(Page 20)

1. title
2. summary
3. introduction
4. main heads
5. summary
6. first
7. last

Application

(Page 20)

Surveying a Book
1. Hebb-neuro
2. response
3. operations
Surveying a Chapter
5 and 8 *not* circled. [Those parts would be ignored by the skilled student, for the present, even though they might be interesting. He does not allow himself to be distracted from the main task, surveying the whole. Remember the forest and the trees.]

LESSON 3: Questions: Einstein, Darwin, and Paul Revere's Horse (1400 words)

(Page 23)

Rate Chart

1:00—1400	3:10—422	5:20—263
1:10—1200	3:20—420	5:30—255
1:20—1050	3:30—400	5:40—247
1:30—933	3:40—382	5:50—240
1:40—840	3:50—365	6:00—233
1:50—763	4:00—350	6:10—227
2:00—700	4:10—336	6:20—221
2:10—646	4:20—323	6:30—215
2:20—600	4:30—309	6:40—210
2:30—560	4:40—300	6:50—205
2:40—525	4:50—288	7:00—200
2:50—493	5:00—280	7:10—195
3:00—466	5:10—271	7:20—191

Comprehension

(Page 25)

1. curiosity
2. question
3. answer
4. longer
5. end
6. before
7. guess

LESSON 4: The First R: Reading (580 words)

(Page 27)

Rate Chart

30—1160	1:20—435	2:20—248
40—870	1:30—387	2:30—232
50—696	1:40—348	2:40—218
1:00—580	1:50—316	2:50—205
1:10—497	2:00—290	3:00—193
	2:10—268	

Comprehension

(Page 28)

1. meaning, information
2. failing
3. selectivity, selection
4. efficient, effective
5. skim
6. anticipated

7. skimming, quick
8. selective
9. thinking

Application

(Page 28)

1. U 2. U 3. U 4. U 5. I

1. U 2. U 3. U 4. LI 5. U 6. I 7. I 8. I

LESSON 5: R2 and R3: Recite and "Rite" (1400 words)

(Page 31)

Rate Chart

1:00—1400	3:10—442	5:20—263
1:10—1200	3:20—420	5:30—255
1:20—1050	3:30—400	5:40—247
1:30—933	3:40—382	5:50—240
1:40—840	3:50—365	6:00—233
1:50—763	4:00—350	6:10—227
2:00—700	4:10—336	6:20—221
2:10—646	4:20—323	6:30—215
2:20—600	4:30—309	6:40—210
2:30—560	4:40—300	6:50—205
2:40—525	4:50—288	7:00—200
2:50—493	5:00—280	7:10—195
3:00—466	5:10—271	7:20—191

Comprehension

(Page 33)

1. continuous
2. underlines
3. questions
4. efficient, effective
5. learning
6. underlining
7. remember
8. recite
9. postpone, delay
10. cue, key
11. memories, thoughts

Taking Lecture Notes

(Page 36)

a. 4 b. 6 c. 1 d. 1 e. 5 f. 5

LESSON 6: Review: The Last Step to Mastery (1140 words)

(Page 36)

Rate Chart

1:00—1140	2:40—428	4:20—263
1:10—977	2:50—402	4:30—253
1:20—855	3:00—380	4:40—244
1:30—760	3:10—360	4:50—236
1:40—684	3:20—342	5:00—228
1:50—622	3:30—326	5:10—220
2:00—570	3:40—311	5:20—214
2:10—526	3:50—299	5:30—207
2:20—489	4:00—285	5:40—201
2:30—456	4:10—274	

Comprehension

(Page 38)

1. forgetting, reviewing
2. use, apply, review
3. relearning
4. reviewing
5. repetition, relearning
6. skill, techniques
7. questions
8. test, question, quiz
9. timing, frequency
10. immediately, right, just

LESSON 7: The Techniques of Test-Taking (1140 words)

(Page 42)

Rate Chart

1:00—1140	2:40—428	4:20—263
1:10—977	2:50—402	4:30—253
1:20—855	3:00—380	4:40—244
1:30—760	3:10—360	4:50—236
1:40—684	3:20—342	5:00—228
1:50—622	3:30—326	5:10—220
2:00—570	3:40—311	5:20—214
2:10—526	3:50—299	5:30—207
2:20—489	4:00—285	5:40—201
2:30—456	4:10—274	

Comprehension

(Page 43)

1. knowledge
2. mastered, learned
3. uncertainty, anxiety, insecurity
4. review
5. security, confidence
6. distribute, space, spread out
7. time schedule
8. cautious, timid
9. knowing, learning
10. showing, demonstrating

Application

(Page 44)

1. Starting the Essay Examination
   Order: d, b, c, a

2. The Essay Question
   a. Misspelling: parasites, plankton, terrestrial
   b. Tautologies:
      1. Marine animals living in the sea.
      2. Terrestrial animals living on land.
      3. Parasites, living on or in other animals.
      (Note: We must assume here that the instructor does not expect definitions of the words denoting the habitats.)
   c. Inexact language:
      It's very small. . . . (microscopic) . . . lives on or in other animals . . . (host)
   d. Circular definition:
      Fleas, lice, and tapeworms are parasites because they live on or in other animals.

3. Taking a Test
   a. intelligence or talent
   b. forgetting
   c. SQ4R
   d. title
   e. main heads, summary
   f. help select important ideas, understand material better, remember it longer
   g. title, main heads, end of chapter questions, technical terms
   h. selective
   i. answer, question
   j. learning, postpones
   k. answers to questions, brief or cues

LESSON 8: Concentration: A Large White Bear and Other Distractions (1140 words)

(Page 46)

Rate Chart

1:00—1140	2:40—428	4:20—263
1:10—977	2:50—402	4:30—253
1:20—855	3:00—380	4:40—244
1:30—760	3:10—360	4:50—236
1:40—684	3:20—342	5:00—228
1:50—622	3:30—326	5:10—220
2:00—570	3:40—311	5:20—214
2:10—526	3:50—299	5:30—207
2:20—489	4:00—285	5:40—201
2:30—456	4:10—274	

Comprehension

(Page 47)

1. concentrating
2. sustained
3. attention
4. needs
5. dominant, predominant
6. attention
7. incentive
8. low, weak, inactive
9. short-term
10. stronger, greater

LESSON 9: Perception: The Foundation of Reading Ability (1584 words)

(Page 51)

Rate Chart

1:00—1584	2:20—678	3:50—414
1:10—1356	2:30—636	4:00—396
1:20—1188	2:40—594	4:10—378
1:30—1056	2:50—558	4:20—360
1:40—950	3:00—528	4:30—351
1:50—864	3:10—504	4:40—340
2:00—792	3:20—469	4:50—328
2:10—732	3:30—452	5:00—317
	3:40—432	

Comprehension

(Page 53)

1. instruction, teaching
2. purpose, motivation, goals

3. perceptual
4, 5, 6, 7: closure, speed, memory, accuracy
8. tension, anxiety
9. rapidly, quickly, faster
10. time

Time-Rate Chart

(Pages 53-55)

2:00—104	1:20—156	40—312
1:50—113	1:10—178	30—416
1:40—125	1:00—208	20—624
1:30—139	50—250	10—1248

Application: Comprehension Checks

(Page 54)

1. b 2. d 3. d 4. b 5. a
1. c 2. a 3. b 4. a 5. c
1. b 2. b 3. d 4. d 5. c

LESSON 10: Comprehension: A New Strategy (580 words)

(Page 58)

Rate Chart

0:30—1160	1:20—435	2:20—248
0:40—870	1:30—387	2:30—232
0:50—696	1:40—348	2:40—218
1:00—580	1:50—316	2:50—205
1:10—497	2:00—290	3:00—193
	2:10—268	

Comprehension

(Page 59)

1. test, measure
2. teach
3. outwit, fool, cheat
4. broad, general (narrow)
5. narrow, specific (broad)
6. sentence
7. problem solving
8. evidence, information
9. hypothesis, guess
10. check, test, evaluate

LESSON 11: Vocabulary: Are Words Important? (1584 words)

(Page 65)

Rate Chart

1:00—1584	2:20—678	3:50—414
1:10—1356	2:30—636	4:00—396
1:20—1188	2:40—594	4:10—378
1:30—1056	2:50—558	4:20—360
1:40—950	3:00—528	4:30—351
1:50—864	3:10—504	4:40—340
2:00—792	3:20—469	4:50—328
2:10—732	3:30—452	5:00—317
	3:40—432	

Comprehension

(Page 67)

1. meaning, significance

2. verbal, word
3. meticulous
4. experiences
5. context
6. curious
7. frustrated
8. technical, specific, special
9. context, setting
10. definition, meaning
11. root, roots

LESSON 12: Critical Reading: How to Avoid the Pitfalls (1600 words)

(Page 70)

Rate Chart

1:00—1600	3:00—533	5:00—320
1:10—1371	3:10—505	5:10—309
1:20—1200	3:20—480	5:20—300
1:30—1067	3:30—457	5:30—291
1:40—960	3:40—436	5:40—282
1:50—873	3:50—417	5:50—274
2:00—800	4:00—400	6:00—267
2:10—738	4:10—384	6:10—260
2:20—686	4:20—369	6:20—253
2:30—640	4:30—356	6:30—246
2:40—600	4:40—343	6:40—240
2:50—575	4:50—331	6:50—235

Comprehension

(Page 72)

1. information, facts, data
2. objective, accurate, straightforward
3. bias, prejudice
4. distorts, changes, modifies
5. critically
6. verified, checked, proved
7. inference
8. judgments
9. slanted
10. ourselves, the reader

Application

(Page 73)

1. The Democrats are caught in a scandal again.
2. To raise doubts about the fitness of Democrats to govern.
3. Their response to the attack was different; Truman said that White was disloyal; the New Republic said: "There can . . . by Miss Bentley."

(Page 73)

a. Loaded word: line
   Connotation: Communist Party "line"
b. Unproved premise: that Truman is an expert witness
c. Unproved premise: that the New Republic is more extreme in its partisanship (thus less likely to admit the facts) than Truman
d. Unproved premise
e. Loaded words

(Page 74)

a. unproved premises
b. linking

c. ridicule
d. over-generalization
e. facts; defense of security; great power; defense of freedom
f. mistake; attack; isolationist; Nazi

TIMED READINGS

(Pages 109-120)

Rate Chart (286 words)

0:20—858	1:00—286	1:40—171
0:30—572	1:10—246	1:50—156
0:40—429	1:20—216	2:00—143
0:50—342	1:30—192	

Rate Chart (1000 words)

0:30—2000	2:10—461	3:50—261
0:40—1500	2:20—428	4:00—250
0:50—1200	2:30—400	4:10—240
1:00—1000	2:40—375	4:20—231
1:10—856	2:50—353	4:30—222
1:20—750	3:00—333	4:40—214
1:30—666	3:10—316	4:50—207
1:40—600	3:20—300	5:00—200
1:50—545	3:30—286	5:10—192
2:00—500	3:40—273	5:20—188

Rate Chart (725 words)

0:20—2175	1:00—725	1:40—435
0:30—1450	1:10—600	1:50—395
0:40—1080	1:20—540	2:00—362
0:50—870	1:30—480	2:10—334

Our New Breed of Knuckleheads

(Page 109)

1. a 2. c 3. d 4. b 5. d

Gateway to the Animal Mind

(Page 111)

1. b 2. a 3. d 4. d 5. c 6. d 7. b 8. c 9. b 10. d

Adjustment in College: Separation from Primary Groups

(Page 112)

1. d 2. a 3. c 4. c 5. b 6. a 7. a 8. a 9. c 10. b

Social Relationships: Dynamics of Friendship

(Page 114)

1. b 2. d 3. b 4. a 5. a 6. b 7. c 8. a 9. a 10. c

Fraternities

(Page 115)

1. a 2. c 3. b 4. c 5. d 6. a 7. b 8. d 9. b 10. a

Don't Be a Pal to Your Son

(Page 117)

1. a 2. d 3. b 4. a 5. d

Teaching Machines: The Coming Automation

(*Page 118*)

1. c 2. a 3. a 4. d 5. b 6. b 7. d 8. c 9. d 10. b

The Mechanical Man

(*Page 119*)

1. c 2. a 3. b 4. c 5. c 6. a 7. a 8. b 9. a 10. d

APPENDIX 3

(*Page 125*)

1. d	1. d	1. d	1. c	1. a
2. b	2. a	2. b	2. a	2. a
3. b	3. b	3. d	3. a	3. c

4. d	4. d	4. c	4. a	4. c
5. b	5. a	5. b	5. c	5. a
6. a	6. d	6. a	6. c	6. c
7. b	7. d	7. a	7. a	7. b
8. c	8. b	8. b	8. b	8. a
9. d	9. d	9. b	9. b	9. c
10. c	10. a	10. b	10. d	10. a
11. d	11. b	11. c	11. d	11. a
12. a	12. c	12. b	12. a	12. d
13. b	13. c	13. d	13. d	13. c
14. a	14. b	14. b	14. b	14. b
15. a	15. a	15. a	15. b	15. c
16. c	16. d	16. a	16. d	16. d
17. d	17. c	17. d	17. d	17. a
18. b	18. c	18. c	18. b	18. c
19. c	19. a	19. d	19. c	19. c
20. d	20. b	20. a	20. b	20. a

SUMMARY OF SQ4R

1. *Survey*

   Determine the structure, organization, or plan of the chapter. Details will be remembered because of their relationship to the total picture.

   a. *Think about the title.* Guess what will be included in the chapter.

   b. *Read the introduction.* Here the main ideas are presented, the "forest" which must be seen before the details, the "trees" make organized sense.

   c. *Read the summary.* Here is the relationship among the main ideas.

   d. *Read the main heads* (boldface type). Here are the main ideas. Determine where in the sequence of ideas each one fits.

2. *Question*

   Having in mind a question results in (1) a spontaneous attempt to answer it with information already at hand; (2) frustration until the question is answered; (3) a criterion against which the details can be inspected to determine relevance and importance; (4) a focal point for crystallizing a series of ideas (the answer).

   a. Use the questions at the beginning or end of the chapter.

   b. Formulate questions by changing main heads and subheads to questions.

   Example: *Causes of Depression.* What are the causes of depression? What conditions are usually present before a depression occurs?

3. *Read*

   Read to answer the question. Move quickly. Sort out ideas and evaluate them. If content does not relate to the question, give it only a passing glance. *Read selectively.*

4. *Recite*

   Answer the question—in your own words, not the author's.

5. *"Rite"*

   a. Write the question (one sheet of paper is to contain *all* the notes for this chapter—so keep it brief).

   b. Write the answer using only key words, listings, etc., that are needed to recall the whole idea.

6. *Review*

   Increase retention and cut cramming time by 90% by means of immediate *and* delayed review. To do this:

   a. Read your written question(s).

   b. Try to recite the answer. If you can't, look at your notes. Five to ten minutes will suffice for a chapter.

   c. Review again after one week.

	MONDAY	TUESDAY	WEDNESDAY	THURSDAY	FRIDAY	SATURDAY	SUNDAY
7							
8							
9							
10							
11							
12							
1							
2							
3							
4							
5							
6							
7							
8							
9							

COURSES	HRS. CREDIT	HRS. STUDY (2×)

TEXT

_____

_____

_____

	MONDAY	TUESDAY	WEDNESDAY	THURSDAY	FRIDAY	SATURDAY	SUNDAY
7							
8							
9							
10							
11							
12							
1							
2							
3							
4							
5							
6							
7							
8							
9							

COURSES	HRS. CREDIT	HRS. STUDY (2×)

TEXT